PHASE LINE GREEN

Phase Line Green

The Battle for Hue, 1968

NICHOLAS WARR

NAVAL INSTITUTE PRESS
ANNAPOLIS, MARYLAND

ISBN 1-55750-911-5

Printed in the United States of America

To the Marines of Charlie Company, First Battalion, Fifth Marine Regiment, in the Vietnam War era, and in the memory of my father, Joseph Packer Warr (1912–1981).

Dad, you were the only one who welcomed me home.
In my newly acquired guilt, I asked you to take the welcome home banner down. Now that I understand, you are gone.
I hope you can read this from where you are.
Thank you.

No evil is greater than commands of the sovereign from the court. . . .

He whose generals are able and not interfered with by the sovereign will be victorious. . . .

There are occasions when the commands of the sovereign need not be obeyed. . . .

If the situation is one of victory but the sovereign has issued orders not to engage, the general may decide to fight. If the situation is such that he cannot win, but the sovereign has issued orders to engage, *he need not do so.*

Sun Tzu, *The Art of War*
China, 500 B.C.

If them dumb mutherfuckin' politician pukeheads would just let us alone and let us do our jobs, we'd be outta here and back to the World in no time at all. Shit! No arty, no fixed wing, no direct support from those dumbshit, poor-ass tank crews; just our damned M-16s and grenades and they want us to root out a regiment of entrenched NVA in a day or two. Well, let them dumb asshole politicians come over here and follow me around for a minute or two, and see what kind of bullshit happens when dumbshit mutherfuckin' politicians start calling the shots on the ground. Jesus H. Christ, why can't they stick to kissing asses and babies?

Obscene mumbling from pinned-down Marines
overheard amid street fighting, Hue, 1968

Contents

Preface

A Ground Pounder's Perspectives on Strategy,
Vietnam War Style

I started writing this book in February 1983, almost exactly fifteen years to the day after this story's events actually occurred.

I must confess that I have an unfair advantage over most writers in that, despite the relatively long duration of this effort, the writing of this story has expended very little actual literary "elbow grease." You see, I lived these events, and in some parts of my mind, I have been living them, every day of my life, since they took place.

To be sure, during the first ten or so of those fifteen years, I had absolutely no conscious realization that I was constantly reliving the days and weeks we spent in Hue during the Tet Offensive.

After having concluded my second consecutive, unsuccessful, five-year marriage, I sought counseling in an effort to understand just exactly why matrimony and I were seemingly incompatible. I spent the better part of six months visiting a very nice, competent psychiatrist twice a week, baring my soul to this capable and sympathetic individual, telling her the story of my life. That was in 1978. In 1983, after the unexpected death of my father and the resulting catharsis that I experienced, I reflected back on that counseling. In a flash I realized for the first time that my attentive and professional counselor, despite her having picked my brain for nearly fifty hours over that six-month period, had absolutely no clue that I was a Vietnam veteran. In 1983 I had to confront the fact that the events recorded in this book were having a devastating and negative effect on my life and on my interpersonal relationships with people, despite my having buried these memories so deeply that I no longer consciously remembered them.

Having been profoundly shocked by the revelation that my wartime experiences were haunting me without my conscious knowledge, I made the very difficult decision to try to consciously remember what had happened and to write it all down as a form of therapy.

Of course, fifteen years is a long time, and certain parts of the memories had eroded. But I quickly found out that my memories of the story were there in vivid and graphic detail, although some dates and names were dim and vague. So I decided to do some basic research.

Through correspondence with several sources of research materials, I began to accumulate a significant stack of documents, including maps of Vietnam, the Command Chronology of the First Battalion, Fifth Marine Regiment, during the period of 1–29 February 1968, and a copy of the Combat After-action Report on Operation "Hue," which I assume was written by 1/5's battalion commander after the battle was over. My readings of these documents were very disturbing, because there were serious discrepancies between my memories and these documents.

Once I started this project, it took on a life of its own. I became almost obsessed with finding anything and everything written about the Vietnam War, especially anything having to do with the Tet Offensive of 1968. I found that much of what was written was very sketchy, and that the limited information available followed the line established by the "official" records.

Let's get to the bottom line.

The battle for the Citadel of Hue, during the Tet Offensive of 1968, is universally considered by writers and historians as *the* most hard-fought and bloody battle of that long and bloodthirsty war. I do not dispute that. I saw it and lived it, up close and personal. It was a devastating confrontation between a large, determined force of North Vietnamese Army regulars and an equally determined force of U.S. Marines. Even given the best of all possible scenarios, under these circumstances, much blood would be lost.

Neither do I dispute the outcome. Although it took nearly a month of hard fighting and personal sacrifice, the Marines achieved a decisive victory, ultimately crushing a numerically superior enemy.

The dispute, here, is over the "rules of engagement" established by higher authorities and placed upon the Marines of 1/5.

Every book I have ever read about the Vietnam War seems to center on three themes. The first is the American politicians' micromanagement of the war effort. The second is how the establishment of extremely strict rules of engagement handicapped American forces by the same politicos who destined our military to ultimate failure in spite of an incredible advantage in firepower and technology. The last theme is about how America's military leadership failed to resist or change this self-defeating scenario.

Is there any other period in mankind's history of warfare during which a war's losing party won virtually *every single battle?* I think not.

The after-action report and command chronology of the battle for the Citadel of Hue create the impression that the military leaders had finally learned their lessons and had avoided these pitfalls. Specifically, these documents state that every effort was made to provide heavy artillery, air strikes, and naval gunfire support to the troops on the ground from the beginning of the battle. The reports further state that American attacks during this battle were made "upon completion of prep fires, walking artillery in front of advancing troops."

When I first read these reports, I was dumbfounded. It was devastating enough to force to the surface my memories of the fighting and the dying of a terrible battle. It was much worse to find that the chain of command, for reasons unknown, had decided to fabricate a more acceptable history than what my memories demanded, and that these "facts" were becoming accepted as the actuality of history. When I read these "facts," I felt that they were a betrayal of the men who fought and died there. This discovery became my motivation, my impetus, to see that history was made accurate.

Quite by chance, in 1986, I was exposed to *The Art of War,* by Sun Tzu. I was attending a professional sales strategy conference sponsored by the computer company I was then working for, and the conference coordinator continually referred to this work. Since it sounded like a fascinating source of information for business strategy, I purchased a copy of it and started reading. I did not expect to find what I found.

There are at least eleven quotations in *The Art of War,* including the four at the beginning of this book, warning military leaders that "interference by the sovereign" is a surefire formula for disaster. Of course, in ancient China, this precept of warfare strategy was particularly important. It could take days or weeks to transmit commands from headquarters to the battle site. In those days, by the time a message from the sovereign arrived at the battlefield, the entire tactical situation could have changed; thus those orders, if executed, could easily result in disasters. The modern-day equivalent of this, the "rules of engagement" that Vietnam combat veterans were forced to deal with, could, and often did, cause their own disasters.

The Battle for Hue, during the infamous Tet Offensive of 1968 at the height of the Vietnam War, was an important chapter in Marine Corps history. The result of over thirty days of devastating house-to-house combat in the largest city in central Vietnam was a completely routed and nearly destroyed enemy force of over two NVA regiments by two battalions of Marines from the Fifth Marine Regiment. The First Battalion, Fifth Marine Regiment—my outfit—was issued a Presidential Unit Citation for our crushing defeat of the large NVA force occupying Hue's Citadel, a huge walled and moated fortress guarding the Imperial Palace, the spiritual and religious center for millions of Vietnamese people.

The Battle for Hue also caused widespread destruction in this beautiful city, high casualties on both sides of the fighting lines, and the deaths of thousands of noncombatants, murdered by Viet Cong and NVA troops during the first few days of the Tet "liberation." The battle was, ultimately, convincingly won by the Marines and was reported by the U.S. press to have been a "great victory" by U.S. and South Vietnamese forces. This battle was, in reality, a very close thing, a near-disaster, which could have just as easily resulted in the complete destruction of the First Battalion, Fifth Marine Regiment as a fighting unit. The Battle for Hue, now another fabled victory in the Leatherneck's long history of major American victories, could have just as easily gone down in history as a major defeat along the lines of the Dien Bien Phu disaster in the French Indochinese War in 1954.

As someone who luckily survived the three weeks of house-to-house fighting inside the Citadel and who has lived to read and study *The Art of War,* I can be certain that several ancient Chinese military strategists rolled over in their graves in February 1968.

Acknowledgments

The many hours of work put into the publication of this book was a team effort. My thanks extend to many people who have, over the past decade, encouraged and helped me complete this work.

In particular, many thanks to my family for putting up with me. To my son, Brent, thanks for your editing. To my mother, Dorothy, thanks for teaching me the lessons of persistence and determination. Without that, I don't think this book would have ever been finished. To my wife, Pamela, thank you is not enough. You saved my life. You are my life.

To Alex Lee, thank you for connecting me with Naval Institute Press, and for your encouragement and guidance. To Ri Van Lam, my friend, thank you for introducing me to Colonel Lee, and for your interest and translations.

My special thanks are extended to Scott Nelson and Dr. Jack Shulimson for their invaluable contributions and assistance with this book. Scott, thanks for being there, and thanks for being who you are.

Introduction

Nicholas Warr's *Phase Line Green* is a first-person account of the struggle for Hue, one of the defining battles of the Communist 1968 Tet Offensive, and indeed of the entire war. As a relatively new Marine platoon leader, just arrived in Vietnam, then Lieutenant Warr participated in the "liberation" of the former capital of the Vietnamese emperors, an event which would have a life-long searing impact. Twenty-nine years later, in this book, he tells his story from the perspective of the small unit leader in vivid prose that has lost none of its urgency or pungency in the passage of time. In the telling, he spares few, including himself.

On 30–31 January 1968, during the Vietnamese lunar New Year, the Vietnamese Communists mounted a surprise offensive throughout all of South Vietnam. Most of these attacks were by local Viet Cong units. There was one place, however, where the Communists committed first-line North Vietnamese units, and that was in the one-month struggle for Hue.

At the beginning of 1968 (nearly three years after the commitment of large American combat forces to the war), the U.S. Military Assistance

Command, Vietnam, under Army General William C. Westmoreland, had intelligence of a massing of enemy divisions in the northern border region, especially in the Demilitarized Zone (DMZ) dividing the two Vietnams and in Laos near the isolated Marine base at Khe Sanh. Westmoreland prepared to reinforce the III Marine Amphibious Force (III MAF), under Marine Lieutenant General Robert E. Cushman, in the five northern provinces of South Vietnam.

In January 1968, III MAF numbered over one hundred thousand Marines, sailors, and soldiers, including one Army and two Marine infantry divisions. In mid-January, Westmoreland rushed yet another Army division, the 1st Air Cavalry Division, north. Worried about the Marine defenses at Khe Sanh and lacking confidence in the ability of the Marine commanders to control the situation, Westmoreland planned to establish a temporary northern forward headquarters under his deputy, Army General Creighton Abrams.[1] Before he could implement this plan, the enemy launched their Tet offensive—everywhere but at Khe Sanh.

As the former imperial capital, Hue was for many Vietnamese the cultural center of the country. It radiated a sense both of its colonial and imperial past. It was, in effect, two cities. North of the Perfume River lay the walled city of the emperors, called the Citadel. (There is some confusion in the term·"Citadel," because it also refers to the Royal Palace grounds, which are also surrounded by a wall.) South of the river was the modern city. The South Vietnamese had dismissed any notion that the enemy had the ability to launch a division-size attack against the city.[2]

Unknown to the allies, two enemy regiments—the 6th and 4th NVA—were on the move. At 0223 on 31 January a four-man North Vietnamese sapper team opened the western gate of the Citadel to the lead battalions of the 6th NVA. By daylight, most of the Citadel was in the hands of the NVA. At the 1st ARVN Division's Mang Ca compound, an ad hoc two-hundred-man defensive force managed to stave off the enemy assaults.[3]

Across the river in southern Hue, the NVA maintained a virtual siege of the MACV advisory compound. While the 4th NVA attack in the new city lacked the cohesion and timing of those in the Citadel, the NVA controlled most of southern Hue.[4]

The first U.S. Marines to bolster the South Vietnamese in the city were from the newly formed Task Force X-Ray, under Brigadier General Foster C. LaHue, at Phu Bai, about eight miles south of Hue. LaHue had barely enough time to become acquainted with his new sector, let alone the fast-developing Hue situation. LaHue later wrote: "Initial deployment of forces was made with limited information."[5]

With this "limited information" Company A, 1st Battalion, 1st Marines received orders to relieve Hue. Although reinforced by four Marine tanks, the Marine company was caught in a murderous crossfire after crossing the An Cuu Bridge into the city. Among the casualties was the company commander.[6]

The Marines reinforced the embattled company with the command group of the 1st Battalion, 1st Marines (Lieutenant Colonel Marcus J. Gravel) and Company G, 2d Battalion, 5th Marines. Gravel's relief column reached Company A in the early afternoon. By this time, the enemy attackers had pulled back their forces.[7]

Leaving Company A behind to secure the MACV compound, Lieutenant Colonel Gravel took Company G and attempted to cross the main bridge over the Perfume River. Two infantry platoons made their way over but immediately came under machine gun fire. Gravel remembered, "We were no match for what was going on. . . . I decided to withdraw."[8]

This was easier said than done. The enemy was well dug in and "firing from virtually every building." Company G lost nearly a third of its men, either wounded or killed.[9]

The American command still had little realization of the situation in Hue. In Saigon, General William C. Westmoreland cabled Washington: "The enemy has approximately three companies in the Hue Citadel and Marines have sent a battalion into the area to clear them out."[10]

General LaHue soon realized the enemy strength in Hue was much greater than he had originally estimated. Shortly after noon on 1 February, he called Colonel Stanley S. Hughes of the 1st Marines and gave him tactical control of the forces in the southern city. Hughes reinforced the two Marine companies in Hue with Company F, 2d Battalion, 5th Marines.[11]

In southern Hue, on 2 February, the Marines made some minor headway and Company H, 2d Battalion, 5th Marines reinforced the Marines in the city. The NVA, however, continued to block any advance to the west toward the province headquarters building.[12]

At Phu Bai, Colonel Hughes prepared to bring his headquarters and that of the 2d Battalion, 5th Marines, under Lieutenant Colonel Ernest C. Cheatham, into Hue. On the morning of the third, Hughes established his command post in the MACV compound and held a hurried conference with his two battalion commanders. While Lieutenant Colonel Cheatham took control of the three companies already in the city, Gravel retained command of Company A.[13]

Establishing his command post at the University, Lieutenant Colonel Cheatham, like Gravel before him, made no headway against the enemy.

On 4 February, Colonel Hughes decided to place the 1st Battalion on Lieutenant Colonel Cheatham's exposed flank and continue the push against the enemy defensive positions.[14]

That morning, Company B, 1st Battalion, 1st Marines joined Lieutenant Colonel Gravel's command. That night, however, North Vietnamese sappers blew the An Cuu bridge, closing the land route into the city. This left the Marine command only two alternatives to resupply the Hue forces—river traffic and helicopters.[15]

With little room to outflank the enemy, the battalion had to take each building and each block one at a time. According to Cheatham, "We had to pick a point and attempt to break that one strong point." After a time, Cheatham and his officers noted that the enemy "defended on every other street." In other words, the battalion would move quickly and then hit a defensive position.[16]

On the morning of 5 February, both Marine battalions resumed the attack in a southwesterly direction toward the city hospital and provincial headquarters. On the right flank, Company H advanced along the river front. The 1st Battalion, 1st Marines secured the left flank. Lieutenant Colonel Gravel remembered, "The going was slow. . . . We fought for two days over one building."[17]

On the afternoon of 6 February, Company H used tear gas to overwhelm the NVA defenders in the provincial headquarters. The capture of the provincial headquarters was more than symbolic; the building had served as the command post for the 4th NVA Regiment. Once the headquarters fell to the Marines, much of the enemy's organized resistance in southern Hue collapsed.[18]

By 10 February, despite some occasional resistance, the Marines were in control south of the Perfume River. With the NVA still holding fast in the Citadel, Hue was now indeed two cities.[19]

In clearing the modern city, the Marines took a heavy toll of the enemy, but at a high cost to themselves. The Americans had accounted for over 1,000 enemy dead and took 6 prisoners. Marine casualties included 38 dead and over 320 wounded.[20]

While the Marines cleared the new city, a South Vietnamese offensive in the Citadel had faltered. By 8 February, Brigadier General Ngo Quang Truong, the 1st Division commander, had inside the Citadel four airborne battalions and the 3d ARVN Regiment, which were able to hold their own.[21]

About ten miles to the west of Hue, the U.S. Army's 3d Brigade, 1st Cavalry Division was having as little luck as the ARVN forces. Having run into well-entrenched enemy forces, the 3d Brigade could not push the NVA out. During this period, the North Vietnamese command maintained its own support area outside the western wall of the Citadel.[22]

In the interim, the South Vietnamese Joint General Staff sent reinforcements from Saigon to Phu Bai, the lead elements of a Vietnamese Marine task force. General Truong proposed to have the South Vietnamese Marines replace the battered Vietnamese airborne battalions in the Citadel. Although one company entered the Citadel on the tenth, the Vietnamese Marine commander refused to insert any more troops until the rest of his command arrived from Saigon.[23]

General Truong also asked for a U.S. Marine battalion. On 11–12 February, the 1st Battalion, 5th Marines, under Major Robert H. Thompson, entered the Citadel to take over the southeastern sector. Like the other 5th Marines battalions, the 1st Battalion remained under the operational control of the 1st Marines.[24]

The 1st Battalion, 5th Marines included Company C, commanded by First Lieutenant Scott A. Nelson, along with Second Lieutenant Nicholas Warr and his platoon of fifty-one Marines.

Apparently when the one Vietnamese Marine company came into the Citadel the previous day, the Vietnamese airborne units departed. Unaware of the departure of the Vietnamese airborne, Major Thompson departed the Mang Ca compound on the morning of the thirteenth to take over the new sector: "There was no Airborne unit in the area and Company A was up to their armpits in NVA." Within minutes the company sustained thirty-five casualties.[25]

Much of the fighting centered around an archway tower occupied by the NVA along the Citadel's eastern wall. Finally after committing its reserve and the extensive use of supporting fire including air, the battalion captured the tower on the night of 15–16 February.[26]

For the next few days the 1st Battalion met the same close-quarter resistance from the enemy. The battalion discovered that the NVA units in the Citadel employed "better city-fighting tactics" than the enemy in southern Hue.[27]

During this period, on the thirteenth, the Vietnamese Marine task force finally arrived in the Citadel and was assigned the southwest sector. In two days of heavy fighting, however, the Vietnamese Marine task force advanced less than four hundred meters. In other sectors of the Citadel, other ARVN units were also at a standstill.[28]

By this time, the enemy also had his problems. On the night of 16–17 February, the allies intercepted an enemy radio transmission relating the death of the NVA commander in the city and the assumption of command of a new officer. The new commander recommended with-drawal but the senior headquarters denied the request.[29]

In the Citadel, General Truong prepared for the final thrust to capture the Imperial Palace. With the Vietnamese Marines on the western flank, he placed the 3d ARVN Regiment in the center. On the left flank, the U.S. Marine battalion renewed its assault. If the NVA in the Citadel were now fighting a rear guard action, they contested nearly every piece of ground.[30]

Generals Abrams (who had established his new headquarters at Phu Bai) and Cushman shared a concern about progress in the Citadel and the resulting American casualties. The *Washington Post* quoted a Marine officer: "We don't have enough men, . . . air support, or enough artillery to do this thing quickly."[31]

On 20 February, General Abrams radioed General Cushman that he considered "the measures so far taken to be inadequate." He also sent a message to General Tolson of the 1st Air Cavalry to clear the approaches to Hue.[32]

Despite the note of anxiety in Abrams's messages, the battle for Hue was in its last stages. By 22 February, after stiff resistance, the 1st Cav-alry's 3d Brigade was within sight of the city walls.[33] In the eastern sec-tor, the 1st Battalion, 5th Marines had once again taken the initiative. Despite heavy initial resistance, by the morning of the twenty-second the Marines had reached the southeastern wall.[34]

To the west of the American Marines, however, the North Vietnamese continued to hold out. Venting his anger at what he considered the slow progress of the Vietnamese Marines, General Abrams complained to Westmoreland that the Vietnamese Marines in the last three days "have moved forward less than half a city block," and even recommended their possible dissolution.[35]

Notwithstanding Abrams's frustrations, the Vietnamese forces were on the offensive. At 0500 on the twenty-fourth, ARVN soldiers raised their flag over the Citadel; by late afternoon, South Vietnamese troops had recaptured the palace with its surrounding grounds and walls. Except for mopping up operations, the fight for the Citadel was over. On 26 February, ARVN forces relieved the Marine battalion.[36]

On the twenty-ninth, the 1st and 2d Battalions, 5th Marines con-ducted a sweep east and north of the city, but the search for significant North Vietnamese forces proved fruitless. Lieutenant Colonel Cheatham observed, "We couldn't close the loop around the enemy. To be honest, we didn't have enough people to close it." On 2 March 1968, the Marines closed out the operation.[37]

The suddenness and the extent of the enemy offensive in Hue caught both the South Vietnamese and American commands off stride. At first underestimating the strength of the enemy in Hue, the allies sent too few troops. Command, control, and coordination remained a problem until the last weeks. The activation of the MACV Phu Bai Headquarters added an additional, unneeded layer of command from above. Task Force X-Ray, the 1st ARVN Division, and the 3d Brigade all fought their own battles in isolation. Aside from General Cushman of III MAF and General Abrams, there was no overall American, let alone single, commander of the Hue campaign. Both Cushman and Abrams were at too high a level to focus much of their attention on the Hue situation. Even General Truong controlled the South Vietnamese effort from his headquarters. As a Marine officer observed, the lack of an overall commander resulted in competition for support and no general battle plan. By the time a U.S. Army general became the Hue coordinator, "He didn't have anything to coordinate."[38]

The battle cost all sides dearly. Allied unit casualties totaled more than 600 dead and nearly 3,800 wounded and missing. Allied estimates of NVA and VC dead ranged from 2,500 to 5,000 troops.[39]

Just as speculative were the size and number of enemy units participating in the one-month battle. Allied intelligence officers initially identified at least three North Vietnamese regimental headquarters. Later they confirmed battalions from at least four more NVA regiments. Allied intelligence estimated that from sixteen to eighteen enemy battalions took part in the battle. Some of these battalions were supposed to have been at Khe Sanh. From 8,000 to 11,000 enemy troops participated in the fighting for Hue in the city itself or its approaches. American intelligence officers believed that a forward headquarters of the Tri-Thien-Hue front under a North Vietnamese general officer directed the Hue offensive.[40]

Given both the resources that the North Vietnamese put into the battle and the tenacity with which they fought, it was obvious they placed a high premium on Hue. The North Vietnamese planners viewed Hue as the weak link in the allied defenses in the north.

Once in Hue, the Communists established their own civil government, and their cadres rounded up known government officials, sympathizers, and foreigners. After the recapture of Hue, South Vietnamese authorities exhumed some three thousand bodies thrown into hastily dug graves. The North Vietnamese admitted tracking down and punishing "hoodlum ringleaders" but denied killing innocent civilians.[41]

Only the failure of the North Vietnamese to overrun the Mang Ca and MACV compounds permitted the allies to retain a toehold in both the

Citadel and the new city. This enabled the allies to bring in reinforcements, albeit piecemeal. If the enemy had blown the An Cuu Bridge on the first day, the Marines would not have been able to bring their initial battalions and supplies into the city.[42]

General Truong told the 1st Cavalry commander that if "I could ever get the Cav to the walls of Hue, the enemy would 'bug out.'" The 1st Air Cavalry Division eventually positioned itself to commit a four-battalion brigade to the battle. The problem was that it took twenty-two days for the 3d Brigade to fight its way there.[43]

Although the Viet Cong and the North Vietnamese harassed ship traffic in the Perfume River, they made no serious attempt to close the waterways. Even with the An Cuu Bridge closed for over a week, the Marines had stockpiled and brought in enough supplies by boat to support operations in both the Citadel and southern Hue. If the enemy cut both the water and land lines of communication, the outcome of the struggle for Hue would have been less predictable.[44]

Although desiring a general uprising during Tet, the Communists may realistically have had a more limited and attainable goal in mind. Perhaps they hoped that the capture of Hue would result in the defection of the South Vietnamese forces and the loss of other population centers in the two northern provinces of South Vietnam. Such a result would have cut the allied lines of communication and left the 3d Marine Division isolated in fixed positions bordering the DMZ and Laos. This would have left the Communists in a strong position for obtaining their own terms.

In any event, Tet served as a benchmark for both sides, forcing them to reassess their strategies. The United States determined the extent of its commitment to Vietnam and began turning more of the war over to the South Vietnamese. After August 1968, the Communists scaled down their large unit war, probably out of both weakness and the expectation that the Americans would eventually withdraw. Tet taught both sides that there was to be no quick fix.

Jack Shulimson

Notes

While I am employed by the Marine Corps Historical Center, the opinions expressed above are my own and in no way represent the views of the U.S. Marine Corps or the U.S. government. — J.S.

1. For Westmoreland's doubts about the Marine command, see Historical Summary, General Entry, 27 Dec 67– 31 Jan 68, v. 28, pp. 19–21, History File, William C. Westmoreland Papers, CMH. See also Diary entry, 26–27 Jan 68, LtGen John R.

Chaisson Papers (Hoover Institution on War, Peace and Revolution, Stanford University).

2. MACV ComdHist, 1968, pp. 881–83.

3. FMFPac, MarOpsV, Jan 68, pp. 18–20 and Feb 68, pp. 8–10; Truong Sinh, "The Fight to Liberate the City of Hue," pp. 90, 93–95, 97; Lung, *The General Offensives,* p. 79; Pham Van Son, *Tet Offensive,* p. 249; Waldron and Beaver, "Operation Hue City," pp. 7–8; "The Battle of Hue," (3dMarDiv ComdC), pp. 2–3.

4. Nolan, *Battle for Hue,* pp. 6–8; Truong Sinh, "The Fight to Liberate the City of Hue," p. 101; 1st Mar AAR Hue City; People's Liberation Army Forces List of Military Objectives in Hue, Jan 68, trans (Hue Folder, Tet Box, A&S Files, Indochina Archives).

5. 1/1 ComdC, Jan 68; 1st Mar Div Sit Rep No. 1, Hue City, dated 3 Feb 68, Hue City Jnl & Msg File; TF X-Ray ComdC, Jan 68; TF X-Ray AAR Hue City; 1st Mar AAR Hue City; LaHue debriefing; "History of Task Force X-Ray," n.d., Attachment to Col A. J. Poillon, Comments on draft ms, dated 30 Oct 69, Donnelly and Shore, "Ho Chi Minh's Gamble," (Comment File). TF X-Ray AAR, pp. 9–10; III MAF Jnl and Msg File, passim., 30–31 Jan 68.

6. Ibid.; Nolan, *Battle for Hue,* pp. 12–13; Gravel interview; Medal of Honor Recommendations, dated 25 May 68, in Sgt Alfredo Gonzalez Biographical File (RefSec, MCHC); Paul Drew Stevens, editor, *The Navy Cross, Vietnam, Citations of Awards to Men of the United States Navy and the United States Marine Corps, 1964–1973,* (Forest Ranch, CA: Sharp & Dunnigan, 1987), pp. 27–28, 54.

7. Gravel interview pp. 5–6; 1st Mar AAR Hue City; 1st MarDiv AAR, Tet, p. 56; 1st MarDiv COC Notes, 31 Jan 68 (III MAF Msg & Jnl File); LaHue debriefing.

8. Gravel interview, pp. 5–6; Nolan, *Battle for Hue,* p. 20.

9. 1st Mar AAR Hue City; Gravel interview, pp. 7–8; Cheatham et al., presentation, p. 23; 1st Mar Div COC Notes, 0001-0900, 1 Feb 68, III MAF Msg & Jnl File.

10. LaHue debriefing; Westmoreland message to Wheeler, 31 Jan 68, Westmoreland Messages, Westmoreland Papers, CMH.

11. 1st Mar AAR Hue City, p. 11.

12. 1st Mar AAR Hue City, p. 13; Cpl George E. Minor interview in Cheatham et al. interview Tape 2511; 1st MarDiv SitRep No. 1, 3 Feb 68 (Hue City Jnl & Msg File).

13. Cheatham et al. presentation, p. 24; 1st Mar AAR Hue City, p. 14; 2/5 AAR Hue City.

14. III MAF SitRep No. 5, Hue City, 4 Feb 68 (Hue City Jnl & Msg File) and 1st Mar AAR Hue, p. 15; Gravel interview, pp. 18–19.

15. TF X-Ray, AAR Hue City, p. 11; 1st Mar AAR Hue City, pp. 15 and 18; 1st MarDiv Sit Rep, Hue, No. 7, 4 Feb 68 (Hue City Jnl & Msg File).

16. Cheatham et al. presentation, p. 17.

17. Gravel interview, pp. 15, 19; 1st Mar AAR Hue City, p. 18.

18. Cheatham et al. presentation, p. 56.

19. 2/5 AAR Hue City; 1st Mar AAR Hue City, pp. 24–34.

20. 1stMarDiv Sit Rep No. 33, 11 Feb 68 (Hue City Jnl & Msg File); Bedford et al. interview, Tape 2673.

21. 1st ARVN Adv Det, "The Battle of Hue;" 1st Mar AAR, Opn Hue City.

22. U.S. Army, 14th Mil Hist Det, 1st Cav Div (AM), "The Battle of Hue, 2–26 February 1968," dated 10 Mar 68 (copy in Nolan Papers), hereafter 14th MHD, "The

Battle of Hue," Mar 68; 1st Mar AAR, Opn Hue City; Braestrup, *Big Story,* vol. I, pp. 316–17.

23. 1st Infantry Division Advisory Detachment, Advisory Team 3, CAAR, Opn NVA/VC Tet Offensive: Hue, dated 30 Mar 68 (copy in Nolan Papers), hereafter 1st InfDiv, Adv Tm 3, CAAR, Hue; TF X-Ray AAR, Opn Hue City; Maj Talman C. Budd II, MAU, NAG, CAAR, Hue City, dated 25 Jul 68; Pham Van Son et al., *The Viet Cong Tet Offensive,* pp. 256–59.

24. 1st Mar AAR, Opn Hue City; 1/5 AAR, Opn Hue City; Col Robert H. Thompson letter to Keith B. Nolan, 16 Sep 80 with attached copy of briefing map (Nolan Papers), hereafter Thompson letter, 16 Sep 80; 1/5 Frag O 6–68, 9 Feb 68, Encl 1, 1/5 AAR Hue City, 15 Mar 68; 1/5 AAR, Hue City.

25. 1/5 AAR, Opn Hue City; Thompson letter, 16 Sep 80.

26. 1/5 AAR, Hue City.

27. Ibid.

28. Budd, AAR and Pham Van Son, *Tet Offensive,* 257–59; Pham Van Son, *Tet Offensive,* pp. 262–66; 1st ARVN Adv Det, "The Battle of Hue," p. 8; Waldron and Beavers, "Operation Hue City," p. 38.

29. III MAF COC message to MACV(J2), 17 Feb 68 (III MAF Jnl & Msg File). See also Hallmark 62 message to Hallmark 6, Hue City SitRep, 17 Feb 68, App 5, Tab C, 1st FAG ComdC, Feb 68 and Alexander W. Wells, Jr., "Synopsis From Combat Report: February 1968—Vietnam," in Alexander W. Wells, Jr. Papers, MCHC.

30. Waldron and Beavers, "Operation Hue City," pp. 42–43; Pham Van Son, *The Viet Cong Tet Offensive,* p. 267; Maj Talman C. Budd II, MAU, NAG, CAAR, Hue City, dated 25 Jul 68; Lung, *The General Offensives,* p. 83.

31. Clark Dougan, Stephen Weiss, and the editors of Boston Publishing Company, *The Vietnam Experience: Nineteen Sixty-Eight* (Boston, Ma: Boston Publishing Company, 1983), p. 30; Clipping, Lee Lescaze, "Shortage of Men, Air Support Slows Marine Drive in Hue," *Washington Post,* 19 Feb 68, Braestrup Papers. The 1st Marine Division responded to obvious concern by higher headquarters. Although not disputing the accuracy of Lescaze's article, a division message explained that weather permitted fixed-wing support only on three days, 14–16 February 68. Because of the need for accuracy, the division stated it used only 8-inch howitzer and naval gunfire in support of the battalion. It admitted that "1/5 casualties have been high. During past week, priority of personnel replacement has been given to the 5th Marines." (1st MarDiv message to CGFMFPac, 21 Feb 68, Encl 14, 1st MarDiv ComdC, Feb 68).

32. Abrams message to Cushman, info: Westmoreland, 20 Feb 68 and Abrams message to Tolson, 20 Feb 68 (Abrams Papers, CMH).

33. 14th MHD, "The Battle of Hue, " Mar 68, pp. 5–6; Waldron and Beavers, "Operation Hue City," pp. 43–47.

34. Thompson letter, 16 Sep 80; AP dispatch, 22 Feb 68, Clipping in Polk Folder (Nolan Papers, MCHC); 1/5 AAR Hue City.

35. Budd, AAR; Abrams message to Westmoreland, 23 Feb 68 (Abrams Papers, CMH).

36. Budd, AAR; 1st InfDiv, Adv Tm 3, CAAR, Hue; 1/5 AAR Hue City; Thompson letter, 16 Sep 80.

37. 1st Marines AAR Hue City; 2/5 AAR Hue City; 1/5 AAR Hue City; Cheatham et al. presentation, pp. 11–12, 28–29.

38. Budd, AAR and LtCol Joseph W. Malcolm, Jr., debriefing at FMFPac, 28 Oct 68, Tape 3453 (Oral HistColl, MCHC).

39. TF X-Ray AAR Hue City; 1st InfDiv, Adv Tm 3, CAAR, Hue; Budd, AAR; 14th MHD, "The Battle of Hue," Mar 68; 1st Bde, 101st Airborne Div, CAAR, Opn Hue City, 23 Mar 68, encl 5, TF X-Ray AAR Hue City; Pham Van Son, *The Tet Offensive*, p. 271. The breakdown of casualties among the Marine infantry battalions are as follows: The 1st Battalion, 5th Marines sustained 67 dead and 403 wounded. The incomplete 2d Battalion, 5th Marines after-action report does not show total Marine casualties but the battalion's command chronology for February shows 65 Marines killed and 421 wounded. It can be assumed that over 90 percent of these casualties occurred during the Hue City fighting. The 1st Battalion, 1st Marines did not submit an after-action report for Hue, but its command chronology for February reflects 17 dead and 154 wounded. Again it can be assumed that the bulk of the casualties occurred in the Hue City fighting. 1/5 AAR Hue City; 2/5 ComdC, Feb 68; 1/1 ComdC, Feb 68.

40. Ibid.; 1st Lt John R. Morse, USA, Thua Thien Sector, S-2 Order of Battle Advisor in Hue, RVN, interview, 8 Mar 68 (U.S. Army, 45th Military History Detachment, Interview Enclosures Folder, Nolan Papers, MCHC); I Corps, Tactical Opns Center to III MAF, Resume of Telecon, 6 Feb 68 (Hue City III MAF Msg & Jnl File); Rand Interview No. 28 in Interviews concerning the NLF, May 68, Folder 2, Tet Box, A&S Files, Indochina Archives.

41. Truong Sinh, "The Fight to Liberate the City of Hue," pp. 105–107; and Pham Van Son, *The Tet Offensive*, pp. 271–84; Westmoreland and Sharp, *Report on the War*, p. 160; Lung, *The General Offensives*, p. 85; Oberdorfer, *Tet!*, pp. 232–33; Braestrup, *Big Story*, vol. I, pp. 201–16. For contrasting views of the Hue "massacres," see Douglas Pike, "Viet Cong Strategy, New Face of Terror," and D. Gareth Porter, "The 1968 Hue Massacre" in Hue Tet Folder, A&S Files, Indochina Archives.

42. Gravel interview, pp. 2–3.

43. 14th MHD, "The Battle of Hue," Mar 68; Tolson interview, p. 5.

44. 1/5 AAR Hue City; Thompson letter, 16 Sep 80.

PHASE LINE GREEN

Chapter One

A Conversation with a Dead Dog

14 February 1968, 1040 hours

The small room in which I stood was as empty as my soul. The room contained no signs of human habitation. It looked as though it had been abandoned long ago. I knew that its previous occupants had probably departed only a few days before I had arrived, having taken all their belongings with them. Now the room was merely a dim, dusty space: four walls, a rude wooden floor, and a badly stained ceiling. The only illumination in the room came from its three doorways, two of which were now permanently open, the doors having been ripped off their hinges. The room was the back one of two rooms that defined a little, nondescript house sitting about twenty-five feet back from phase line green, or Mai Thuc Loan (pronounced "My Took Low-an") as the Vietnamese called it.

For the first time in many days, I was alone. My only company was the scratchy static and the staccato voices of radio traffic coming from the "Prick-25" (PRC-25) that had been hastily strapped to my Marine Corps–issue backpack.

As a platoon commander for Charlie Company, First Battalion, Fifth Marines, I was unaccustomed to carrying the heavy radio, which, under normal circumstances, would be lugged around by a Marine radio operator. But nothing that had happened in the past two weeks could be considered normal. On the contrary, virtually everything that had happened recently could only be described—quite tamely, I might add—as completely abnormal.

At that exact moment, standing in the dim and empty room, I had become the most contemptible of human characters, a commander with no one to command. As of the previous day, 13 February 1968, the platoon of Marines that I had been commanding for the past three months, the group of young men called Charlie One, was history. Charlie One had been virtually destroyed on the street called phase line green, by a combination of a large force of determined NVA regulars and the rules of engagement established by American and South Vietnamese politicians.

Although my mind was filled with the horrors that had befallen Charlie One yesterday, I didn't have time to dwell on them, since I still had a job to do. Charlie Company's commanding officer, 1st Lt. Scott Nelson, had handed me the damnable Prick-25 and had given me the mission of moving up to this house to act as a company forward observer, or FO, for the sixty-millimeter mortar crews, in an effort to keep the NVA's heads down as Alpha Company assaulted them across phase line green.

I guess Scott Nelson wasn't too terribly worried about me, or his own problems were more important than worrying about a young second lieutenant who had just had his platoon wiped out. Or perhaps he gave me this assignment because he *was* worried about me. Whatever his motivation, he had come to me early that afternoon and had asked for my help.

"Charlie One," Nelson had said, his struggling mustache quivering slightly as he spoke in his young but clear and forceful voice, "Alpha Company is preparing to assault across phase line green in a couple of hours, and Charlie Company is going to provide a base of fire on their right flank. You know the ground on phase line green better than anyone else, and I'd like you to get up as close to their attack positions as possible to act as forward observer for the sixty-mike-mikes (sixty-millimeter mortars). I want to drop some sixties in on top of the gooks, just across the street in front of Charlie Three, to keep their heads down during Alpha's assault."

Nelson pointed to a spot on his 1:10,000 map and continued, "I figure you can work your way up behind this courtyard wall, just behind the houses on phase line green. The wall will give you decent cover and still put you in a good position to call in the sixties. Take the spare Prick-25 and start directing fire as soon as you get into position."

What the hell, I had thought. I was tired of breaking down sixty-mike-mike ammo crates and tired of ignoring the sidelong glances of the mortar teams. Despite the horror of the previous day and my instinctive efforts to find shelter, to try to survive, I just felt funny hanging out in the rear. I rigged up my pack so that it rode on the back of the Prick-25, picked up Estes's M-16, and took off in the direction of phase line green.

Although I was somewhat hindered by the combined weight of my still-full pack and the heavy Prick-25, I made steady progress, moving as quickly as possible from house to house, back toward the street that had been the scene of Charlie One's destruction. I had to stay inside the buildings as much as possible, because this block was dominated by open courtyards, and the houses on the other, enemy, side of phase line green were all two-story structures, giving the waiting NVA soldiers excellent fields of fire.

I had arrived at this small house within a few minutes, entered through the rear door, and made sure it was empty. The house consisted of two empty rooms, both unoccupied. The small house's front room offered little protection from enemy fire. The front of the house was lined with many windows, their glass panes long since shattered and useless, offering excellent visibility for the enemy and little safety for the Marines. And because it sat about twenty feet back from the street, occupants of the house had a poor view of the street. That was why it was empty.

Forcing myself to address the task at hand, I ventured a couple of quick peeks out the side door of the back room and then sat down just inside the empty portal, with my back against the wall, facing away from the enemy. Grabbing the Prick-25's handset, I called in my first fire mission: "Charlie Six, this is Charlie Five. Fire Mission, over."

The reply came immediately: "Charlie Five, this is Six. Ready for Fire Mission, over."

I said, "Six, this is Five. One round Hotel Echo, map coordinates 76202299. Request call shot, over."

Although I didn't have a lot of experience calling in supporting fire missions, I did know enough to do four things right. First, I remembered to use the eight-digit map coordinate and not to use the reference points that we used to call in our own positions. If we were being monitored by the enemy, it would be very simple to break our reference point codes if we used them to call in fire missions. The enemy could start with the obvious impact point of the fire mission and work backward, reverse engineering our reference points.

Second, I knew that "Hotel Echo" is military jargon for "H. E.," or high explosive. If I had wanted a white phosphorus round, I would have asked for "Whiskey Poppa," but this was definitely a Hotel Echo situation.

Third, I knew enough to call in a single first round, to make damned sure that the sixty-mike-mike gunners and I were coordinated. The maps we used in Vietnam were suspect at best. Although my new 1:10,000 map showed the actual locations of each house on the street, I didn't want to make a rookie mistake and call in a "fire for effect" only to find out the hard way that the map coordinates were off by just a little bit. Our front line troops were very close to the enemy, within twenty or thirty meters, and I would hate like hell to call in a fire mission that ended up with friendly casualties. High-explosive rounds are very effective when called in correctly on the enemy. High explosives can screw up your whole day, however, if you don't get it right.

Worrying about that aspect of my new job, my mind flashed briefly back to late November 1967, Charlie One's Hoi An days. When I had first arrived in the Hoi An area, located about forty kilometers south of Da Nang, I had already heard of many incidents where young platoon commanders had called in supporting artillery fire during a firefight and, in the heat of battle, skipped the first "spotter" round. They called for an immediate "fire for effect" and accidentally dropped four or six or eight 105-mm or 155-mm artillery rounds on their own position, making a bad situation terrible.

So I had been extremely careful calling in my first artillery fire mission. Unfortunately, the results had become an often-told joke in Charlie One. Worse, it could easily have been a tragedy. It took place during my first month in country. I was learning the ropes, so to speak, and one of the most difficult challenges at that point was to make damned sure that I always knew exactly where we were, in case we needed to call in artillery support or other heavy firepower. This had been especially important in the Hoi An area, which was geographically dominated by rice paddies and low, rolling sand dunes. The area around Hoi An had very few distinctive terrain features that could be used as reference points to determine either your own or the enemy's positions. Our 1:50,000 terrain maps were at least ten years old, and the trails and streams marked on them were often hopelessly incorrect.

To pinpoint our location, I called in a fire mission, asking for a single smoke round from a 105-mm battery, to be detonated at a map location that I had estimated to be at least one kilometer away from Charlie One's location. The theory was that when I saw the smoke round detonate, I could point my compass at its location and then run a "back azimuth" to our location. I could then estimate our distance from the smoke round, thereby pinpointing our location on the map.

The 105-mm smoke round detonated right above our heads, and the heavy, expended canister struck the soft ground exactly in the center of our hasty perimeter. It scared the shit out of me, and generated many uneasy sidelong glances from the Marines of Charlie One over the next few days.

Sitting in my open door inside that small house within the Citadel of Hue, within fifty meters of the enemy and knowing that friendly troops were very close to the intended impact point, I cautiously called in a single first round. The map coordinates were the location of a house just across phase line green that was, we hoped, a currently occupied enemy position.

The fourth thing I did right as I now sat within the Citadel was to ask them to radio me with the message, "Shot," when they fired. A few moments passed, and then the familiar thunking pop of a sixty-millimeter mortar round being launched from its tube punctuated the sounds of sporadic small-arms fire that had been our background music throughout the day. My Prick-25 squawked the confirmation that this was a friendly mortar round. "Shot, out."

The next five seconds slowed maddeningly and refused to tick off. Since the Charlie Company mortar positions were less than a hundred meters behind my position, the trajectory of this mortar round was nearly vertical. And, although our gunners were well trained and had a good reputation for accuracy, until the first round exploded, you just never knew where the damned thing was going to land. Waiting for those slow seconds to tick off, my still-numb mind perversely returned to the fire base at Phu Loc 6. I relived the long nights of constant terror, of hearing the firing of incoming enemy mortar and rocket fire, and waiting for the inevitable explosions. I remembered the persistent, inescapable question: Would this be the one that would land right on top of my head, or worse, in my lap?

None of these thoughts prepared me for the shattering explosion that ripped apart the shrubbery just outside my door and threw violent chunks of shrapnel, dirt, and brush through the open door. The sharp, powerful flame from the high-explosive mortar round illuminated the dim room, and the concussion of the mortar round's detonation shoved me away from the door and deafened my left ear. Instantly, dust, small chunks of dirt, and cordite fumes filled the small room.

Rolling back upright and without thinking, I looked out the door and immediately saw the sixty-mike-mike's tailfin sitting in the middle of a newly blasted hole in the ground about two feet outside the door and slightly toward the street. I reached out the door and retrieved the explosion-hot tailfin with no difficulty. Tossing the tailfin gingerly back and forth between my hands like a hot potato, I then dropped it onto the floor between my legs and keyed the handset of the Prick-25 with my right hand. In a completely detached voice that I cannot possibly attribute to my real self, I said, "Add fifty, fire for effect."

The Charlie Company mortar team answered immediately, confirming my adjustment, "Roger, add fifty, fire for effect," and within moments they started pouring sixty-millimeter high-explosive rounds just across the street, right on top of the enemy positions. I told them to walk the rounds left and right and away from us, but not to fire anything closer than my initial adjustment, "Add fifty, fire for effect." My adjustment dictated that they add fifty meters to the trajectory of the first round and start firing as rapidly as possible for as long as possible. The mortar team's response was accurate and continuous over the next several minutes.

A few minutes later, Scott Nelson burst through the back door of my hide hole, took one look at me, and said, "Jesus, Charlie One, what the hell happened here?" Nelson was having as hard a time terminating my Charlie One call sign as I was, but I let it go without comment. In fact, I said nothing but simply handed him the sixty-mike-mike tailfin and pointed out the side door to the small crater, and he understood everything.

Nelson grinned at me and said, "Jesus, that was close. Good shooting, though. The sixties are blasting away at the gook positions just on the other side of the street."

Never one to allow anyone to rest on his laurels for long, Nelson let me know right away that this was not a pleasure visit. He wanted me to get closer to the corner, so he pointed out the opposite door to a low wall surrounding a courtyard about fifty feet away. "I'd like you to get over behind that wall and monitor the battalion frequency. Alpha Company is going to assault across phase line green in a few minutes, and I want you as close as possible."

I started to make some lame commentary about snipers and machine guns in the enemy positions in the second floors of the buildings just across phase line green, about their great fields of fire looking right down our throat, and about having to run across fifty feet of open ground to get to the questionable safety of the low wall. But from the look on his face, Nelson had pretty much decided that I was going over there, so I just nodded. He looked in my eye for a long moment and finally grinned again and said, "Hey, no big deal. I'll go with you. It's not very far, and we'll catch them sleeping up there. Ready?"

We stood in the doorway for a moment, each of us grabbing the door jamb on our respective sides. Thinking, "What the hell, over?" we pulled ourselves out of the doorway and ran into the open courtyard.

If the enemy gunners were sleeping, they woke up very quickly, as the rate of fire increased with each long stride we took. Hellishly, inevitably, the scene ratcheted down into an agonizingly lethargic slow motion. It seemed like the faster we ran toward that low wall, the slower we went and the more the enemy shot at us. I was again trapped in a recurring nightmare of frustration, trying to run as fast as possible to avoid the NVA gunners' fire, and feeling as though my feet were wrapped in concrete boots.

I started giggling. I don't know why. I just couldn't help myself. There was nothing funny about any of this, but a bad case of the insane giggles took hold of my mind and refused to release me. The giggles probably saved my life, because they bent me over double. I was still running as fast as I could, however, neck and neck with Scott Nelson, when something tugged at my back, and I started to stumble and turn. Laughing, choking, stumbling, and finally crash-rolling to the ground, I scrambled the last couple of feet to the safety of the wall.

Winded but temporarily safe from enemy gunfire, Scott Nelson and I took inventory of each other for a few minutes as we caught our breath. The enemy gunners were shooting the hell out of the wall and surrounding area, but the Charlie Three Marines were returning their fire and the Charlie Company mortar team was still raining high explosives on them as well. The wall turned out to be thicker and more protective than it had seemed from a distance, so we were pretty safe in our new position, as long as we kept our heads down.

Scott Nelson caught his breath first. He looked over at me and asked, "You okay, Charlie One? That was freaking unbelievable. What the hell were you laughing at, anyway?" Nelson persisted in calling me Charlie One, and I didn't make any effort to correct him.

I grinned for a moment myself and said, "I have no idea, Skipper, I just couldn't help it." I really did have no idea what had started the laughing fit, but I knew why I was grinning now; we had made it across, and neither of us had been hit. "Yeah, I'm fine. Thanks for the company."

Nelson stayed with me for a few more minutes while I dialed in to the battalion frequency and made sure that the Prick-25 was in good operating condition. Then he took one more look in my eyes and said, "Okay. Keep your head down, and check in with me every hour or so."

With that, Nelson gathered up his bulky frame and took off across the open ground back toward the house we had just abandoned. The enemy gunners opened up on him again right away, and dust kicked up at his feet from the impact of several AK-47 rounds, but he was just too damned fast for them. Scott Nelson was a two-hundred-pound giant, but he could really move fast when he needed to!

I spent the remaining daylight hours of that day, 14 February 1968, hunkered down behind the low but protective wall, constantly monitoring the battalion and company radio nets. My only company for the rest of the day was a dead dog. Its bloated body was several feet further down the wall and I had not noticed it at first. Soon after Scott Nelson left, however, the unmistakable scent of death wafted across my nostrils and drew my attention toward the remains of this unfortunate animal.

The dog hadn't been dead more than a couple of days, because it wasn't completely bloated like many other animals I had seen that had cooked for days on end in the relentless Vietnam sunshine. The terrible heat and humidity of Vietnam caused their bodies to swell to two or three times their normal size, forcing their legs to stick out stiff and straight. The overall effect of this postmortem process made them look like obscene pincushions. In this case, the smell of death emanating from the dog, although not very pleasant, was not intolerable, and the dog was not a pincushion yet.

Upon closer inspection, I found that I was not the first person who had visited this dog after his death, because he had a plastic C ration spoon sticking out of his mouth. This was someone's idea of dark humor, I supposed, but I did nothing to change the scene. Somehow it looked right, and if you had eaten more than a few C ration meals, the humor was inescapable; this dog had obviously been done in by some bad Ham and Lima Beans. Ham and Lima Beans, or Ham and Lunkers, or Ham and Mutherfuckers, as they were often called, were universally reviled as the worst C ration meal ever.

I looked over at the dog and said, "Hey, dog, what the hell happened, over? Didn't anyone teach you about Ham and Lunkers? Shit, man, you should have listened to your squad leader." My mind was in a place that allowed for this kind of conversation—no, that *required* this kind of conversation. It was a diversion from the previous day of horror, and as long as I was having a conversation, I wasn't thinking about any of that. I sometimes think that without that dog to keep me company during that long and hellish afternoon, I would have lost my mind, gone totally bonkers. I might have even started shooting Estes's M-16 at the enemy positions. Because the hell that Charlie One had endured the previous day was happening all over again. Alpha Company had started their attack across phase line green, and they were being slaughtered.

As the cycle of death on phase line green began once again, my mind went into a sort of hibernation while my external self went through the motions of living in a combat zone. Ignoring the dead dog for a while, I mentally traveled back in time to the night when it all had changed.

Chapter Two

The Longest Night

31 January 1968

An entire generation of Americans remembers exactly what they were doing on the morning of 7 December 1941. Another generation remembers exactly where they were when they heard that President Kennedy was assassinated. Like them, for every American serving in South Vietnam at the time, 31 January 1968 is a date that will "live in infamy." During the late night hours of 30 January and the early morning hours of 31 January, another generation of Americans was shocked to learn that the world as they knew it had been changed, dramatically, literally overnight.

Although American forces had been deeply involved in the civil struggle between the North and South Vietnamese since the early 1960s, up until that fateful night the Vietnam War was largely a pastoral war. It was an unbalanced clash between the world's strongest military power and a poorly armed but deadly and elusive enemy force of ragtag soldiers called the Viet Cong.

Before 31 January 1968, most stateside Americans believed that it was only a matter of time before the pesky VC would be subdued. The notion of defeat was simply inconceivable. Although a few antiwar demonstrations had spontaneously erupted across the nation before that pivotal date, the demonstrations would now grow into intense and organized public resistance to a war that was escalating dramatically with ever-mounting casualties. As the public attitude toward the Vietnam War was dramatically changing, the reality for those fighting the war was also changing.

Prior to 31 January 1968, the Marines of Charlie Company, First Battalion, Fifth Marine Regiment (1/5), had become somewhat accustomed to long periods of boredom, shattered occasionally by a few minutes of the terrors found in the "battles" that the Viet Cong chose to fight. Long, strenuous, and unproductive patrols throughout the South Vietnam countryside were the order of the day. Throughout the long months of November and December 1967 and January 1968, the Marines of Charlie Company spent all their time conducting long, strenuous, somehow boring and yet terrifying patrols in the Hoi An and Phu Loc 6 areas of operations, or AOs. And then it all changed.

In the very early morning hours of 31 January, I awoke abruptly, my mouth fouled with the nasty taste of Southeast Asian humidity and not enough sleep. A strong feeling of panic welled up inside my guts. Although I was not wide awake, I was fully aware that something was wrong, badly wrong. Numerous explosions had rudely awakened me. I was not yet sure if they were real or the audio components of a vivid, very bad dream.

I checked the luminous dial of my Marine Corps–green, standard-issue plastic wristwatch; it was 0100 hours, an hour before Benny Benwaring, platoon radio operator for Charlie One, was supposed to wake me for my part of the watch. A myriad of conflicting thoughts rushed through my sleep-addled brain as I struggled to clear the cobwebs. These explosions were definitely not dream-generated explosions, because I was fully awake now, and they were still shattering the night. There was no particular pattern to them, no consistency like what you would expect during a mortar or rocket attack. About the only thing that I knew for sure was that the explosions were very large and, fortunately, quite a distance away from our present location. Although the sounds of distant explosions are often tricky in this type of terrain, it sounded like they were at least a few kilometers to the south, up Highway One on the Hai Van Pass.

As my eyes adjusted to the early morning blackness, I automatically scanned my surroundings. Although I couldn't see many of them, I knew that the Marines of Charlie One were there, silent and invisible, quietly sitting in their two-man perimeter positions surrounding the Charlie

One Command Post (CP). The Charlie One CP group included myself; Benny Benwaring, my radio operator; SSgt. John A. Mullan, our platoon sergeant; and "Doc" Lowdermilk, one of the two Navy corpsmen assigned to Charlie One. The CP was situated roughly in the center of Charlie One's perimeter, which was about a hundred meters in diameter. We were located about five hundred meters south of, and roughly one hundred meters above, the Lang Co Bridge. We were dug in on a low scrub- and jungle-covered "finger" of the towering, threatening mountain range that dominated the Dam Lap An Bay. The finger was covered with a thick scrub brush that afforded us some cover and concealment but was low enough to provide us some visibility of the surrounding terrain.

Our mission was to protect the Lang Co Bridge. The Lang Co Bridge was the longest bridge between Da Nang and the DMZ. It was also one of the few bridges along Highway One not protected by a cordon of barbed wire. Because of the bridge's exposure, I had chosen to stay mobile and remain off the bridge during the long, dark nights, instead of taking up positions on the bridge itself.

For the past few days, since we had arrived in the Lang Co area, Charlie One had set up in platoon-sized ambush positions in a different location each night. Our mission was to stop any enemy approach to the strategically important bridge. Another Charlie Company platoon, Charlie Three, had the job of protecting the bridge structure itself. They typically stayed on the bridge with the Charlie Company CP group, or in the village of Lang Co, on the other side of the bridge.

The explosions continued relentlessly. Finally fully awake, I successfully pushed back the initial rush of panic that loud explosions in the night always caused. I reached out to touch Benny Benwaring, who was lying down about a meter to my right in a shallow depression on the damp ground. Benny crawled over to me immediately, his PRC-25 radio already mounted on his back, ready to move out if necessary. It was easy to see, even in the "zero dark thirty" gloom of the early morning hour, why all Marine radio operators referred to their PRC-25 radios as "Prick-25s." The bulky, uncomfortable attachment to Benny's Marine Corps–issue backpack added at least twenty-five pounds to his load, not including the added bulk and weight of several spare batteries. Somehow the tall, skinny Marine managed without a lot of complaining, but I was sure as hell glad that he—and not I—had to carry the Prick-25.

"Nothin' comin' over the company net yet, Lootenant," Benny whispered in his nasal Tennessee twang.

I peered at Benwaring in the dark and asked, "How long has this been going on, Benny?" I had been sound asleep and couldn't be certain that the first explosion had been the one that woke me up.

"Jist a couple a minutes, Lootenant. Sounds like they're all coming from up the Hai Van Pass, but, shit, they ain't nobody much up there tonight except Charlie Two. Jist that antiaircraft missile site at the top of the pass and them damn ARVN gooks at the French compound halfway up. Don't sound like mortars or rockets, more like sappers is havin' a shitpile of fun. And, they ain't a single rifle blowin' caps, at least not raht now." For Benny, this was a long speech, perhaps even a filibuster. To those of us who knew him, speech for Benny Benwaring seemed to be almost painful. Benny was a man of very few words unless he was speaking into the Prick-25, doing his job. When he did talk with his buddies in Charlie One without the assistance of the Prick-25, his speech patterns were quiet and slow, and his face would scrunch up as though the utterance of a few words was somehow more difficult than weight lifting. When the shit hit the fan, however, like when Charlie One got into a firefight or some other scrape and we depended upon Benny's skills as our only link to larger forces or the necessary supplies for a Marine combat platoon in the bush, his speed and volume would increase considerably. But it still seemed to hurt him to talk.

I thought about Benny's assessment of the situation for a few minutes and agreed. We knew that one of our sister platoons, Charlie Two, was on its own up in the Hai Van Pass tonight and was broken down into squad-sized ambushes. They, or more likely the antiaircraft missile site on the pinpoint-sharp mountaintop just above the summit of the Hai Van Pass, which protected the northern air approaches to Da Nang, were probably being hit by Viet Cong sappers. The sappers were the terrorists who sneaked up on you and tossed a few satchel charges at you in the dark of the night.

The Hai Van Pass was aptly named. The Vietnamese word *hai* means "ocean," or "sea," and *van* means "cloud." The Hai Van Pass was definitely a place where the ocean meets the clouds. The Vietnamese highlands, which dominate the western regions of this long, skinny country, thrust eastward toward the sea in this area only a few miles north of Da Nang. The mountainous highlands protruded into the South China Sea north of Da Nang Bay. The Hai Van Pass allowed travelers on Highway One to proceed north to Lang Co and beyond via a twisting, turning two-lane road.

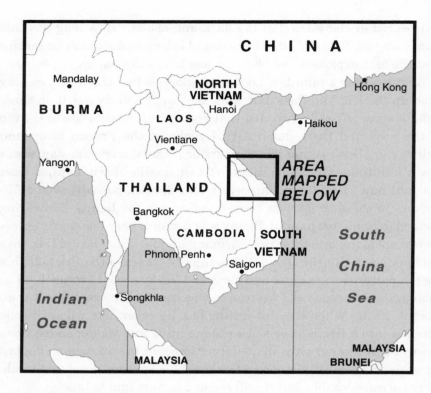

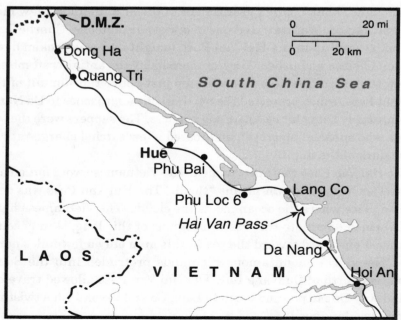

During the past couple of weeks, since moving out of the battalion fire base at Phu Loc 6 in mid-January, Charlie Company, 1/5, had been assigned to the Lang Co AO. The Lang Co AO was a territory that started at the base of the mountain pass about eight kilometers north of the Lang Co Bridge and extended south past the Lang Co village and bridge, up the Hai Van Pass, another ten kilometers, to the top of the pass. The primary mission of Charlie Company in the Lang Co AO was to protect Highway One, the critical, and only, land supply route between Da Nang and the DMZ. If the enemy were allowed to shut down Highway One in the Lang Co AO, the only methods of resupply for the vast American forces north of us would be through the air, or possibly by sea.

The Lang Co village at the north end of the bridge was populated predominantly by Catholic Vietnamese villagers considered friendly to American and Army of the Republic of Vietnam (ARVN) forces. But the area south and west of the Lang Co Bridge, and the entire Hai Van Pass area, were constantly exposed to attacks by the Viet Cong.

From Lang Co, travelers on Highway One crossed the Lang Co Bridge, then proceeded south toward Da Nang. Once across the thousand-foot-long bridge, the road turned sharply left and headed east toward the South China Sea. After meandering east a couple of kilometers along the inlet to the bay, the two-lane dirt highway then made a sharp hairpin turn back due south. At that point, even in daylight, travelers on Highway One were lost from view to those remaining behind on the bridge. The big, lumbering convoys of Army and Marine Corps "six by" trucks and the small, gaudy, overcrowded "gook buses" dominating the constant flow of vehicular traffic north and south on Highway One were seemingly swallowed up by a rugged mountain range that flanked the winding dirt road almost all the way into Da Nang. The ramshackle huts so common on the outskirts of Da Nang began to appear about thirty kilometers south of our position on the bridge.

Well-built reinforced concrete bridges had been erected over the mountain streams crossing Highway One by the French during their many decades of occupation. Between each large stream were several small streams. Culverts in the small streams allowed Highway One to continue steadily, although steeply and precariously, to the top of the pass. The vertical rise from the Lang Co Bridge to the top of the Hai Van Pass was over seven hundred meters. This may not sound like much to the uninitiated, but to those who humped and drove it, Highway One through the Hai Van Pass was like a highway through hell.

Since I had grown up driving the dirt logging roads and back country roads of Southwestern Oregon, I was accustomed to nasty back roads and steep drop-offs. But along Highway One through the Hai Van Pass, I definitely preferred walking. The terrain was extremely rough. The once-paved, now mostly dirt two-lane road rose over six hundred meters (nearly two thousand feet) in just the last three kilometers approaching the top of the pass. The many switchbacks and hairpin turns along the Hai Van pass had terrorized truck drivers for years as convoy after convoy slowly moved their critical supply loads north from Da Nang toward Phu Bai and the critical American and ARVN outposts along the DMZ.

Over the past few weeks, attacks on the convoys in the Hai Van Pass, which seemed to be the Viet Cong's favorite ambush area, had been steadily increasing. Before the end of 1967 only about one in ten convoys had been attacked and damaged at some lonely hairpin curve of the steep and uneven roadway. In early 1968 that percentage rose sharply. The convoy truck driver's mentality was to always maintain as high a speed as possible (with the belief that a fast-moving target is much more difficult to blow up than a slow-moving target), but that was just not possible on this section of the highway. At best, the heavily loaded six-by trucks were forced to shift into a very low gear as they made their way up the steep road at about twenty miles per hour or slower. At a couple hairpin turns they had to come nearly to a stop to stay on the road. In short, the trucks were easy prey for a well-prepared, well-hidden team of Viet Cong equipped with a nasty and deadly variety of high-explosive devices. After detonating their mines or shooting off their rocket-propelled grenade (RPG) rockets, the Viet Cong had an easy escape route up into the high reaches of the silent, jungle-covered mountains.

Since arriving here, Charlie One had spent many long hours patrolling up and down this tortuous section of the Hai Van Pass and the area west and south of the Lang Co Bridge. We never actually *saw* an enemy unit during those two weeks, but several truck convoys were ambushed in broad daylight and suffered spectacular destruction. Even while keeping their feet stomped down on the gas pedal, many convoy truck drivers and those riding "shotgun" with them were killed. Viet Cong ambushes were causing severe damage by hit-and-run tactics and were beginning to disrupt the critical flow of American supplies from Da Nang northward, and they were usually getting away with it.

Charlie Company's new commanding officer, 1st Lt. Scott Nelson, had assumed command from the previous company commander only a couple of days before. So far he had spent most of his time in and around Lang Co village with Charlie Three, leaving the security of the Lang Co Bridge and the Hai Van Pass to Charlie One and Charlie Two. The Delta Company of 1/5 occupied a small artillery firebase that dominated a smaller mountain pass to our north, and they were responsible for their own security. They were important to us, however, since the 105-mm and 155-mm guns at the Delta firebase were the only artillery in range of our positions in the Lang Co AO.

The distant explosions to the southeast continued their sporadic clashing choruses, keeping me on edge. I was very aware and concerned that if Charlie Two was getting hit, we would probably have to react quickly and go to their aid. From this distance, it didn't sound like a fixed position was getting overrun, but rather like H&I (harassment and interdiction) fire. The only problem with that supposition was that the enemy in this area was not supposed to have any heavy artillery or rockets. My mind went back to Benny's theory that we were hearing the results of sappers.

Benny interrupted my thoughts: "Radio traffic from Charlie Two to Six. Wait one." Benny listened in as 2nd Lt. Richard L. Lowder, platoon commander of Charlie Two, communicated with Lieutenant Nelson (Charlie Six). I waited about thirty seconds before Benny spoke again. In a stage whisper, he said, "Shit, them gooks is blowin' the bridges all the way up the Hai Van. Now we'll never get up to that mess hall at that antiaircraft missile base. Damn me all to hell!"

I had heard about the famous mess hall at the antiaircraft missile base, which, due to its proximity to Da Nang and the supposed importance of the base's mission, was constantly supplied with fresh eggs and other culinary delights. I could empathize with Benny's concern. But I was starting to get annoyed with him, since I wanted to know what the hell was going on up in the Hai Van Pass. Marines in combat could think about the strangest things at the most awkward moments, and Benny was no exception.

I grabbed Benny's arm and, in a loud whisper, got his attention: "Dammit, Benny, stop worrying about that skinny gut of yours for a minute, and tell me what's going on!"

"Raht away, Lootenant. Charlie Two Actual says that all the bridges and culverts on our side of the Hai Van Pass has been blowed up! He had Charlie Two broke down into three squads in ambushes, and they were settin' about a hundred meters above Highway One, just off the streams, hopin' to catch Victor Charlie comin' down the mountain. It 'pears that Charlie snuck around all of his ambushes after dark, crossed the road *between* the bridges, and came in from below. Them gooks set charges on all the bridges and culverts, and now there's nothin' left of Highway One. Charlie Two estimates at least twenty major explosions. No contact with any gooks. They just blew the bridges and di-di mau'd." Since I knew that *di-di* means "go," and that *mau* means "fast," I knew that the VC had made themselves scarce.

From my own firsthand experience of the Hai Van Pass, if what Charlie Two had just reported was true, this was not good news. There were at least six or seven large mountain streams that cut across Highway One between our present location and the night ambush sites of Charlie Two. While the destruction of Highway One's bridges and culverts would not pose a problem to Charlie Two's Marines, since they were on foot and could ford the streams without too much difficulty, the loss of those bridges would cut off our food and ammunition supply. Up until this point, our supplies had come via trucks from Da Nang or Phu Bai, the locations of the two largest concentrations of U.S. military personnel in I Corps. If the enemy had succeeded in closing down Highway One even for a short time, it would put a major crimp in the logistical plans of American forces in the northernmost corps (I Corps) of the four designated corps zones. (The "eye" in I Corps is really the Roman numeral one, but no one ever called I Corps "One Corps." The others are called II (two) Corps, III (three) Corps, and so on, but I Corps was always called Eye Corps.)

In the three southernmost corps areas—II Corps, III Corps, and IV Corps—Highway One was an *important* artery of motor vehicle traffic, but it was not the *only* route available. Several other east/west highways were linked by other north/south routes in the highlands of II and III Corps and the Mekong Delta that dominated IV Corps. In I Corps north of Da Nang, Highway One was the *only* north/south route for ground transportation.

My thoughts were rudely interrupted by more distant explosions. But this time, the explosions were louder and were coming from the exact opposite direction of the fireworks that had interrupted my sleep. These explosions were coming from the Delta Company firebase, several kilometers northwest of us. Since we were on relatively high ground and Delta Company's firebase was on even higher ground, with nothing between us but the broad, dark water of Dam Lap An Bay, this fight was clearly visible as well as audible. It was immediately apparent that

Delta Company had come under heavy enemy attack. This time the explosions were accompanied by the syncopative percussion of enemy mortar and rocket fire interspersed with an increasing volume of small-arms fire. Enemy 82-mm mortar rounds and the enemy's deadly RPG rockets were easily distinguishable as they impacted various points within Delta Company's firebase. Red and white tracers from small-arms fire erupted with a surprising intensity, the red tracers emanating from the position we knew to be Delta Company's firebase; the white or light green enemy tracers tracking inward from the enemy positions above and westward of the firebase. The shit was hitting the fan big time at the Delta Company firebase.

"Jesus H. Christ. What the fuck is going on?" I thought I was thinking this, but I must have muttered it out loud, because Benny answered, "I don't know, Lootenant, but it sure as shit looks like the whole fuckin' area around us is gettin' blowed away."

"No shit, Benny." Turning away from Benny, I found Staff Sergeant Mullan lying prone a few feet away in the gloomy darkness and whispered to him, "Get word to the squad leaders to put everyone on one hundred percent alert until further notice, and then have them come in here for a quick briefing." Sergeant Mullan grunted acknowledgment and quietly scurried away. I looked over at Benny and said, "Benny, get me Charlie Six Actual on the horn."

The order I had asked Sergeant Mullan to pass on to our three squad leaders was probably unnecessary, but I wasn't taking any chances. I had gotten to know the people around me very well during the past few months, walking with them down the jungle trails and back roads of Vietnam. Our nights in the bush were constantly sleep-impaired, and I was sure that every one of the fifty-one Marines of Charlie One was wide awake and watching the show. It was the nature of the combat Marine in Vietnam to be sound asleep, dreaming exotic dreams of the World one moment, and then the least little noise in the bush, and most certainly any explosion, no matter how distant, would bring him wide awake. But, again, I wasn't taking any chances. Based on what was going on all around us, an attack on the Lang Co bridge could happen anytime.

I also wasn't sure I could tell the squad leaders anything they didn't already know when they got to the platoon CP in a couple of minutes for my briefing, but maybe Lieutenant Nelson could enlighten me.

Benny prodded me with the telephone-receiver-like handset from the Prick-25 and muttered that Charlie Six Actual was on the horn. I grabbed the handset, squeezed the activator, and verbally confirmed that I was listening. "Six Actual, this is Charlie One, over."

The back-and-forth banter of tactical radio conversations had by now become second nature to me in my two and a half months in Vietnam, but it always reminded me a little of playing combat when I was a child, and it made me feel slightly self-conscious. If it were light enough to see, I'm sure that a slight grin would be evident on my face.

I knew that Scott Nelson was grinning as well. I knew he was grinning because over the past several days I had gotten several chances to observe him using the radio since he had assumed command of Charlie Company. Every time I had watched him he had worn this unerasable shit-eating grin, as if he were going out to play a big football game. He looked excited, anticipatory, and seemingly not the least concerned with any threat whatsoever.

First Lieutenant Nelson was a big man, at least six foot two and over two hundred pounds, but he had a baby face and nearly transparent blonde hair, with very few whiskers or mustache hairs. When we were first introduced, after he had extracted himself from the CH-34 helicopter that had dropped him off on a dirt landing zone just south of the bridge, I had experienced instant pangs of doubt and concern. As quickly as possible I had veiled the shocked realization that this seemingly overgrown adolescent was now Charlie Company's "skipper," although no one would refer to him as that until he proved himself in the bush. He had seemed okay over the past several days, but not much had happened, either.

"Charlie One, this is Six Actual. Sit rep, over." Nelson's squawking voice broke my reverie and brought me back to the present.

I answered back, "Six, this is One. We're sitting tight. No contact, but we can see Delta's firefight. We're hearing multiple explosions south of us up the Hai Van Pass. What's Charlie Two's status, over?"

Nelson's voice responded clearly through the squelch of the radio, "Charlie Two has no contact at this time, but they report major damage to bridges and culverts on Highway One. They'll sit tight until first light, and then assess damage and report in. Millbrook Delta is under heavy attack with mortars, rockets, and small arms. Delta should be able to hold their position. You're to sit tight, restrict radio traffic, and maintain security on the bridge. You may come under attack. Adjust your positions as you see fit. I'll be staying over on this side of the bridge with Charlie Three, and we'll protect your backside if things start happening over there. Lang Co Bridge must not be destroyed. You must hold your positions and defend the bridge at all costs. Don't expect much in the way of artillery or air support, it appears all the firebases north and south of us are under attack. I'll let you know when I know more. Over and out."

Nelson sounded as frustrated as I felt. The shit was definitely hitting the fan all around us, but we knew very little about what exactly was going on. The situation in the Lang Co AO had changed dramatically, that was certain. It felt something like being in the eye of a hurricane, but a hurricane whose rain and wind were steel and fire. It was quiet and calm in our immediate vicinity, but the winds of war were raging all around us. As I waited for my squad leaders to report in, I reflected back on the events that had occurred since I had arrived in Vietnam three months earlier.

I arrived in South Vietnam on 15 November 1967, wet behind the ears and scared nearly speechless, although I tried very hard not to let anyone know that dismal fact. My fearful condition had been formulated by a combination of my training experiences and by some information I got, quite by chance, just before I left Quantico for WestPac duty.

I was one of a handful of young men who went through both the Marine Corps' boot camp and the Infantry Training Regiment (ITR) in San Diego and Camp Pendleton, California. I had also gone through Officer's Candidate School and Basic Infantry Officer's Training (Basic School) in Quantico, Virginia. A Marine recruiter convinced me that if I enlisted in the Marine Corps for four years, I could put in for the Marine Corps' MarCad program, where enlisted men were sent to Pensacola, Florida, given Marine Cadet status, and taught how to fly jets. If I got my wings, I would also get a commission.

After three weeks in boot camp, I finally scrounged up the courage to actually speak to a drill instructor, beyond a response to his question or instruction. I provided this particular drill instructor, an E-5 sergeant named Callahan, with a few minutes' entertainment when I asked him, very respectfully, how I could sign up for the MarCad program. When he finally stopped laughing and had wiped the tears from his eyes, he looked at me and, in that singular fashion that only Marine Corps drill instructors can demonstrate, said, "Get the fuck outta my face, shitbird. There ain't no such thing as a MarCad program, and hasn't been since 1962."

Although I had been terribly deceived by my recruiter, I had been in boot camp long enough to see what happened to dissenters. Their punishment was to be sent back to the dreaded "Day 1." I decided to keep my mouth shut and do what I was told. I made the best of it.

A few days before graduation from boot camp, Sergeant Callahan called me into his office. After I went through the now-automatic and obligatory rituals of reporting to the drill instructor, Sergeant Callahan asked me if I had been serious about wanting to fly airplanes. He looked at me with his typical disdain and said, "Although you are still only a shitbird, you have kept your mouth shut and your nose clean. You will graduate as a squad leader, and we will put you up for promotion to PFC outta boot camp. If you really want to fly them damned planes, I'll make you a deal."

I was wary of any "deal" being offered by a Marine DI, but since he seemed sincere, I decided to take a chance. Shouting as loudly as possible, I said, "Sir, the Private is very interested in going to Pensacola, sir."

Sergeant Callahan said, "Okay, shithead. Here's the deal. I give the PFC promotion to one of these other poor slobs who will need it more for his enlisted career, and I recommend you for the Enlisted Commissioning Program. You gotta go to OCS in Quantico, get a commission, and then you gotta put in for Flight School in Pensacola. That's the deal. You wanna try?"

I was well aware that the vast majority of my peers in boot camp would be getting orders to the other OCS (Over the Choppy Seas) as infantrymen, so I figured I had very little to lose by trying. I accepted the deal, and Sergeant Callahan was good for his word. I was accepted into the Enlisted Commissioning Program, completed OCS in the prescribed ten weeks, and got my commission as a second lieutenant in March 1967. I immediately put in a request for Flight School and was told that I would have to complete the twenty-one-week Basic Infantry Officer's School for new Marine officers and that I could request Flight School from there.

It was about halfway through Basic School, in the hot and sweaty summer of 1967, that I was finally told that I was physically unsuitable for Flight School, due to a sinus blockage (having had my nose smashed several times in football games). That was it. I was destined to be a ground pounder.

Although I was never a top scorer in OCS or Basic School, I competed well enough in the challenging physical and mental games of OCS and Basic School to be given my first choice of military occupational specialty (MOS). I decided on Supply. After a year in the military, I had learned two very important things about a profession in logistics: first, a supply sergeant or supply officer was everyone's best friend; second, and probably more importantly, supply officers very seldom left the comfort and security of a rear area.

That was when Capt. Jack Kelly made a significant impact on my life. Captain Jack, or Smilin' Jack, as we called him when he wasn't listening, was our Basic School platoon commander. He was an early veteran of the Vietnam War and had been awarded the Silver Star for his part in Operation Starlight, the largest American combat operation of the war thus far. He was also a very convincing motivator.

During my fifteenth week in Basic School, after I had submitted my request for a Supply MOS, our platoon of forty or so new second lieutenants was on a run out on some deserted dirt road in the back woods of the Marine Corps base in Quantico, Virginia. Since I am over six feet tall, I was running in the front of the platoon, in the position of a squad leader. About halfway through our run, Captain Jack surprised everyone by hollering at me and ordering me to fall out and drop behind. He wanted to have a little chat with me. I dropped out of the formation and fell about fifty feet behind the running platoon, where Captain Jack was trailing.

As I fell into position beside the still-running Smiling Jack, he didn't waste any words. He said, "You've put in for Supply, Lieutenant Warr?" It was a question, but it wasn't a question.

"Yes, sir. I want to be in logistics, sir," I replied.

"Okay, you've earned the right to be given your first choice of MOS, so if that's what you want, that's what you'll get." I continued to look straight ahead, not understanding why we were having this conversation. "But I just want you to consider this one fact before you make up your mind."

"Yes, sir."

"See that shitbird college graduate up there at the end of the formation, Warr?" Kelly didn't have to point for me to understand whom he was talking about. At the end of the formation, a short, very unmilitary young second lieutenant was struggling to keep up with the rest of the men. Every four or five paces, he would get out of step and would either threaten to step on the heels of the man in front of him or fall behind a couple of paces. The increasing human demands of the Vietnam War had resulted in an erosion of the Marine Corps' normally very high standards. Men were being given commissions in the Marine Corps then who, a couple of years before, would never have made it through the first couple weeks of OCS, let alone Basic School. I knew what Kelly was talking about.

"Yes, sir," I said.

"Well, if I give you Supply, that shitbird is going to get Infantry. You have friends from boot camp who are already in the 'Nam, don't you, Warr?" Kelly knew that I had been through boot camp.

"Yes, sir," I replied.

"Well, if that shitbird takes over a platoon in the 'Nam, he's going to get some people killed, if you get my drift. That's the guy that should be a supply officer." Kelly kept up his steady, "recon shuffle" pace, never looking at me during this conversation.

"Yes, sir. If you say so, sir."

"It's your choice, Lieutenant. If you request Supply, I'll give you Supply. On the other hand, I've been watching you, and I think you could make a fine career for yourself in the Marine Corps. Only a few of these men will be given 'regular officer' status when they leave here; most will be reserve officers, and they will get out after their tour is up. Regular officers get their choice of duty assignments and get put on the fast track for promotion. So here's the deal: You request an Infantry MOS, and I'll put you in for a regular commission. Think about it. Now, fall back in with the others."

The next day I requested an Infantry MOS, and true to his word, Captain Kelly put me in for a regular commission. I was a ground pounder and was headed for WestPac.

None of this would have mattered a bit if it hadn't been for one more, seemingly insignificant thing that happened to me while I was still in Basic School. I took a test and didn't fail it. It was called the Army Language Aptitude Test (ALAT), and unlike the vast majority of my peers, I didn't get a rock bottom, 0/0 score. I think I got a 1/2 out of a possible 5/5 score, which indicated some aptitude for a foreign language, at least in comparison to my peers. My now "proven" ability lead to my being assigned to a six-week high-intensity language training program at Quantico right after Basic School, along with eleven other second lieutenants.

For six weeks, eight hours a day, the twelve of us struggled to learn Vietnamese. We didn't think anything of the fact that our instructors were Americans, staff NCOs who had spent tours in Vietnam, or that we were learning the Hanoi dialect. After a few weeks, my classmates and I babbled away at each other and actually seemed to communicate. A two-star general showed up at our graduation and told us that we would be put into strategically important positions where our newfound language skills would help make a difference.

Still, none of this would have made any difference in my military experience whatsoever. In my fifth week of the language school, however, something seemingly insignificant made a serious impact on my state of mind. I just happened to pick up a copy of a military newspaper that reported, every week, the deaths of American fighting men in South Vietnam. I had read this information many times before, had seen the ranks and names of the dead many times before, but until this moment that's all they were: the names and ranks of dead people. Since I didn't know any of them, their death had been totally unreal to me. However, this particular issue listed the names of four or five second lieutenants who, a short five weeks ago, had been my classmates in Basic School. One of them had been the top man in our class. These five young men had left Quantico five weeks ago, had taken their obligatory thirty days' leave, had said goodbye to their friends and families, and had been promptly killed during their first week in combat.

This was not possible. These were all guys who knew what they were doing, and now they were dead. It was a moment that I remembered long afterward. It was the moment that the first seed of doubt entered my mind. I was shocked and no longer fearless. I began to think, for the first time, that maybe, just maybe, we were not prepared for this war.

I graduated from the language school, took my thirty-day leave time, and flew, via Okinawa, to South Vietnam. After going through processing in Da Nang at the First Marine Division Headquarters, I was assigned to the Fifth Marine Regiment, who were then stationed in the Hoi An area, about thirty kilometers south of Da Nang.

When I arrived at the Fifth Marines' compound, decisions were being made as to which battalion would be my new home, and I found myself with a little time on my hands. Seeing a Vietnamese farmer walking across a grassy area inside the regiment's compound, I decided to try out my newly learned language skills. Approaching this farmer, an old man with his mouth filled with betel nut, I said hello.

"Chao, Ong," I cried out, remembering to make the phrase sound like "Chow Om," as we had been taught.

The man looked at me with fear in his eyes and tried to continue on his way, muttering something that I couldn't understand. I tried again, several times, smiling so that he could see that I was no threat to him in any way, that I was only interested in a little conversation in his native language.

We never communicated. After about five minutes of trying and failing to use the most basic greeting, "Hello, sir," the panic in his eyes made me understand that he hadn't understood a word I had spoken. As he hurried away from me, I finally realized that the words he was saying to me were that he was sorry, but that he didn't understand English.

That was my first and last attempt to use my Vietnamese language training. The South Vietnamese dialect was as different from the Hanoi dialect as was the language used by a rural farmer from Alabama and a fifth-generation Bostonian. Further exacerbating the situation, try as they did, our instructors had not succeeded in making us understand just how important inflection is to the Vietnamese language. We had talked about inflection, but we really didn't understand that a single word in Vietnamese could mean five different things based upon how it is spoken, its inflection.

The only benefit that I received from the Language School was reading that newspaper and seeing the names of the dead men. Reading their names shook the foundations of my confidence in our tactical training and opened my mind to the fact that how we were trained had not prepared us well for how the war was being fought. Thus, when I was finally assigned as the platoon commander of Charlie One a couple of days later, I had made up my mind to "hide and watch" for a while.

Oh, to be sure, for all appearances I immediately assumed command of Charlie One and called all the shots from the beginning. There was no way that I could act otherwise and not be instantly castigated and possibly prosecuted for dereliction of my duties. I was assigned as the platoon commander of Charlie One, and Charlie One had to fight the war on the day that I had taken over. The problem was that deep down inside of me, I was terrified that I was not ready to be in command and that I would do or say something that would get people killed. I decided to approach Staff Sergeant Mullan quietly and ask for his help.

Charlie One had been operating in the Hoi An area of operations for several months. I had gotten my assignment because the former Charlie One Actual had been killed by a command-detonated mine a month before I arrived. Sergeant Mullan, the platoon sergeant, had been acting as platoon commander since that day, and it was immediately apparent that the men respected him and that he had what I needed, experience.

I asked to speak privately to him, and simply and quietly explained my concerns. I told him that I was afraid that I would do something out of ignorance of the situation that might end up hurting one or more of the men, and I asked him if he would be willing to help me without the rest of the men knowing. After briefly thinking over what I had said, he agreed that it would not be right if the men knew what I had suggested, but that he would do everything he could to help me get up to speed. We worked out an "on the job" training program that would have all the appearance of my being totally in charge while the training period lasted, and we worked out a way to have a few minutes alone together at least daily. I told Sergeant Mullan that it would be up to him to let me know when he thought I was ready to take command in both name and actual fact. After about four weeks, Sergeant Mullan took me aside, thanked me for my concern, and let me know that he thought that I was totally ready for command. This arrangement proved to be one of the best decisions I made while in Vietnam. I don't think any of the men ever knew how much I had relied upon Sergeant Mullan during those early days.

My thoughts of those long Hoi An days were interrupted momentarily by another update from Benny Benwaring. According to the information that he had overheard on the battalion net, the bridges had all been blown between here and Da Nang, and it looked like everyone north of us was fighting for his life. Helpless and frustrated, I couldn't stop the constant mental exercise inside my brain. I continuously asked myself, "How the hell did I get here, and what should I do next?"

Waiting in the dark and shattering night for my squad leaders to arrive, it was difficult to think about anything except the awesome display of the firefight at the Delta Company firebase across the empty waters of the bay. I couldn't change or even remotely influence the explosive events of this unforgettable first night of what would soon be called the Tet Offensive of 1968.

On Christmas Day, 1967, 1/5 moved en masse from Hoi An to Phu Loc 6, located about fifty kilometers north of Da Nang. The fighting in early January at Phu Loc 6 had been intense, especially in comparison with our contacts with the VC in the Hoi An area, but even at Phu Loc 6 our enemy was elusive, reluctant to show itself, seemingly content to lurk in the jungle and throw rockets and mortars in our direction. But now, from the sounds of the fighting north of us, the enemy had apparently decided to attack massively. I was having a hard time understanding why the Lang Co Bridge hadn't been hit.

Lang Co was the largest bridge by far between the DMZ north and Da Nang to the south, a distance of nearly one hundred kilometers. It was also the only bridge that could not have been replaced with a pontoon bridge or other temporary bridge structure had it been destroyed, because of strong tidal currents running back and forth from the Dam Lap An Bay and the South China Sea. The bridge's span covered mud and water for nearly a half kilometer from shore to shore. Although during low tide much of the bridge covered mud flats, the channel under the center span was unusually swift and very deep. During high tide, the entire half-click (half-kilometer) span was under another ten or more feet of water. Strangely enough, although the destruction of this one bridge would have dealt the most severe blow to U.S. and ARVN supply lines, it was the only bridge not blown up, at least so far, between the top of the Hai Van Pass and the Delta Company firebase. We would find out soon enough that the Lang Co Bridge was the only significant bridge left standing between Da Nang and the DMZ when that long night ended.

Chapter Three

Lang Co Village: In the Eye of the Storm

31 January to 10 February 1968

The ten days that followed the first terrifying night of 30 January 1968 were long, tense, frustrating, and very unproductive for the Charlie Company Marines. We were now effectively marooned in the Lang Co area of operations. The atmosphere of the area around the Lang Co Bridge turned sour and damp. The unusually bright and breezy late January weather dissipated, as though it was trying to stay in synch with the forces of conflict building up throughout Vietnam. As the pleasant weather gave way, so the first terrifying night of the enemy's Tet Offensive gave way to daylight on the morning of 31 January 1968.

The firefight at Delta Company's firebase was continuing, although its intensity had diminished somewhat shortly after dawn. The morning air along Highway One in the Hai Van Pass was still and silent. Ominous stacks of dark, boiling cumulus clouds began building up against the steep mountains that dominated the area.

Charlie Two returned from their night ambush and patrolling activities in the Hai Van Pass about midmorning. Rich Lowder reported in

29

to Scott Nelson, telling him in detail of the extensive damage to the bridges of Highway One by the Viet Cong sappers during the long and explosive night. Although Charlie Two had spent a sleepless night up in the Hai Van Pass and had been surrounded by violent explosions during the darkest hours, they had seen none of the enemy, nor had they engaged in any firefights with the enemy. The Hai Van Pass chapter of the Viet Cong apparently wanted to blow the bridges without detection. The extent of their success had been spectacular.

Scott Nelson decided that there was no further reason to patrol the Hai Van Pass. Highway One had been effectively eliminated as a supply line for American and ARVN (Army of the Republic of Vietnam) forces, so Nelson surmised that the VC would probably desert their vigilant watch over the area, at least for the time being. There would be no convoys agonizing up the Hai Van Pass for quite some time.

The antiaircraft missile battery at the top of the Hai Van Pass had weathered the storm reasonably well, although we heard a couple of days later that Viet Cong sappers had overrun the high-tech base during the long night and had succeeded in destroying several million dollars' worth of missiles and supporting equipment. Casualties had been low, however, and the situation had not turned into a pitched battle. A few VC sappers had gotten inside the wire, had blown up some expensive hardware with satchel charges, and then had simply disappeared into the misty gloom that shrouded the mountaintop facility. No further attempts had been made to attack the missile site. Charlie Company was thus ordered to withdraw from the Hai Van Pass. There was nothing left up there worth defending.

By midmorning, a noticeable difference in the attitudes of the Marines of Charlie Company was detectable by anyone paying attention. The normal high volume of daily road traffic was completely shut off. Normally, long columns of green military trucks, interspersed regularly with straggling coveys of the highly colorful Vietnamese buses and punctuated by the occasional Vietnamese family stuffed into old, beat-up Renaults, Fiats, or Citroens left behind by the French, made their way over the tortuous Hai Van Pass. Today, there were none. All bridges north and south of the Lang Co Bridge were completely destroyed, so no one was going anywhere unless he could walk or fly.

Resupply, never a problem before, was now a major question mark: When would we see our next case of C rations? When would we be getting more ammunition and the other supplies required to stay alive in the bush? It appeared from our monitoring of the battalion and company radio networks on Benny's PRC-25 that the troops from Delta Company north of us (and presumably everyone from Da Nang south to the Mekong Delta) were all fighting for their lives.

We didn't know it yet, but during the previous night the combined forces of Viet Cong and the North Vietnamese Army (NVA) had attacked every major population center throughout South Vietnam. They had attacked American and ARVN forces with an intensity and determination never before seen from the enemy. Major combat bases were hit hard, and many of them had been overrun. Countless small outposts had been overwhelmed, many completely wiped out. Large segments of Saigon, Da Nang, Hue, Quang Tri, and other large cities throughout South Vietnam were now suddenly under the complete control of enemy forces. After many years of being the elusive prey, the VC and NVA now seemed to be saying that *they* would hunt for a while.

As the long and tense day of 31 January 1968 wore on, we learned more from our constant monitoring of the company and battalion radio frequencies. The Citadel in Hue was reported to be under control of the NVA. The firebase in Phu Bai had been hit hard; damage and casualties had been high, but friendly forces in Phu Bai had thrown back the enemy attacks. The 1/5 battalion firebase at Phu Loc 6 had been hit especially hard. Phu Loc 6 had come under ground attack. This had never happened before despite the enemy's constant bombardment, but the Marine defenders had successfully repulsed the attacks. The Second Battalion of the Fifth Marines (2/5), our sister battalion who had been operating around Phu Bai about thirty kilometers to the north, was given the mission of moving into the south Hue area. The 2/5 battalion was the first American force committed to start the process of recapturing Hue, an important city because it was considered the cultural center of the Vietnamese people. The Marines of 2/5 were heading north.

The situation in South Vietnam had changed dramatically overnight, and the Marines of Charlie Company could sense the changes being explosively forged all around us. None of these changes would be welcome. Like the weather, the outlook of the men turned cloudy.

Late that afternoon, the Vietnamese first lieutenant in charge of ARVN forces in the Lang Co area of operations (AO) came to our company command post (CP) overlooking the southern approaches to the Lang Co Bridge. Scott Nelson and the Charlie Company CP group had relocated to the old, abandoned railroad station sitting about a hundred meters west of the southern tip of the Lang Co Bridge. Although the Vietnamese railroad system hadn't run this far north in years, it had once been an extensive system. The railroad tracks that ran parallel to Highway One took an equally spectacular but lower route around the Hai Van Pass area. However, the tracks didn't cross the Dam Lap An Bay entrance as Highway One did at the Lang Co Bridge. Instead, the railroad continued west for several kilometers and then turned north and worked its way around the perimeter of the bay, a detour of several kilometers, before it finally rejoined Highway One at a tunnel just below the Delta Company firebase. Since Lang Co had long been a thriving village and was a significant population center, a large railroad station had been constructed there many years before. Standing inside the old concrete hulk that was the remnant of the railroad station, one could still imagine the villagers as they walked across the bridge from the village, paid for their tickets to Da Nang or Phu Bai, and fought for seats on the train waiting to leave the station. The Lang Co train station had once been a center of commerce and travel, but had long since been abandoned when the railroad system died, probably during the early years of the French Indochinese War.

The ARVN lieutenant knew a little English, and he managed to get his message across to Scott Nelson and the hastily assembled officers responsible for Charlie Company (2nd Lt. Rich Lowder of Charlie Two; 2nd Lt. Travis Curd, our artillery forward observer; 2nd Lt. John R. Aamodt of Charlie Three; and me). The ARVN lieutenant had received some intelligence information that indicated that the VC and the NVA would combine and attack the bridge at Lang Co, probably that very night.

The ARVN lieutenant was normally a very calm person. Scott Nelson and I and a couple of the other platoon commanders had enjoyed a Tet celebration dinner in late January at his home in the village. The Vietnamese officer had seemed very nice and well in control of the situation in the Lang Co AO. Now he was obviously on edge and very tense. "Boocoo VC an' NVA, numbah fuckin' ten, come to bridge to-ni'; boom-boom bridge, many VC come to-ni'. Numbah fuckin' ten."

The pidgin English was easy to translate, and his message was very easy to believe, given the shattering explosiveness of the previous night. Most of us had been wondering and worrying about the fact that the VC hadn't touched the Lang Co Bridge last night. It was obvious to all of us that if the VC and NVA could take out the Lang Co Bridge, they could conceivably destroy our capabilities for ground transportation and resupply by truck convoy indefinitely. The railroad track around the bay might have been an alternate route, but our recent daytime patrols down the railroad tracks had confirmed that the tracks and bridges had been long since destroyed, and there were many signs of the elusive VC no more than a couple of clicks (kilometers) down the tracks. Those daytime patrols had been just too damned quiet. Trying to use the railroad track as an alternative route would be ten times worse than the Hai Van Pass, and that had been a nightmare.

So, we obviously had to protect the Lang Co Bridge. Charlie Company was left in the Lang Co AO to make sure of that. Every other unit of the Fifth Marines was fighting the enemy in pitched battles all over Northern I Corps. But in the nearly two weeks that we were marooned at Lang Co, nothing happened. The bridge was never attacked. However, every single afternoon during our nervous stay there, the ARVN lieutenant came to Lieutenant Nelson, told him that the NVA and VC would most definitely attack the bridge that night. We would respond with varying tactics to defend against the impending attack. The attack never came, however. All three platoons of Charlie Company were put on full alert during the night: two platoons out in the bush blocking the approaches to the bridge on both sides, and the third set up in defensive positions on the bridge itself. The Lang Co Bridge literally bristled with firepower each night during early February, but other than a brief skirmish with an inept VC mortar team that left us alert but intact, nothing ever happened.

I mean that literally: nothing happened, including resupply. Most Marines of Charlie Company had maybe one or two days' supply of food and four days' supply of ammo left when the shit had hit the fan during the early morning hours of 31 January. We had never before had to think about stocking up on a three- or six-day supply of C rats at Lang Co like we normally did while out on an extended patrol. We didn't worry about it, because we could always get a nearly instant resupply of food from Phu Loc 6 or Phu Bai via the daily truck convoys. Now, there were no trucks, and the only available method of resupply was via helicopter. Charlie Company's problem was that during the first weeks of February, all American helicopter resources were needed for moving tactical units into battle and for critical resupply for fighting forces, not to mention medevac usage. We would end up waiting seven days before we were finally resupplied with a pallet of C rations slung under a CH-46 helicopter.

Despite the lack of food (we probably wiped out a year's supply of rice from the village, and we bought out the fresh vegetables in the market whenever we could), those first two weeks in February in the Lang Co AO were unforgettable, because for the first time in nearly three months, I started relaxing a little. The constant worrying about stepping on a mine or booby trap or getting hit by mortar shrapnel or a sniper round started to dissipate. The war really did stop for Charlie Company during those long days at Lang Co, although in the pit of every man's stomach was a certainty that this heretofore pastoral, guerrilla war had gone through a metamorphosis. Everywhere else, the war had really intensified.

We knew with a perverse conviction only known by a combat infantry-man that we were not long for this quiet, peaceful life. We could easily see the daily and nightly firefights at the Delta Company firebase, and we could hear the distant but constantly rumbling sounds of men being killed in the war all around us.

We spent a lot of time patrolling in the daylight and explored the small, abandoned villages that were little more than dots on my map, scattered sparingly along the approaches to the old railroad tracks a couple of clicks to our west. We never saw a human being on any of those patrols, but we could feel the presence of the enemy, who for some rea-son in the Lang Co area were hiding and watching. Perhaps they were simply biding their time.

During those ten confusing days, Charlie Company pulled in tighter in both formation and in personal contact. Ever since we had left Hoi An and landed at Phu Loc 6, Charlie Company had operated in platoon- and squad-sized missions. The one exception was our "reconnaissance in force" from Phu Loc 6 to the Lang Co AO in late January. We hadn't spent much time with our new company commander, Scott Nelson, nor had the Charlie Company platoon commanders had much opportunity to spend time together. Now, because of the relatively small geographic area that we had to cover, namely the Lang Co Bridge and the Lang Co village area, it was decided that Charlie Company's CP group and all three platoon CP groups would set up in the old railroad station for ease of command and communications. Daytime activities would be platoon and squad patrols, and nighttime ambushes would be focused on the approaches to the bridge and the railroad station.

There is an old saying, "Familiarity breeds contempt," which I had always wondered about. But after those ten days in the Lang Co rail-road station with Scott Nelson, Rich Lowder, John Aamodt, Travis Curd (our recently assigned second lieutenant forward observer from 11th Marines), The Gunny (our gunnery sergeant), and our related radio operators and platoon sergeants, I quickly gained an appreciation of the adage. The closeness can be especially difficult when there is a severe shortage of food and when there's not a lot to do. A group of Marines without food, and with no real prospects for resupply, can get to be a pretty ugly situation.

The war was still raging all around us. The Delta Company firebase continued to be the focus of daily mortar attacks and small-arms fire-fights, as did the Phu Loc 6 firebase (we had heard that the replacement 1/5 battalion commander had been wounded and evacuated already). The 2/5 battalion was already fighting in the southern sections of Hue. They were in heavy contact with NVA forces who occupied and con-trolled almost the entire city. Meanwhile, we were peaceful but hungry at the Lang Co Bridge.

We ventured into the village as often as possible; the first couple of days of our forced fasting was made bearable by the village kids' sell-ing us plates of rice. A small serving of rice, at which no respectable Marine would have given a second glance a week before, let alone pay money for, was now going for five dollars or more. A couple of times fights broke out between Marines bidding for rice.

Seven days went by. We kept our minds off food through constant daytime patrolling, nighttime ambushes to protect the bridge, the occa-sional bowl of rice from the village, and the inevitable back-alley bridge games. Back-alley bridge was very popular in Charlie Company, with some of the games continuing, nonstop, for weeks. The only thing that disrupted the games were patrols, ambushes, and death. If someone left a game permanently, there was usually some new guy who would step in and take the vacant position. Although no one discussed it, back-alley bridge games carried a disturbing parallel to the war we were fighting. There did not appear to be an end to it.

At the end of that agonizingly long week, some of us began to chuckle at the black humor of being sent to fight a jungle war, being afraid of being blown to bits by mines, booby traps, mortars, and rockets, and now it appeared that we would most likely die of starvation.

Finally, early on the afternoon of 7 February, an Army CH-47 Chinook twin-rotor helicopter made a brief stop to drop a pallet of C rations off at the railroad station by the Lang Co Bridge. Food had arrived, and we didn't even care that it was the Army that delivered it.

It turned out that the lack of food was the most significant thing that happened to us during those ten days. Fortunately for us, The Gunny took control of the situation and prevented us from mutiny or some other such hunger-motivated acts of violence.

I am sure that at some point I was told The Gunny's last name. But to my recollection The Gunny's last name was never used within Charlie Company. When you needed to talk with him directly, he was simply "Gunny." When you referred to him when talking with others, he was "The Gunny." The capitalization of the word "The" was always heard; it was put there instinctively through respect, through the reverence of a nearly godlike figure.

During my four years in the Marine Corps, I had contact with many fine staff NCOs, the men who are truly the backbone of the Corps. All of them had a last name. I remember Staff Sergeant Mullan, Charlie One's platoon sergeant who handed me the reins and the responsibilities of platoon commander of Charlie One; I can still see "Top" Stanford clearly, doing handstand pushups outside the Charlie Company headquarters tent in Phu Bai, looking for all the world like Popeye after he had consumed a can of spinach. I remember Gunny Portner, Alpha Company's gunnery sergeant, as he stood in the middle of the dirt road called Highway One late one night and cussed out the battalion commander at the top of his lungs. These men remain, along with their names, etched in my memories forever. But The Gunny was simply The Gunny.

The Gunny was a man of very few words. Those words he did speak were so low in volume that any listener had to concentrate to hear what he was saying. All the Marines of Charlie Company, officers and enlisted alike, always paid very close attention when he spoke.

He was small and slight, standing no more than five foot six and weighing about 130 pounds soaking wet. It was very difficult to determine his age, and when we were not in his presence, this question was frequently debated. We knew that The Gunny had fought in some of the worst battles of World War II in the South Pacific and that he had seen action in the Korean War as well, so he had to be at least forty years old. He had the deeply sunken eyes and facial wrinkles of a much older man or of a man who had simply seen too much of the deaths and mutilations of young men.

The Gunny always had a Lucky Strike cigarette hanging out of the corner of his mouth, and his eyes were so distant that it was nearly impossible to see their color. They were a light shade of dusty gray, but they could have been blue and covered by a film of cigarette smoke residue. But no one in Charlie Company seemed to care about any of this. The Gunny was The Gunny, and any man in Charlie Company would have followed him anywhere.

As the next couple of days crept by, the food situation was alleviated somewhat by the pallet of C rats. Nevertheless, The Gunny made sure everyone understood that he had no idea when we would get resupplied and that he would not issue any of the remaining few cases of rations until he, The Gunny, determined that we were either seriously starving to death or that we would be moving out, whichever came sooner. The Gunny posted armed guards on the remaining pile of C rations cases, and we understood why he did this: because you could never underestimate a hungry Marine. But I believe that this was totally unnecessary, because no one in his right mind would ever consciously cross The Gunny. Soon regretting that I had scarfed down half of my newly issued food in the first ten minutes, I determined that I would not eat another meal that day, and that of the remaining three C rations, I would eat one per day and hope we got resupplied soon.

2nd Lt. Rich Lowder, Charlie Two, had also taken his six meals into a lonely corner of the dusty, empty railroad station and had claimed this dank corner as the Charlie Two CP. In all the time I knew him in Vietnam, covering over a year, Rich Lowder never once complained about anything. Hailing from a rural area in South Carolina, he had adopted a very southern approach to life. He talked slowly and softly and seemed to be a very gentle man in spite of his large size. Rich was at least five foot ten and probably weighed over two hundred pounds. Although he had a somewhat chubby appearance, it was deceptive. He was solid muscle. I had found out from our many conversations from Hoi An to Lang Co that Lowder had played college football. He was a guard or a tackle and strong as a bull, but he wasn't an intimidating individual. Quite the contrary, Rich got results because you couldn't help but like him. His men worshipped him, and they would go anywhere and do anything he asked of them. His gentle, melodic southern drawl made you smile in spite of yourself. He smiled a lot and seemed to find life in general to be his personal amusement park. Even after nearly three months in Vietnam, having patrolled the booby-trap-infested area around Hoi An, having experienced the terrors of the Phu Loc 6 firebase, and having been wounded in the neck by shrapnel from a Chinese Communist command-detonated claymore mine that detonated only fifty feet in front of him (fortunately, this particular ChiCom claymore was either old or defective and only a small portion of its explosive power had been unleashed), Rich still seemed unaffected by the war.

There was no way you couldn't like Rich Lowder, and under normal circumstances, you would never suggest that Rich could do anything dishonest or underhanded. But, as I have mentioned, these were not normal times, and we were no longer normal people. Lack of food and our proximity to the war raging all around us—living in the eye of the hurricane, so to speak—had changed us into near-animals.

As the next three days progressed and my remaining three meals were reduced to two and then one, it seemed to me that Rich Lowder was eating all the time, but that despite that, his hoard of C rations never seemed to diminish. I can remember several times having muttering conversations with both John Aamodt and Travis Curd, wherein we discussed this phenomenon. It was as amazing to us as Jesus' miracle of the loaves and fishes must have been to those who had partaken of that feast.

Rich Lowder continued to eat, and he seemed to always have six meals remaining. Travis and I speculated that perhaps one of his men, or his radio operator, had given him some of theirs because Rich was so likable, but this made no sense at all, since those Marines had been just as starved as we had been.

In retrospect, I shudder to think of what might have occurred in that remote railroad station had we remained there past 10 February. In my worst nightmares I can see us lynching poor Rich Lowder, who was obviously innocent of anything except perhaps wise conservation of his meals. I can see Rich look down at us from the gallows with a gentle smile on his face, eating yet another spoonful of beans and weenies.

But the war saved us from committing this insane, paranoid act. On the evening of 9 February 1968 we got word that we would be relieved of our responsibilities in the Lang Co AO early the next morning by an Army unit. We would be transported by helicopter back to Phu Bai for resupply and then trucked northward to Hue.

Charlie Company was leaving the "eye of the hurricane" and venturing into the storm of death yet again. By all standards of human behavior, we should have been terrified about what was about to happen; we were headed north toward some of the fiercest fighting of the war. Yet I can honestly say that the only thing I was thinking about at that moment was that there was a mess hall at Phu Bai and that we would soon be getting a hot meal.

Chapter Four

Phu Bai: Mess Hall Chow

10–11 February 1968

Charlie Company was picked up the following morning, 10 February 1968, by several Army Chinook CH-47 helicopters, after the dual-rotor workhorses disgorged their loads of fresh Army infantry troops. A quick briefing was conducted by Scott Nelson for the benefit of the Army officers who would now be responsible for the Lang Co AO.

As the Army filed off the helicopters and the Marines prepared to board for the short hop to Phu Bai, a longstanding tradition in the American military establishment took effect. A loud, dull roar of many disparaging remarks between the two groups erupted. While most comments were made in fun and not to be taken too seriously, the trash talk would have made an outsider blush.

"Yeah, this is typical. After the Marines have cleaned out an area, they send in the Army to babysit the civilians."

"Oh, yeah, we heard you Marines got your butts handed to you up here, so they had to send the Army in to straighten out the VC."

"Hey, get some, you scumbag doggie! Keep yo' head down!!"

"Yeah, right, leatherface, leave just while the fun is starting."

And so on. . . .

Despite my desire to see the inside of the Phu Bai mess hall and to get out of the Lang Co area (the scene of much hunger and other forms of anxiety), I found myself rather reluctantly boarding the CH-47. Somewhere in the back of my mind my instinct toward self-preservation was beginning to assert itself. There was a logical connection between leaving the eye of the hurricane and subsequently having to go right into the substance of the deadly storm.

I looked around the loaded helicopter at the Marines of Charlie One to see if I could read their expressions, to see if I could figure out what they were thinking at that moment. Their faces were masks; they were the faces of well-trained actors, of men who had been indoctrinated with the history of the Marine Corps. I could see reflected the macho reputation of the infantry Marine and a great belief in the Marine Corps' unequaled history of overcoming great odds. These men totally accepted their destiny as active participants in a battle that would result, for the Marines, in certain victory. They seemed to project no doubt that whatever challenge lay before us was easily conquerable. They all seemed to be looking forward to whatever came next. There was no fear, no uncertainty, painted on those young faces. Was I the only one who worried about what would happen, now that we were venturing into the storm?

Maybe they were simply thinking about the mess hall. Perhaps, for them, nothing else on this earth mattered as much as the prospect of some Marine Corps chow, served hot on a dented and scratched metal tray. Any mess hall chow was better than the best C ration meal, and it beat the hell out of village rice any time.

Unable to read anything significant on the young faces of Charlie One, my thoughts turned inward as the CH-47 tilted forward and lifted off in a great cloud of dust, and the Lang Co Bridge rapidly became small and insignificant. For a couple of minutes I craned my head around and looked out one of the small circular portholes that lined the sides of the aircraft. From this aerial vantage point, I could clearly see what my map had been telling me for weeks, that the Lang Co Bridge was by far the most important bridge in this part of I Corps. One well-placed satchel charge underwater in the main span would have wrecked the bridge and rendered Highway One unusable for a long time. Why did the NVA and VC destroy everything around the Lang Co Bridge, and yet leave it untouched?

For a brief moment, my mind had an answer, but I refused to even consider it until many weeks later, after the impact and implications of the Tet Offensive had become fully evident. That thought was, What if they left the Lang Co Bridge alone because they fully expected to conquer South Vietnam as a result of the Tet Offensive, and they didn't want to have to bear the expense and difficulty of repairing it themselves? By blowing up lesser bridges and culverts, they had achieved the same goal (disrupting resupply of American and ARVN forces via Highway One), and they could repair those smaller spans in no time at all. My mind refused to consider this, the only rational explanation, because it spelled victory for the VC and NVA and doom for America and our allies in South Vietnam.

I chased those rueful thoughts away as though I were swatting at an unwanted bee buzzing much too close to my mind. I forced myself to concentrate on thoughts of the hot food waiting for us at Phu Bai.

Admittedly, it was not difficult to put this unwanted thought behind me, because, at this point in my Vietnam tour, it was still impossible to consider that America would fail in Southeast Asia. Troop strengths were at their highest peak of the war, over 500,000 strong. Every single significant confrontation with the enemy had been decisively won by American and ARVN forces. To be sure, the VC were a dangerous foe, not to be underestimated, and they used terrifying tactics and crude but deadly weapons. But, from a purely military point of view, the VC were really a joke, sentenced by the American presence and awesome firepower to hiding in the daylight and then sneaking out in the middle of wet, dark, oppressive nights to perform nasty, cowardly acts of violence. The VC were, in our minds, not much of a fighting force, and we had been confidant that they would never engage us in force.

No, this war was all but over, victory was assured, and we would go home, if not heroes, then at least as respected fighters who had done our parts to ensure that democracy would reign in Southeast Asia, and that communist aggression would be contained within the confines of North Vietnam. We would most certainly stop those often-described dominoes from falling at the DMZ.

By now, American military strategists, stung by the surprise and scope of the enemy's attacks, clearly felt the impact of the Tet Offensive. But because of our isolation at Lang Co, we had little understanding of what was about to happen to us. We would stop in Phu Bai for a couple of days, stock up on food and ammo, and then go north to help 2/5 secure Hue.

Piece of cake. It sure beat the hell out of patrolling in the Hoi An area and the Hai Van Pass, where ambushes, booby traps, command-detonated mines and snipers were the rules of the game. At least in Hue we would be fighting the NVA, a more conventional enemy force, where our vastly superior firepower would dominate and take us rapidly to victory.

From my seat in the CH-47, I had a clear view of the countryside. As we descended into the Phu Bai area, the beauty of Vietnam struck me once again and commanded my immediate attention. If you could just ignore the bomb craters and the defoliation, the mountainous triple-canopy jungles dominating the western approaches to Phu Bai were spectacular, looking more like a travel poster advertising some exotic Club Med resort than a war zone. Vivid expanses of green rice paddies, almost painful to look at because of the brightness of the light emerald sheen that growing rice became, surrounded Phu Bai on its remaining three sides, south, north, and east and stretched as far as I could see from three thousand feet above the landscape.

Vietnam was definitely a paradise. Since my first day "in country," I had often found myself thinking, Why don't they stop fighting, build some airports, hotels, and golf courses, and bring in the international tourists? The money they could make from tourism alone would shortly turn them into another Hawaiian Islands. If they would only stop fighting. . . .

Reality rushed in as I felt the CH-47 lose power for its rapid, circular descent into the Phu Bai complex. A few hundred feet above the earth, our pilot pulled back on the reins, and the CH-47's rotor blades grabbed hold of the air. Our descent slowed rapidly, and then we came to a bumpy stop in another cloud of dust. As the back ramp dropped down, I and about twenty other Marines of Charlie One ran out into the swirling dust, surrounded by the chopper's chaotic racket. Running out the back hatch of a just-arrived CH-47 helicopter was like running with your eyes wide open into a nasty dust storm. Not smart. Some small, innocuous piece of Vietnamese soil found its way into my left eye almost immediately. Running blindly from the helicopter's rotor wash, I joined the rest of Charlie One at the edge of the landing zone inside the Phu Bai firebase and blinked the dust out of my eyes.

Phu Bai. Mess hall.

First Sergeant Stanford, Charlie Company's "top sergeant," met us at the landing zone and burst our first bubble for the day. The troops would have to make do with their existing "shelter halves," and the officers would be squeezing into the company's administrative office, where we had two fewer cots than officers. After being in the bush for well over a month, sleeping on the ground, living more like wild animals than human beings, we had all been looking forward to a cot and a blanket and some hot food. As it turned out this time, being in the rear provided little in the way of creature comforts for the Marines of 1/5.

Top Stanford looked me in the eye as only a Marine first sergeant can and growled, "Sorry, Lieutenant, but that's the breaks in this man's Marine Corps. All available shelter has been commandeered, and even though I called in all my markers to get some dry bunks for the men, this was the best I could do. You won't be here long, anyway."

"Shit, Top, I know you worked hard and you did the best you could, but isn't there anything for the men?" I asked.

Top Stanford's look of disgust was all the answer I got. He changed the subject, "Well, at least the mess hall is still standing, no thanks to Mr. Victor Fucking Charles. A couple of 140-millimeter rockets made a direct hit on the mess hall two days ago, killed a couple of Marines who were in there early cooking up breakfast, and blew away half the damned roof. We convinced the mess sergeant that we would definitely have hot chow, holes in the roof or no holes in the roof. Your platoon is scheduled for a hot meal in about an hour. I'll let Sergeant Mullan know where Charlie One is to bivouac. Bring your gear up to the company office; you'll have to draw straws with the other lieutenants to see if you get a cot."

First Sergeant Stanford was a Marine's Marine. He had been in the Corps for almost twenty-five years and had seen combat in World War II and the Korean War. He had a lean, tough body and large, hairy forearms. I had seen him do twenty "handstand" pushups once, standing upside down on his hands, pumping his body up and down just for the hell of it. As mentioned earlier, I was always expecting him to pull out a corncob pipe and a can of spinach. He was another enlisted man whom I had to remember not to call "Sir." The truth was that Top Stanford scared the shit out of me, and I tried really hard never to cross him, even though I (theoretically) outranked him. So, I shut up and told him that Staff Sergeant Mullan would be in on the next chopper with the rest of Charlie One, and I trudged off toward Charlie Company's administrative office.

Later that morning, I rejoined my platoon outside what was left of the mess hall and lined up at the back of the line, eager to get at the long-awaited hot chow. The mess hall had several large gaping holes in the roof, hastily covered with sheet plastic, the obvious results of being in the impact zone of several 140-mm rockets. It was amazing to me that the mess hall still stood or had not burnt to the ground, and I could not help but wonder what would happen if another 140-mm rocket came down on us right then. It would be poetic justice: damned near starving to death at Lang Co, dreaming of hot chow since we were told we were going back to Phu Bai, finally getting there, and then getting blown away between bites of shit on a shingle.

The officers of Charlie Company met with all the other officers in 1/5 at about 1500 hours that afternoon for a briefing on the mission we were about to undertake, the retaking of the Citadel fortress of Hue. We learned that our sister battalion, 2/5, had been in south Hue since 2 February and had been engaged with the enemy constantly since then. During the briefing, 1/5's battalion S-3, Maj. L. A. Wunderlich, told us that 2/5 was initially not allowed to use heavy weapons, that they had taken high casualties on the first couple days of the fighting, but that the Marines of 2/5 had persevered. They had finally completed their first sweep of south Hue, only to find out that the NVA had slipped around them and had come in behind them. Consequently, 2/5 had to do it all over again. Before south Hue had been totally secured, 2/5 had been forced to "sweep" the city five times to eliminate all pockets of resistance.

The fighting had been fierce. It was close-in fighting. Going from house to house and without heavy weapons, 2/5 took fearful casualties. After they were finally given permission to use air strikes, artillery, and, ultimately, their tanks and Ontos, naval gunfire, and anything else they could get their hands on, the tide had turned. Casualties had been high, but the enemy was now on the run, and south Hue was considered to be under control.

The job of 1/5 was to pass through 2/5's positions and cross the Perfume River by landing craft (the huge bridge approaching the Citadel across the Perfume River had been blown up during the night of 31 January, and all traffic north had to go by boat). The 1/5 Marines were then to enter and reoccupy the Citadel, a mile-and-a-half-square fortress that, according to military intelligence, was currently occupied by a couple of reinforced NVA companies.

The briefing was short, no longer than a half hour, and did little to improve my morale. The bottom line was that we would mount up on a truck convoy at "zero dark thirty" the next morning, 11 February 1968. We would be driven as far as possible to the first blown-up bridge on Highway One north of Phu Bai, which prior to 31 January 1968 had crossed a small tributary about two kilometers south of the Perfume River. From

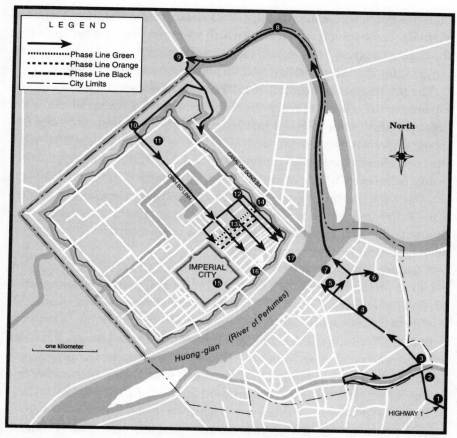

Map reference points: (1) Highway One, the approach route from Phu Bai (approximately eleven kilometers south of this point), 1000 hours, 11 February 1968. (2) Dismounted truck column due to blown bridge, two-kilometer detour. (3) Site of destroyed M-48 tanks, results of fighting involving 2/5. (4) Site of destroyed civilian family. (5) MACV compound. (6) The stadium. (7) The boat ramp area; here, 1/5 departed on Whiskey boats, 0800 hours, 12 February 1968. (8) Site of the Viet Cong sixty-millimeter mortar attack on 1/5, while the battalion was on board Whiskey boats en route to the Citadel. (9) Ferry and boat landing site. (10) 1/5's entrance into the Citadel. (11) First ARVN Division Headquarters compound. (12) Site of Alpha Company's first contact with the NVA inside the Citadel. (13) Phase line green, Mai Thuc Loan, 0900 hours, 13 February 1968. (14) Dong Ba Porch (the tower). (15) The Imperial Palace, or City— the sacred inner city within the Citadel. (16) Thuong Tu Porch (the southern tower), 1/5's exit point from the Citadel. (17) The departure boat ramp area, 1000 hours, 27 February 1968.

there we would hoof it into the MACV (U.S. Military Assistance Command Vietnam) compound in south Hue (which had been nearly overrun during the chaotic night of 31 January) for a final briefing before boarding landing craft for the river crossing and ultimate entry into the Citadel.

The briefing broke up, and we all took off. There was no banter or joking among the officers of 1/5, none of the usual verbal camaraderie or the expected dark humor. We all just left and went by ourselves to our platoons, where we would brief our NCOs and do the best we could to make sure our Marines were as prepared as possible for the upcoming battle.

My mind was blank of independent thought; all my motions and actions were at that moment military, ingrained, necessary, unquestioned. Being a product of my training, I was afraid to let any other thoughts filter in. I found whatever solace there was that dismal afternoon by concentrating on my duties.

I had lost the straw draw and tried to sleep wrapped up in my poncho liner on the hard wooden floor of Charlie Company's administrative office, which consisted of a GP tent with a wood floor, but I was completely unable to fall asleep. It was, therefore, perversely comforting to hear the sirens go off around 0100, signaling an imminent rocket attack. I took off with my pack and gear, found my platoon's tent city in the pitch-black darkness, and dropped into a muddy trench with Benny Benwaring and L. Cpl. Ed Estes, one of the three squad leaders of Charlie One.

Benny and Ed were having a quiet conversation about waterboo, or water buffalo, as they are more accurately and less emotionally named. Waterboo were often the subject of these late-night discussions. Marines were not exactly afraid of waterboo, but they were leery of them. They knew from firsthand experience that most waterboo definitely did not like Marines. No sir, for the young Marines who had to patrol through the paddies and villages of South Vietnam, waterboo were definitely number ten. In Vietnam, if something was good, it was often described as "number one." If it was bad, it was number ten. It was either good or bad; number one or number ten. There were no shades of in between. Everything that happened was at one extreme or the other.

Benny's whining complaint was very familiar: "Fucking kids can whack them waterboo over they heads and they don't give a shit, but let a Marine even look at him, and that fuckin' waterboo goes damn near crazy. Sheeit, I hate fucking waterboos." Benny Benwaring hated water buffalo.

Estes laughed and said, "Shit, Benny, if you'd take a bath more'n once a month, those damned waterboo wouldn't care about you no more. They think they smell a Missus Waterboo in heat, and they just naturally come down your direction. Then they get really pissed off when they expect to see Missus Waterboo and they get your ugly face. No wonder they get that wild look in their eyes."

I finally dozed off about 0300, with the sounds of the gloomy banter about waterboo bouncing around in my mind. I came abruptly awake at 0500 hours. The huge, sprawling combat base of Phu Bai was silent. The large "hard point" bunkers, built with huge timbers and many layers of sandbags, stood out in the dim light of the early morning gloom. If there was going to be an attack that day, this was the likely moment. Silence. Stillness. No noises save the minor singing of early morning insects. The sun lightened the eastern sky again over the shattered landscape of South Vietnam.

Thankfully, the rockets never came on that morning.

Although the mess hall was open, all the Charlie One Marines opened C rations and either ate them cold or heated them halfheartedly over a heat tab or two. We were all lost in our thoughts, and none of us wanted to see the half-destroyed mess hall again. I can remember feeling like I couldn't wait until the truck convoy came to pick us up, so at least I would be doing something, anything, so as to get my mind off of what lay ahead.

Finally, Top Stanford, The Gunny, and Lieutenant Nelson came over from the company HQ hooch and told us where to go to mount up on the trucks. Scott Nelson took me aside and said, "Keep your head down, Charlie One, and don't ride in the front cab of your truck. There've been a bunch of vehicles blown away north of here during the past couple of weeks. An entire ARVN convoy was cut off a few days ago not too far from Hue City, and it was completely wiped out. There are sandbags lining the truck beds, but they don't do too much good. Get at least one M-60 machine gun into each of your three trucks, and keep your eyes open. You'll be on point after we dismount by the first blown-up bridge, so let me know if you have any questions about our route."

I had studied my new maps (each company commander and platoon commander had been issued a brand-new map, a 1:10,000 street map of Hue and the surrounding area, at the battalion briefing the previous day), and I knew from reviewing the map casually the night before where we had to go. So I simply acknowledged Scott Nelson and told him I'd see him at the MACV compound or in hell, whichever came first. It was a poor attempt at humor, something out of a bad movie, but Scott Nelson responded simply with his ever-present grin.

Top Stanford looked in my eyes and said, "Get some, Lieutenant. We owe these bastards."

After the normal confusion associated with getting an entire battalion of Marines correctly situated on a long line of trucks, the truck convoy slowly departed Phu Bai at about 0700. I had been on several truck convoys in Vietnam by now, but this was an entirely different experience. Always in the past, when Army or Marine truck convoys went north or south on Highway One, the two-lane dirt road had the usual mix of military and civilian traffic. Whenever we had stopped before, a rowdy group of Vietnamese kids and old ladies would instantly appear to beg for food or generally just to harass us. Now there were no civilian vehicles at all and no traffic coming south toward us whatsoever. Although villages hugged both sides of the highway all the way from Phu Bai to south Hue, some twelve kilometers north of us, no one came out of the villages. It was as though the Vietnamese civilian populace had all died of a sudden, virulent disease. Other than the diesel sounds of our struggling trucks and the occasional sounds of explosions in the distance north of us, the countryside was silent and still. No noise. Bad news. Number fucking ten.

I don't know how long it took us to traverse the twelve clicks, but I know I didn't breathe deeply during the entire ride. It seemed like the big six-by trucks that carried us stayed in low gear the entire trip. Since Charlie One was on point for the company, and since Charlie Company was on point for the battalion, I was in the second truck back, with only the lead truck and the mine-detecting engineers in front. And although I had recently started riding in the front cab during trips on truck convoys (having become "salty" before my time and giving more importance to comfort than common sense), I took Scott Nelson's advice and rode in the back like everyone else. I had seen destroyed truck cabs too often, and it was just too damned quiet right now.

The engineers and the lead truck finally ground to a halt without incident about a hundred meters short of the first blown-up bridge, our "jumping off point." We stopped at the end of a short line of military trucks and jeeps parked in the roadway. We had been told that there was a makeshift footbridge constructed and that I would decide if we would cross it or go around. Going around meant a two-kilometer detour. We would have to walk about a click to the west, where another bridge crossed this particular river, and then proceed north across the bridge to the other side of the river, resulting in about an hour's lost time.

Adding to our uncertainty, we had no current word on friendlies or enemies in that area.

However, one glance at the supposed footbridge, which was little more than ropes and bamboo suspended by support poles on both sides of the swollen river, convinced me that the two-click detour, even if we had to fight every step of the way, was much more desirable than attempting to cross the dangerous "footbridge." Any Marine who didn't make it across the footbridge would undoubtedly drown, as most of us were carrying at least sixty pounds of weapons, radios, packs, and ammunition. So, without hesitation, I called Scott Nelson on Benny's PRC-25 to give him my assessment. Nelson acknowledged and, without questioning my judgment, approved the detour.

Charlie One dismounted and, with Charlie One Alpha (Estes's squad) on point, we headed slowly and cautiously west toward the still-intact bridge. It took us more than an hour to make the detour, as we had to proceed slowly. The vegetation along the river was thick; we saw more and more hooches and even some concrete houses. We finally made the bridge without incident, checked it out, determined it to be safe, and moved across. We then started back east along the northern bank of the small but swollen river, which was a tributary of the larger Perfume River.

Signs of fierce street fighting began to appear on the northern side of the river, as we moved back toward Highway One and our jump-off point. The hooches and houses grew gradually into a small business district. Although we couldn't read the signs, their presence over the buildings indicated that they were stores and shops. Gradually, as two-story buildings began to dominate, we came to the intersection where all the changes in the war during the past few days came into clear, devastating focus.

For over three months I had been walking through the green, rural beauty of South Vietnam. Landscapes that I could have only imagined in dreams had gone by in wave after wave of green paradise. Every imaginable shade of the emerald color had assaulted my senses and had constantly threatened to rip my attention away from the threats of warfare. Vietnam was just simply green and beautiful.

Now, at this unlucky intersection, as I turned finally back onto Highway One, my vision turned to black and white. There was no more "living color." My eyesight had been suddenly switched to "monochrome viewing only," with shades of only black, white, and gray. Charlie One had arrived at the edge of the hurricane.

Chapter Five

Wading through Deep Shit

11 February 1968

Now I knew without a doubt that we were in deep shit. For a lingering, uncomfortable moment, I felt as though we had accidentally stumbled into the twilight zone. The view was radically different from any other that I had experienced in Vietnam. We had walked through an invisible curtain from an achingly green, vividly living world, into a black and white madness of destruction and death.

Having spent all my time in firebases, rural villages, and "the bush" (except for my fast passage in a jeep through Da Nang from the airport to the regimental firebase in Hoi An), this was the first time since arriving in country that I had spent any time in a business district. Two-story concrete structures commanded the view in all directions. We had stumbled into the Vietnamese version of the "mini-mall."

Or rather what was left of it. . . .

A thick, dank pallor of smoke shrouded the entire disrupted scene. The air was heavy with the conflicting, gagging smells of battle and death. The lingering smoke from the battle had begun to thin out now, allowing us a view of ruined businesses and destroyed lives. The usually faithful breeze from the South China Sea was utterly still, seemingly reluctant to remove the stench of war, the odorous evidence of man's stupidity. Movement, what little there was of it, was tentative and cautious. The few residents of south Hue who had ventured outdoors resembled zombie cattle immediately after a fierce summer storm. In a dazed stupor, they picked their way through the rubble that surrounded the intersection. They moved slowly, but there was a hysterical nervousness about them, as though they were about to burst into a panicked stampede, to get out of there, anywhere. I was convinced that if anyone made a sudden noise, the small handful of Vietnamese citizens picking through the rubble would quickly vanish and would never be seen here again.

As I walked further into the shattered intersection, the main focus of my now totally monochrome vision forced me to look at something my mind had a hard time dealing with. In the center of the intersection, an American M-48 tank was standing on its turret, upside down. It had obviously been blown up and turned over by a large, powerful explosion. The crew never had a chance. The tank's hull was totally burned out. Its companion, another M-48 tank, sat close by, also out of action, with a small but obviously unauthorized hole in its turret and one damaged tread. The second tank appeared to be otherwise unharmed, but it was also abandoned, as though reluctant to leave its destroyed mate behind.

All the buildings that congregated at the intersection had been damaged, some reduced to burned-out hulks, shells of their former selves. Rubble covered the streets, making it difficult for me to walk without looking at the ground right in front of my feet. Watching your feet was not a good thing to do where the enemy might still be holed up. The intersection, then, had been the focal point of one of the many battles that 2/5 had fought during the past two weeks to clear south Hue. The unwelcome, unmistakable smell of death permeated both the air and my thoughts.

We didn't stop; it would have been like crashing a funeral. L. Cpl. Ed Estes's point man, a private first class named Robert Lattimer, continued through the obstacle course slowly, steadily, quietly, and cautiously, his M-16 rifle persistently scanning the area ahead of us. We kept moving, hoping to put these scenes behind us and out of our minds. It didn't take much imagination to consider what it must have been like to have been in the middle of *that* firefight.

We could hear sporadic gunfire and a few muffled explosions in the distance, the noise coming from the northwest, where, we were told during the Phu Bai briefing, the Marines of 2/5 were still "mopping up." The violent sounds of the distant battle, strangely enough, gave me some comfort. If there was fighting just a couple of clicks away, then the bulk of the enemy was most likely over there and not hiding here, watching us walk through the fruits of their labor, waiting for the right moment to strike again.

We kept putting one foot in front of the other, and eventually the scene was left behind. Like all good Marines throughout history, we had a mission to accomplish; to stop our inexorable forward progress for more than a moment would be like taunting history.

Proceeding north from the shattered intersection and out of the business district, Highway One made its way into some open land, in what appeared to be long-unused rice paddies. I knew from reading my map that this was the last vacant land until we reached the south shore of the Perfume River, where the MACV compound was located. The point element of Charlie One was about five hundred meters past the blown-up tanks when Scott Nelson, Charlie Six Actual, radioed us to hold up and "take five." I think he had just reached the blown-up tanks and wanted to check everything out before we went much further.

Staff Sergeant Mullan was bringing up the rear element of Charlie One, and I was in my normal position with Estes's point squad, following behind the first fire team, the four men comprising one of the three fire teams of Charlie One Alpha. I had Benny call Sergeant Mullan to make sure that the Marines of Charlie One were spread out and had taken whatever cover the side of the road afforded. I then had him tell them to take five, but not to get comfortable. I could tell from their actions that my words were unnecessary; the blown-up tanks had gotten everyone's attention. No one spoke, no one grab-assed. Everyone silently fanned out and took up temporary firing positions. Many of us automatically engaged in "Sawaya surveys," a technique for visually surveying the surrounding terrain, which had been refined by, and named for, a Charlie One squad leader who had died in the Hoi An area of operations.

Behind us was an amazing scene of widespread destruction, and ahead of us apparently would be much more of the same. Seventy-five meters further north on Highway One, a large explosion had blown away the front of a formerly large and substantial two-story home. The house could have been built by dairy farmers in rural southwestern Oregon where I had grown up, or it could have been built by the owners of a French vineyard. A huge, gaping hole shattered both illusions.

Banners and South Vietnamese flags, once strung gaily across Highway One and other large city streets in celebration of the Tet New Year holidays, now hung askew, draped at crazy angles across the road. Concrete chunks and other litter were randomly spread across the street. My Sawaya survey stopped abruptly as my eyes reluctantly but inescapably focused on several bodies lying near the center of the blast site. There were at least four, perhaps five, bodies lying there. From my viewpoint, it looked as though a small family had died as a result of the rocket or artillery round, satchel charge, or whatever had devastated the front of their home. At least two bodies were obviously children.

Three Vietnamese men were slowly encouraging an old, worn-out water buffalo pulling an ancient wooden cart to get into position beside the dead family. With handkerchiefs tied around the lower part of their faces, they were a surreal imitation of the outlaws of the old American West.

As my insides played host to conflicting emotions, my body unconsciously shuddered in response to the carnage, and I forced myself to break the hold that the scene of death had established over my consciousness. Quite deliberately, I turned away and continued the Sawaya survey. Only now I took my time and focused on my platoon.

My men, the fifty-one Marines comprising the First Platoon of Charlie Company, were not acting normally, if there ever was such a thing as "normal behavior" for a Marine infantryman in the bush. Every man was quiet, crouching but ready in his assigned temporary firing position, watchful, thoughtful. They were obviously taking very seriously the blatant warning of the two destroyed M-48 tanks and the continuing gunfire off in the distance.

This was not at all like any of our previous experiences in the jungles and the villages, on patrols and in night ambushes, when you *had* to be quiet or quite possibly die a violent death. Here, today, upon entering the ravaged shell of south Hue, everyone just *was* quiet. It was broad daylight, a little before noon, the time of day when the inevitable grab-ass of a Marine unit was usually at its height. Now, everyone seemed to sense that we were on the edge, the "cusp," of something that none of us wanted but toward which we were incessantly driven, as though we were all components of one large, ungainly Marine Corps–green organism. We were being drawn forward, toward Hue. The Citadel. I couldn't see it yet, but I knew it was there. It had a palpable presence in my mind. Its image on my maps only served to cause further discomfort.

As I stood in the middle of the street, witnessing the vast destruction around us, I felt unable to fully comprehend and appreciate what the fighting had been like on this side of the Perfume River. I couldn't help wondering what would it be like inside the Citadel, which was reportedly 90 percent under control of NVA forces. If we could get inside the Citadel in the first place . . .

Shaking off those unwelcome thoughts, I continued my slow survey of Charlie One. Satisfied that there was nothing I could do about anything I was seeing, I forced myself to break the silence. "Benny, call Charlie Six and give him this position report: We're on the street located at: From reference point Los Angeles, right two-point-two, down one-point-five." Benny began to call in the position report immediately in his Tennessee twang. Charlie Six's radio operator could pinpoint our location by going to the "cities" reference point that was marked and maintained on Scott Nelson's command and control map and by traversing east (right) 2.2 clicks and then south (down) 1.5 clicks. Since the command map was a duplicate of the one that I was carrying, and since the reference points were changed, like any good code, on a frequent but irregular basis, we could radio our positions quickly and easily without worrying that the enemy was monitoring our radio traffic. Since they didn't have the reference points, they had no way of pinpointing our location quickly using our own position reports.

The spot that I was indicating on the map was about a click south of the MACV compound, our next objective, which was situated approximately one hundred meters from the southern bank of the Perfume River. There was a large bridge on the map where Highway One went across on its way north, and just on the other side of the river was the huge, intimidating square that represented the Citadel on my map. According to the map, the damned thing was almost a mile and a half square, had walls thirty feet high, could only be entered through one of ten gates, and even had a water-filled moat all the way around it. It was like something out of medieval Europe, only grotesquely huge. From this point of view—from the outside looking in—taking the Citadel back from the NVA forces that had seized it the night that hell broke loose was going to be numbah fuckin' ten!

As I shook off that thought, yet another in an unending series of increasingly uncomfortable ponderings since leaving the Lang Co Bridge, I forced myself to study my new 1:10,000 map of the Hue area, looking for whatever information I could glean, searching for something to be confident about. But scanning the new, still foreign map did nothing to instill confidence.

The map was another problem in itself. It really bothered me. I had never been issued any other map like it during my entire lifetime-long three-month tour in Vietnam. The maps we had used humping through the rice paddies and mountainous jungle terrain of I Corps had always been 1:50,000 terrain maps.

Peering closely at my new 1:10,000 map, I could clearly see the house just north of us, the one that had its front blown off, the one with the dead family. There it was on the map, that little dot. I wondered briefly if I should cross it off or try to erase it.

"Sheeit, Lootenant. Lookit the size of that damned thang. What the fuck is that, over?" As I already described, Benny Benwaring, standing just behind me and looking over my shoulder, was normally a man of few words except when on the radio. And when he did have a normal conversation, he often stayed within the radioman's language, letting you know when he was done talking by saying, "Over," or "Out." Like me, he must have been startled to see so large a structure as the Citadel on a map of Vietnam, and that had started this unusual burst of conversation.

I glanced back at Benny and said, "It's called 'the Citadel,' Benny. That's where we're headed. Don't worry about it. I'll be briefing all the squad leaders later on when we get to our objective for the day, and you can sit in. I'll tell you everything that I know, but I've got the feeling that we're all gonna' learn a lot about the Citadel real soon. I hear it's not too healthy in there right now." Hoping I had covered the tremolo in my voice, unconsciously still striving for the "command presence" drilled into me during OCS and Basic School, I continued, "Call the squad leaders up for a brief powwow, Benny."

Turning away from Benny, I began another survey of the situation in front of us. My attention was immediately drawn back toward the dead family. The scene had almost been played out. The three masked men had loaded up all the bodies except one. Only the father was still on the street, having not yet joined his family on the simple, two-wheeled cart. The water buffalo stood placidly waiting orders to proceed to the next death stop.

Two of the masked men quickly adjusted their handkerchief masks over their mouths and noses in a vain attempt to block the stench of death. They then reluctantly but stoically bent down on either side of the father and, grasping him by the arm and leg on their side, began to hoist him up onto the cart. I tried to turn away, to force myself to think about my men, our tactical situation, anything, but it was futile. Something inside of me had to see it all.

The father must have been killed by a direct hit of something large and metallic in his face, because he had no face; he only had a large, bloody cavity where a face and forehead should be. As the men picked him up, his brain fell out of his face and onto the street. Both of the workers lurched violently, managing to throw the father onto the cart, on top of his shattered, eternally waiting family, before they staggered away. Both of them fell to their knees right there in the middle of the street, tore off their masks, and began vomiting violently and convulsively.

And then it happened again. It had happened before a couple of times, but never as distinctly and as forcefully as now. I felt time stopping, with my normal self and everyone else around me instantly freezing, unable to move, not caring if I ever moved again. And then another part of me, that being with whom I would become very well acquainted in the next few weeks and months, the personality that I eventually came to know as "the observer," stepped out of my body and moved several feet away from me. The observer was able to tear his eyes away from the bloody mess in the street, and with a distinct note of humor tinged with disgust, he said, "Don't worry about it, guy. This is not real. It doesn't hurt, does it? What's the problem, anyway? Those aren't real people anymore, right? This is just like in the movies, so don't worry about it." The observer was loose and relaxed, chuckling with the obvious humor of the moment. "The lieutenant," that scared-stiff automaton, the other personality inside of me, the one that's supposed to know what to do, could not move a muscle or make a sound. If I had moved at that moment I would have joined the two now-recovering Vietnamese vomiting in the middle of the street.

If it hadn't been for Estes, I would probably still be frozen in time, standing in the middle of the damned street, still contemplating that moment's horror and trying to understand it. But Estes, Sawaya's replacement as squad leader of Charlie One Alpha, had walked up behind me quietly, as was his way. He had either not noticed my frozen discomfort or had not cared. In his quiet South Texas voice, Estes reunited the observer and the lieutenant abruptly, allowing my eyes to break away and finally focus on something not full of horror.

"You okay, Lieutenant?" asked Estes. "You look a little pale. Shouldn't bother you at all, just some more dead gooks. The sooner *they* all die, the sooner *we* go back to the World." Anyone who by chance met Ed Estes

at this point in his young life and heard him make a cold-blooded state-
ment like that would have thought that he had always been an all-out,
no-holds-barred ultra-bigot toward Asians, especially the Vietnamese,
because he no longer spoke with any distinction between friendly or
enemy Vietnamese. To Estes now, they were all just gooks. But, that's
not at all what Ed Estes had been like just three months ago, when I
met him for the first time.

L. Cpl. Ed Estes was a typical Marine enlisted man, just nineteen or
twenty years old, but he was the exception to the rule because he was very
mature for such a young age. Although my memories of Ed Estes have
faded over two and a half decades, I remember that he was married, and
if my memory serves me at all, he had a child, or perhaps even two young
children, when he left home to serve his country in South Vietnam.

Although, to my discredit, I never got to know Ed personally very
well, I remember him as having lived in South Texas, perhaps in a rural
area. On the surface, he was a quiet, nice, likable young man. A typical
Marine, he was about five foot seven, wiry and strong, but not aggres-
sively so. His light brown, wispy hair was kept reasonably well trimmed,
but not "gung-ho" short, and he was currently sporting an attempt at a
mustache. Smart and very professional, he had been promoted to E-3,
lance corporal, after only fifteen months in the Corps and had been one
of Sawaya's fire team leaders. Yes, Ed Estes had been a very likable
young man. Until the night Sawaya and three other Marines of Charlie One were blown away by a command-detonated mine only a few feet
outside of a "friendly" Vietnamese village just outside Charlie Company's combat base at Hoi An.

Up until that explosive and deadly moment, Estes was not at all
bigoted and had always reserved the title of "gook" to describe obvious
enemies, Viet Cong and NVA soldiers. He had been respectful of the local
peasants and had not gone out of his way to trouble them.

But the night Sawaya and the others were killed had changed all
that. Estes never forgave the local villagers for not warning us. He
blamed them for the fact that two squads of Charlie One were ripped
apart and shredded by a "daisy chain" of two 105-mm artillery rounds,
command-detonated by the local VC cadre, who, of course, immediately
disappeared, melting into the shattered night. Estes had been there, on
point. His fire team had walked right over the top of the booby-trapped
artillery shells. The VC didn't detonate their little surprise until the center of the night ambush patrol was directly over the killing ground.

Three men died instantly, and Sawaya, the fourth, died on the mede-vac chopper. It had been amazing that Sawaya had not died instantly, as he had been standing right over the top of one of the shells, and the initial explosion had caused several of the five dozen M-79 shells that Sawaya always carried on patrol to explode as well. Most of Sawaya's lower body was in shreds, and in spite of the constantly worn flak jacket, huge holes had been gouged into his back by the force of the secondary M-79 round explosions.

Three more Marines had been severely wounded and medevacced. Although he had been knocked down by the force of the explosion, Estes had been otherwise physically unharmed. But he had never been the same after that night.

Now, to Ed Estes, *all* Vietnamese were just gooks, regardless of their walk of life. After Estes took over Sawaya's squad on the strong recom-mendation of Sergeant Mullan, Charlie One Alpha had patrolled the next day under Estes's leadership for the first time. Their daytime patrol route took them into the same area where the command-detonated explosion had occurred. For several days, I had been blissfully ignorant of what had happened. Later, after hearing some muttered rumors from another platoon commander, I confronted Sergeant Mullan, who reluctantly filled me in. Charlie One Alpha, with Ed Estes in command, had conducted its own "search and destroy" that afternoon. Although no one had been killed, it was only because the villagers were not stupid, having lived and survived in a battle zone for most or all of their lives; they all took off, and they stayed as far away from the Marine patrol as possible.

Most hooches that Charlie One Alpha went through that afternoon mysteriously went up in smoke. Charlie One Alpha had turned into a group of "Zippo warriors" on that sad afternoon.

Since none of the villagers had been hurt or killed, since there had been no repercussions or complaints from those who undoubtedly had known that the VC were planning something explosive in their neigh-borhood before Sawaya and his men were slaughtered, and since Estes seamlessly assumed command of Charlie One Alpha and had, except for that one event, done an outstanding job as a squad leader ever since, I never spoke with him about it. It was very difficult to look Estes square in the eyes these days.

Now, as I forced myself to stop looking at the lumpy reddish gray spot on the ground where the father's head had been, I finally reacted to Estes's quiet commentary. "Sure, Estes. I'm just fine. No problem. Where are the other squad leaders?" Unfortunately, my question needed no answer, because the other two squad leaders and Sergeant Mullan were all standing just behind Estes. Seeing the looks on all their faces, I was without a doubt that they had witnessed the tail end of the body-dumping episode as well.

I mentally shook the tragic picture from my mind and addressed the squad leaders. "Okay, listen up. I want you squad leaders to talk to your people and remind them that this area was no-man's land just a couple of days ago. All they have to do is look around to know that this is a whole new deal. The shit could hit the fan at any time. No grab-assing. No horseplay. No nothing, except be alert and keep your heads down. We should be moving out any minute now, when Charlie Six gets done sifting through the rubble back there. Any questions?"

Usually, at least one of the squad leaders had some kind of a question or a comment, if for no other reason than to converse or to be a smart-ass. This time, no one had anything to say. Estes and the other two squad leaders turned away without a further thought or glance in my direction and walked back toward their troops, leaving me with Benny Benwaring, Sergeant Mullan, and my thoughts.

It was then that I noticed that I was sweating profusely and that my back under my pack, my hair, and my brow were soaking wet. The armpits of my utility blouse, the name given by the Marine Corps for the shirt part of the combat uniform, looked like I had been lounging in a sauna all morning. That could be understandable given the weight of my pack and the normal heat and humidity of Vietnam most of the year. But it was February, and it was overcast and downright cool. Although it was decidedly humid, the temperature couldn't have been more than sixty degrees. And I was soaked with sweat.

I decided not to look over in the direction of the now-departing cart. In the still morning calm I could hear the rusty old wheels groan and creak in protest as the water buffalo trudged away and the Vietnamese men carried their countrymen away.

Benny's nasal twang interrupted my perverse reverie and broke into my consciousness once again, "Lootenant, Charlie Six says to move out, and to let him know when we reach the MACV compound."

Glad to have something else to do, another direction to focus on, and happy to get out of this area and its haunting spots on the pavement, I gave the command. "Move out. Keep your eyes peeled, and don't bunch up."

Chapter Six

The Citadel

11 February 1968

The street was unnaturally quiet. It was nearly noon, and there was no one in sight on Highway One as far as I could see past my point element. Expecting the worst, but seeing nothing that would give me any reason to slow or delay our progress toward the MACV compound, I kept pace with the point fire team at a ten-meter interval and plodded methodically forward.

Sporadic and now diminishing artillery fire off in the distance to the west gave me some measure of unwarranted comfort again, making me think that perhaps this entire area *was* now secure, with the remnants of the enemy force on this side of the river being finally chased by 2/5 back into the mountains to our west. But my mind stayed paranoid and would not let me relax: What happens if some of them slipped through 2/5's lines, as they have already done five times? We could be walking right smack into an ambush. We couldn't put any flanks out, since they would have to climb over fences and through the large houses that now lined both sides of the road. Oh, well, battalion said this sector is now totally secure, so I'll just have to take their word for it.

The lieutenant/automaton part of my personality had continued to plod along steadily, and I realized that we had to be getting pretty close to our destination, the MACV compound. As my eyes recaptured their focus on my point element, I realized that our pace had slowed considerably in the past few seconds. The point fire team was still walking forward, but they were moving very slowly now. Their body language gave me no immediate cause for concern, since they hadn't indicated a hazard ahead of us or some other reason for their slowing. They carried their rifles at a ready position, but not yet in a position that indicated that they were about to fire. And then I looked beyond them and saw what had slowed the point fire team down.

There it was. The Citadel. Even after perusing and pondering the vastness of its two-dimensional image on my 1:10,000 map over the past twenty-four hours, and even though I already knew how huge it had to be, nothing had prepared me for this first three-dimensional view.

Hue's Citadel fortress was still over a kilometer away, and because of the cluster of two-story buildings sitting at its feet and the homes that lined Highway One on our left flank, only a portion of the Citadel's actual structure could be seen from our present position. But even from this limited and restricted viewpoint, it was simply awesome. The Citadel dominated all the other buildings in sight with its sheer enormity. The walls of the fortress were at least thirty feet high, but even the walls were made small by the huge tower that stood guard over the one entrance we could see. Battalion intelligence and our new maps had told us that there was a deep water-filled moat totally surrounding the outside walls of the Citadel, and although we couldn't see the moats from this position, they were easily imagined. I wondered briefly if they had drawbridges like the castles in King Arthur's era.

Just look at it! My God. The Citadel's sheer size and immense architecture just kept on going! I still couldn't see either end of the fortresslike walls, only what appeared to be the southeastern corner. It looked like all the castles I had ever seen in movies and read about in books, all rolled into one. The ancient Vietnamese emperor who built the Citadel must have employed the same architect and builders who had erected the Great Wall of China.

The immense fortress called the Citadel now commanded my entire attention, sitting regally above the comparatively insignificant commercial buildings just across the river. Those commercial buildings were not, in fact, insignificant; they were much larger than the ones we had recently passed through at the site of the destroyed tanks. It was only in comparison with the dominating walls of the Citadel that they appeared to be insignificant.

The imposing aspect of the Citadel was so riveting that I had completely failed to notice the tallest and most imposing bridge I'd seen since arriving in South Vietnam, sitting now totally useless in the middle of the Perfume River, its back broken. A huge expanse of empty space between crumbled concrete supports now allowed the waters of the Perfume to flow by unmolested and unconquered. After a quick double-take between the bridge and the Citadel, the bridge finally captured my attention. Without thinking I gasped out loud, "Number fucking ten! How the hell did they blow that big mutha bridge? That must have taken one hell of a big pile of C-4!"

The main bridge across the Perfume River, one of the largest rivers in I Corps, was now totally destroyed. It had once been a very large and obviously important bridge, since this was the only way for Highway One vehicular traffic to continue north. There was another bridge shown on my 1:10,000 map about a click to the west, but we had been told that it had been blown away years ago. The only other bridge across the Perfume River was a railroad bridge about three clicks further to the west, at the southwestern corner of the Citadel. If this railroad bridge was like any other part of the Vietnamese railway system in northern I Corps, it would also be useless.

The bridge across the Huong Giang River, or River of Perfume, had been a vital link in the resupply chain from the major American I Corps supply depots in Da Nang and Phu Bai to the combat bases in Quang Tri, Dong Ha, Khe Sanh, and the other northern outposts that kept the DMZ reasonably intact. Although this bridge had survived the NVA's Tet Offensive on the night of 31 January, the attacking NVA had blown the huge concrete and steel bridge away a couple of days later. This occurred after a point element of 2/5 had actually crossed it and had then returned to the south shore of the Perfume after making heavy contact with the NVA on the north side.

It looked as though in its heyday this bridge had supported at least two lanes of traffic in each direction, but it was now completely useless, yet another grotesque "ornament" of the war. Once-proud girders were now a spaghetti of twisted metal, and the main road surface of the bridge was completely broken in half, with a major segment of the bridge's roadbed now sloping at a near-vertical angle into the jade-green waters of the Perfume River. Whatever explosives had been used for the job had nearly disintegrated one of the reinforced concrete support structures holding the bridge's span in the center of the river. With one quick glance, it was obvious that the only vehicles going north from this point would be amphibious. Like the bridge at Lang Co, this one could not easily be replaced by a pontoon bridge because of the Perfume River's width and strong current.

But as amazing and riveting a scene that the sight of this blown-up bridge was, my attention was inevitably and persistently drawn back to the Citadel. The blown-up bridge was just one more piece of visual evidence that the Vietnam War had escalated dramatically on the night of 31 January 1968 and could never again be thought of as a "pastoral guerrilla conflict." On that long, terrible night, the Vietnam War had graduated into a full-scale conflict that would take America's full commitment and a large quantity of its tremendous firepower to get back under control.

The Citadel fortress of Hue was our final objective. That's where 1/5 was heading, across the river and into the Citadel, where we had been told the NVA had overrun and taken control of all but one tiny corner of this massive edifice. Our job was to take it back from the enemy.

Questions, all of them unanswered, swarmed through my mind. How would we get across the river, first of all? Further, if the NVA controlled nearly all of the Citadel, how the hell would we ever get inside, let alone destroy an already-entrenched enemy force? The enemy had now had nearly two weeks since the start of the Tet Offensive to get dug in and ready for our inevitable assault. If they controlled all the towers and therefore all the fortress's entry points, this was going to be one hell of a fight just getting inside the damned thing!

As these questions crowded my uneasy mind, my eyes focused again on the Citadel's entry-point tower. It was massive, at least fifty feet high and thirty feet square, made of the same large, reddish brown bricks as the walls. The tower appeared honeycombed with fighting positions, which would easily provide excellent cover for a couple of squads of fighting men by itself. I felt that if the fifty-one men of Charlie One occupied that tower and the adjacent wall, we could hold off an enemy force several times our size virtually indefinitely, given the beans, bullets, and Band-Aids that any fighting unit required to keep fighting.

As my survey of the tower continued, I noticed something that had previously escaped my attention. There was a large, red flag flying on top of the tower, and now that my eyesight finally focused on the flag, my blood ran cold and my entire body raised instant goose bumps. It was a flag, all right. It was big, it was bright red, and it had a yellow star in the center. It was the flag of the NVA.

The enemy was here, right across the river, and they were taunting us, waving their flag in our faces, saying that they were in there and that now the tables were turned. The enemy was no longer the hunted, no longer an elusive but deadly prey. The gods of war had wickedly changed the rules. The NVA had taken a great prize, and it looked like they intended to keep their prize for a long, long time. If we wanted them out of there, we could just come right on ahead and try our best to evict them, and the gods of war would decide who would prevail.

Without realizing that I was speaking just above a stage whisper, I started to tell Benny Benwaring to radio Staff Sergeant Mullan, who was still with our rear element, to come up and join me. As I began speaking, I was surprised and a little embarrassed to hear that I was whispering, so I cleared my throat, pretending like I had a frog, and forced myself to speak loudly and clearly, emulating our instructors in Quantico who had continuously emphasized the need for the command presence, to be an effective Marine Officer. Benny immediately made the radio call and told me that Sergeant Mullan had acknowledged and was on his way. It was my excuse to tear my eyesight away from the dominating presence of the Citadel, and I turned around and surveyed the trailing elements of Charlie One as I waited for "Mother" Mullan to arrive.

In referring to Staff Sergeant Mullan in conversation with my troops, I never used his well-earned nickname, because it would violate several command dictums that we had learned in Quantico. According to tradition and protocol, a marine officer should never refer to any other Marine by his first name. In Vietnam, officers and NCOs commonly referred to their troops by their last names only, simply because it was faster to say "Estes" than it was to say "Lance Corporal Estes." Enlisted men were sometimes referred to by nicknames, such as "Benny " or "Chief" (which seemed to be the nickname for every Marine I ever met who had even a small portion of Native American ancestry). But staff NCOs and officers were always referred to with both rank and last name or, in a pinch, just by their rank.

The chain of command, and the respect that the Marine Corps demanded for both rank and the chain of command, had been drummed into me for nearly two years, as it had been to every other Marine, enlisted and officers alike. Thus, it was *Sergeant* Mullan, and *Lieutenant* Warr, and *Major* Wunderlich, and *Private* Lattimer. No, I never referred to Sergeant Mullan as Mother Mullan, or Mutha Mullan, but I definitely thought of him in both those ways.

The nickname "Mother" Mullan was well earned, because SSgt. John A. Mullan definitely took his job as platoon sergeant of Charlie One very seriously. After fourteen years in the Marine Corps, Sergeant Mullan loved his men and his Corps, and he took all aspects of his job seriously, although not without a great sense of humor. Every man in Charlie One respected him and followed his orders to the T and jumped when he yelled, "Jump." And it wasn't just because they had to. In Vietnam, especially in a combat situation, you could not depend 100 percent on blind faith in the military system of obedience and courtesy. Experienced bush Marines did not instantly give their undying obedience to staff NCOs and officers, just because of their higher rank. During the Vietnam era, that respect had to be earned. Although this was not spoken of universally among the ranks, it was prevalent, and I believe it was accepted and understood as a significant but minor refinement of the rules made necessary by the shattering realities of combat in Vietnam.

In the Vietnam War, there were too many occurrences of new NCOs and officers, fresh from stateside training and ignorant of the realities of combat in the rice paddies and jungles of Vietnam, getting people needlessly hurt or killed because they took themselves too seriously and failed to listen to the experienced hands. The "rumor mill" made sure that everyone knew about these incidents. Each new NCO or officer arriving in Vietnam for the first time had to show that he had his act together before most experienced bush Marines would follow him and obey his orders blindly and instantly. The Marines' respect for the chain of command, one of several important aspects of Marine training that had made them legendary, now had to be earned by each new small unit commander that entered the fray in I Corps. In most cases, if a new Marine NCO or officer was considered potentially dangerous because of his conditioned belief in the conventional tactics he had been trained to use, yet he was likable, the experienced Marines of lesser ranks had subtle but effective methods to perform the required "on-the-job training."

"Mother" Mullan was taller than the average infantry Marine. Around my height of six foot two, Sergeant Mullan was of medium build and could hold his own physically with most younger Marines in the platoon. Although quiet by nature, he could be very loud when necessary.

God protect the Marine who screwed up within Mother Mullan's areas of responsibility. When he was riled, his long, drooping mustache, slightly outside Marine Corps regulations but not uncommon in Vietnam, would start twitching, and he would unconsciously pull one corner of it into his mouth while his light blue eyes would narrow and sparkle dangerously. He never had to revert to physical threats or even violence, as I understood sometimes occurred (although it was never tolerated) between staff NCOs and enlisted men in the Marine Corps. All he had to do to straighten out any Charlie One Marine who had the temerity or bad luck to screw up was to give that poor hapless soul the "jaundiced eyeball" that staff NCOs are so good at and let loose with a few selected motivating words and phrases.

The men of Charlie One, almost to a man, loved Sergeant Mullan as they loved their own mothers, although if you suggested that to any of them you would want to get into the next county really quickly. Furthermore, Sergeant Mullan, like the classic Marine staff NCO that he was, loved the Marines of Charlie One and took care of them in ways that even the finest of America's mothers could not measure up to. That they sometimes referred to him sarcastically and somewhat fearfully as "Mutha Mullan" was understandable and was probably the result of feeling his wrath. But even when they castigated him, it was with much respect.

Mother Mullan very seldom said anything to me in greeting in situations like this. He just walked up to me and looked me in the eye, a slight grin of acknowledgment and confidence on his face, and I knew that he was ready to take on anything I could assign him. One of the first rules learned upon arriving in Vietnam is that saluting officers is verboten, especially outside the wire (outside the protective defenses of a combat base). VC and NVA had sniper scopes, too.

I quietly gave Sergeant Mullan some quick and probably unnecessary instructions to keep the men alert and ready for anything and to take over while I went into the MACV compound and checked in. As I turned to enter the compound, I observed once again that Mother Mullan didn't have to speak to make men move. He just did his version of a Sawaya survey, gazing in each squad leader's direction with his "jaundiced eyeball" expression, and the men of Charlie One reacted instantly, taking up firing positions with whatever cover was available. Highway One quickly became the dusty, empty center of an elongated perimeter of Marines ready to fight. Confident that Charlie One was in good hands, I turned away and entered the MACV compound.

The MACV compound was an old two- or three-story hotel reinforced by stacks and rows of sandbags and many strands of barbed wire. It was the last building on the east side of Highway One and was just two hundred meters from the entrance to the destroyed bridge. From my vantage point just outside the sandbagged entrance to the compound, I could easily see the Perfume River, and the bridge that could no longer perform its duties. On the river's south shore just to the east of the bridge, I saw what looked like a very busy, hastily prepared boat docking area. Obviously, bulldozers had scraped away any vegetation that had lined the edge of the river to allow boats to load and unload their cargoes.

There were a few Vietnamese sampans hovering just offshore, but there was no room for them to dock. Several U.S. Navy LCMs, or "Mike boats," the middle-sized landing craft associated with the landing forces of the Marine Corps since late in World War II, were dominating the rudimentary docking area. Landing craft were not new to us. As a trainee in Camp Pendleton and again in Quantico while going through Basic School, I had participated in amphibious warfare exercises and had hit the beach with forty-nine other second lieutenants just south of Virginia Beach early one morning from the ramp of a Mike boat.

There were two other types of landing craft used by Marines. The small Poppa boat was the original landing craft that appeared during the height of the Pacific War after the Marines learned the hard way that the Higgins boat was more trouble than it was worth. The Higgins had no convenient front ramp to protect its passengers from small-arms fire until it dropped down to become the bridge from the boat to the (theoretically) dry shoreline. As passengers on the Higgins boat, the World War II Marines were offered little protection from enemy small-arms fire, because the Higgins boat was made mostly out of wood. And there was no front ramp, so that when a Higgins boat ended its journey on an enemy-held shoreline, its occupants had to crawl over its sides, into the sometimes shallow, sometimes deep water at the shoreline.

The Poppa boat and its larger sibling, the Mike boat, were a great improvement over the Higgins boat. About twenty Marines could squeeze into a Poppa boat, while the much larger Mike boat could handle about fifty combat-ready Marines. The steel construction of these improved modes of combat transportation provided much more protection; their large, powerful diesel engines could often push the bow of the landing craft right up onto the beach, and the front ramp would then drop down, allowing easy egress onto the beach. At least, this was usually the case. A few times during the South Pacific island-hopping campaigns, the designated landing beaches did not cooperate, and their protective coral reefs prevented the landing craft from making it all the way to the beach. The Navy personnel had no choice but to drop their ramps and watch as the Marines assaulted into chest-high water several hundred meters from the shoreline. But still, these boats were great improvements over the Higgins boat.

The third in this family of amphibious warfare landing craft was called the LCU, or landing craft utility. The Navy personnel referred to them as Whiskey boats. Perhaps they were a more current version of the LCU, or LCW. (The word "Whiskey" is used in the military alphabet.) Although I had not yet laid eyes on one personally, I had heard a few things about these craft. According to the rumor mill, a Whiskey boat made a Mike boat look like a rowboat by comparison.

Amid the confusion of the Mike boats clustered around the Perfume River's chaotic shoreline, two Whiskey boats stood, ramps down, disgorging a stream of supplies carried by a motley group of Marines. The Whiskey boats were huge. It looked as though we could get the entire company on board and have room left over. The crew of Marines tending to the Whiskey boats' hoard of much-needed supplies were scurrying like ants between a huge pile of ammunition and other supplies stacked up above the high-water mark and the boats. Several pallets of C rations had been off-loaded from the Whiskey boats and were stacked neatly side-by-side next to the more deadly supplies. Still somewhat affected by our shortage of food at Lang Co, I found this a comforting sight. At least we're going to have chow for a while, even if it was only C rats, I thought. The Gunny will be happy.

The scene was made unusual and captivating by the obviously frenetic pace of the platoon of Marines off-loading the supplies, and for a moment I mused that they must have been engaged in a race of some sort. Normally, Marines assigned the duty of carrying any mound of supplies from one point to another resembled reluctant, two-legged mules with helmets instead of ears. Their progress was usually steady (especially when the jaundiced eyeballs of their gunny or their platoon sergeants were within range), but there was nearly always much complaining about the unfairness of not only having to face danger and death fighting for their country, but having to do the work of beasts as well. This time, although I was within easy hearing distance of the work, I could tell that no one had any time to bitch. These men were nearly running back and forth between the Whiskey boats and the temporary supply dump, each with a case of small-arms ammo or mortar rounds or some other form of death.

I was about to ask myself why they were in such a hurry when the NVA manning the Citadel's tower across the river made my question superfluous. A single shot from an AK-47 rang out loudly, and the working party hit the deck. Someone screamed, "Sniper, sniper! Get down, get your heads down!" Another frantic voice out shouted this alert with, "Where the fuck did that one come from? Is it still those assholes on the tower?"

After a few seconds went by and there were no following shots, the work party started to move quickly again, and I decided that I didn't want to ask too many more questions. Without choice, my mind asked another, inevitable question: I wonder how long this has been going on? That made it easier to tear myself away from the action and to go into the MACV compound.

As I stepped into the MACV compound's sandbagged entryway, I was blinded for a few moments as my eyes slowly adjusted to the gloomy light typical of an American command bunker in Vietnam. Command bunkers in Vietnam were often dug into the ground several feet and then covered with three or four feet of timbers, metal runway sections, and layer after layer of sandbags, the Marine's constant companion. This one was inside a building that could have once been a large home or a small hotel. The main part of the working areas were at ground level, but there appeared to be a second, perhaps even a third floor. The inside walls were all reinforced by a layer or two of sandbags, and the entryway was double-reinforced by sandbags. Walking into command bunkers always left me with a vaguely claustrophobic feeling, like I was crawling inside a cave.

Of course, a command bunker's size, permanency, and resources were in strict proportion to the command group that they contained. Divisional command bunkers were near-duplicates of stateside "puzzle palaces," with a myriad of communications devices, status boards, and tactical maps dominating the decor. Regimental and then battalion command bunkers were scaled-down versions of this theme, with their size somehow always matching their position in the chain of command. Company and platoon command bunkers were most often hastily prepared, offering little in the way of shelter or resources.

Yet regardless of their size and importance, command bunkers all had some things in common. The plastic-covered tactical maps critical to command and communications at every level were the most obvious similarity; one or more Prick-25 radios and other larger, more powerful communications devices took up nearly every square inch of available desk space. The strange breed of men who filled the airwaves with their constant, absolutely necessary babble of information took up most of the sitting spaces. And the darkness. There were no windows in command bunkers, for obvious reasons, so even during the brightest hours of the day, command bunkers were smoke-filled dungeons making even those with the best vision strain their eyes to see every detail.

The other thing that all command bunkers had in common was that they were either totally becalmed with bored silence sporadically stirred gently with a quiet situation report or request for supplies coming in over the radio network from a subordinate unit, or they were a place of shattering chaos. When one or more field units were in contact with the enemy, the bored silence of command bunkers quickly deteriorated into a nightmare of tension, frantic cries for help in the form of fire missions or medevac requests, or requests for reinforcements, resupply, or reaction/maneuver forces to help them get back into control of their situation.

The MACV compound matched the image of the normal command bunker in every way. At this particular moment, it was quiet, although there were probably twenty people inside its gloomy walls. After walking further inside the sandbagged room that served as the main command and control point for the MACV in Hue, I began picking up bits of quiet conversations between radio operators and each other, and between the officers. These officers had the job of making the decisions that would keep them and the American and South Vietnamese forces firmly in control of the conflict now raging out of control throughout South Vietnam.

The dim, smoky light gave the brightly colored arrows, boxes, rectangles, and other assorted symbols on the maps a muted, fluorescent hue. These symbols indicated the locations of enemy units, friendly positions, and suspected avenues of attack. I easily recognized the baseball-diamond-shaped Citadel fortress in the center of the large wall map that immediately grabbed the attention of any person who entered the room. None of the occupants of the command center had yet noticed my entry, so I had a few moments to study the map, to see if I could learn anything about what we were up against.

Most symbols that represented military units inside the Citadel itself were one color, red. Red was the color reserved for enemy positions.

There were several red symbols crowded inside most of the Citadel, and one black symbol, alone by itself in the northeast corner of the diamond-shaped Citadel. I was already aware, from the briefing we were given in Phu Bai on the previous day, that this symbol represented the head-quarters group of the First ARVN Division and some infantry units who were providing security for them. There sure as hell were a lot of red symbols on the tactical map, both inside and outside that damned Citadel. After nearly two weeks of constant fighting with large elements of a pre-viously elusive enemy, the Viet Cong and the NVA still had a strangle-hold on the Hue area. There was little comfort in the black symbols that now dominated south Hue, because my eyes were forced back to the blotches of red. How many of them were there waiting for us inside Hue's Citadel fortress?

As these questions crowded my mind with the fears and uncertainties that had constantly been present since my arrival in Vietnam, I noticed someone break away from the group of Marine and Army officers deep in discussion and map-gazing and head in my direction. I quickly recog-nized him to be Maj. L. A. Wunderlich, 1/5's battalion S-3, or operations officer. Major Wunderlich had been our S-3 and effectively third in com-mand (after the battalion commander and executive officer) of 1/5 since I had arrived in country, and I had experienced several brief but confidence-building encounters with him. Major Wunderlich always seemed to remain calm, no matter how difficult the present crisis; he had a great strategic and tactical mind. The Marines and officers of 1/5 liked him a lot, and we were all expecting him to take over as the new battalion com-mander, since our last CO was killed a few days before in Phu Loc 6. Although the battalion executive officer, Maj. P. A. Wilson, was techni-cally second in command, as the battalion S-3, Major Wunderlich was the de facto second in command of the forward elements of 1/5.

Major Wunderlich had the same relaxed, almost bored expression he always carried around. Only the much-deepened bags under his eyes dis-played the stress weighing down on his shoulders since I had first met him in Hoi An. In the four or five weeks between 1/5's move to Phu Loc 6 on Christmas Day 1967 and the night of the Tet Offensive, 1/5 had undergone the new command of, and then the loss of, two new battalion commanders.

I greeted Major Wunderlich in the required traditional manner (Marines do not wear any "cover" while indoors, and we do not salute without a cover, or hat, on, unlike our Army brethren) by simply com-ing to attention as he approached. He responded in his normal, quiet but strong voice, with a small, amused smile on his face. "How are you doing, Charlie One? Keeping your head down?"

I tried to shake off the persistent nagging fears and questions about the impending operation and forced as much confidence into my manner and voice as possible. "Just fine, sir. Charlie One is the point platoon for the battalion, and we were instructed to make contact with you here and then await further orders. My men are strung out down the street. I had Benny contact Charlie Six Actual and let him know that we're here, and he should be up here pretty soon, sir." I had never been able to develop the knack of being, or even acting, totally calm when addressing someone two or more grades higher in rank than me.

Major Wunderlich replied, "OK, Lieutenant. Go ahead on back out there with your people and tell them to keep spread out and to keep their fool heads down, hear? I'll fill Lieutenant Nelson in on the scoop when he gets here. But thanks for letting me know that you're here; I feel safer already." I wasn't sure if he was serious, or if he was mocking my attempt to be militarily proper.

"Aye, aye, sir. Major Wunderlich?" I knew I'd been dismissed, but I couldn't help asking just one more question.

"Yes, Lieutenant Warr?" was his wistful reply.

"Sir, are you taking over 1/5 permanently this time, sir? The men are all speculating that they will let you take over as skipper, sir. We all feel pretty comfortable with you running the show." This was the major topic of scuttlebutt in the rumor mill, and the odds were heavily in favor of Wunderlich, a very senior major who had been with 1/5 for many months, taking over as battalion commander.

Wunderlich cast me a weary glance and said, "No, Lieutenant. 1/5 has a new skipper. He joined us this morning. You'll be meeting him down by the loading ramps later."

I persisted, asking, "Down by the loading ramps, sir? What's the colonel's name, sir? Do we know him?" Discretion was never one of my strong points.

Major Wunderlich replied, "Uh, he's not a lieutenant colonel quite yet, although he's up for the promotion right now. His name is Major Robert Thompson."

Continuing in my no-thought mode, I asked further, "Major Thompson, sir? I don't recall a Major Thompson in any of the other battalions' S-3 slots. Is he new in-country?" I tried hard to keep any of the constantly present fear out of my voice. Breaking in a new battalion commander could be very hazardous to the health of the troops, especially if this was his first combat experience in Vietnam.

"No, *Lieutenant,*" Major Wunderlich subtly emphasized my rank as a gentle reminder of just exactly who I was. "He's not new in-country. He's been the Fifth Marine's Regimental S-4 for several months." Wunderlich was beginning, obviously, to tire of this conversation.

I couldn't stop. The bald edge of fear egged me on. "S-4, sir? You mean he's the regimental *supply officer,* sir?" I had not at all intended for my voice to crack when I said the word "supply." Nor had I considered for even a moment that everyone else in the bunker would stop their tense, whispered conversations to breathe a collective breath. But it happened, as it had happened that time in my Junior English class when I had tried to silently squeeze out a persistent fart. Just as I thought that the gas would pass without notice, everyone in the room stopped talking and my attempt at stealthy gas-passing failed miserably. Most of my high school classmates had burst into loud and long raucous laughter at what became mildly famous at Marshfield High School in Coos Bay, Oregon, as "Warr's Salvo." Now, however, the gallows-humor laughter was stifled. Most of the Marines and Army personnel in the bunker were experienced in combat. They could thus immediately identify with my reaction to this information, that 1/5 would go into combat with a brand-new commanding officer who was a supply officer. Flashing looks of fatalism crossed the few sets of eyes visible in the gloom.

Major Wunderlich was less amused. "Lieutenant Warr, *must* you be reminded that we are *all* trained to be infantry officers *first* in the Marine Corps? That no matter what our particular assignment may be, that being an infantry officer is our number-one priority in any situation that dictates it?" From my present position at point-blank range, Wunderlich's quiet but firm voice slashed me unmercifully, but fortunately, the others in the room were oblivious to, or ignoring, my dressing down as he continued his tongue lashing. "Major Thompson is going to need 125 percent effort and confidence from everyone, especially from someone in your position. I don't want to hear another comment or question of that sort again. You understand me, Mister?"

I reflexively came to attention and said, "No, sir. I mean, yes, sir. I mean, aye, aye, sir." Clumsily, hastily, I began a tactical withdrawal and started edging toward the door and freedom. Like a brand new "boot" Marine, I erroneously but instinctively saluted Major Wunderlich while "uncovered," breaking a long-standing Marine Corps tradition and acting like just any other dog-face soldier. Then, of course, realizing my error and now attracting the attention of everyone in the MACV command post, I made a bad situation worse by tripping over my feet as I turned abruptly and nearly lost my balance. I barely recovered and stumbled, red-faced, back out into the gray morning.

Although the sun was mostly blocked by the persistent overcast, the daylight momentarily blinded me as I emerged from the MACV compound, the low sounds of quiet, bitter laughter completing my humiliation. It still didn't matter much. The single dominant thought in my mind at that moment, and one that ruled my thoughts continuously through the days and weeks ahead, was that 1/5 was now in the hands of a *logistics* officer. Now, I don't want to belittle the importance of supply or logistics, because this is obviously a critical aspect of successful military campaigns. However, S-4s were usually people who wanted to be in logistics, and not necessarily in command. Further, Major Thompson might have been the most exemplary officer in the history of the Marine Corps, but if he was an S-4, chances are that he had little or no combat experience, specifically little or no infantry combat experience. As I continued to think about it, however, I realized that fact was not rare. The United States had not fought a significant war since the end of the Korean conflict fourteen years previously. One result of that happy fact turned out to be usually unhappy for junior officers, NCOs, and enlisted men in the Vietnam War. It meant that their company and battalion commanders usually had no combat experience. It took between four and six years to reach the rank of captain, then another four to six years to be promoted to major, and then another six to ten to achieve the rank of lieutenant colonel. This meant that the average lieutenant colonel or senior major, like Majors Thompson and Wunderlich, had been commissioned after 1954 and thus had little or no combat experience. This situation did not sit well with combat Marines who knew too well the realities of the battlefield in Vietnam.

These unsettling thoughts vaporized as the image of 1st Lt. Scott Nelson and The Gunny came into focus, my eyes finally adjusting to the gray gloom once again. It was immediately obvious that the company CP group was all there, obvious because of the cluster of "whip antennae" that surrounded Nelson and The Gunny as they approached the MACV compound. There were three fifteen-foot-high antennae, indicating that the Charlie Company radio, Travis Curd's FO radio, and a forward air controller's radio were dueling for the airspace over Scott

Nelson's head. They really do look like aiming stakes, as we often labeled them, using the pervasive black humor of Vietnam. I had to be careful with that name around Benny, though, because he would go into a black funk if you referred to his whip antenna as an aiming stake. Benny in a black funk was not to be tolerated.

As usual, Scott Nelson had his map in one hand and the phonelike radio receiver of his command PRC-25 in the other, holding it gingerly to his right ear. He looked, for just a moment, like an overgrown child using a telephone for the first time in his life. As he approached the entry to the MACV compound, tucking the map packet back into the left leg pocket of his Marine Corps–issue utility trousers, he flashed his patented, boyish grin briefly in my direction and then concentrated on finishing his radio conversation.

"Roger, Millhouse Six, I'm at the MACV compound now. I'll make contact with Millhouse Three and await orders. Charlie Six Actual, out." The Prick-25 squawked a distant, "Millhouse Six, out," and went dead in Nelson's ear. Nelson slowly pulled the phone out of his ear, continued to listen for just a moment longer, seemingly reluctant to believe that his new experience with a telephone was over, then gave up, handed the handset to his radio operator, and directed his solid frame toward me and the MACV compound. More than anything else, Nelson resembled a football player, probably a center, breaking eagerly away from the huddle, ready to kick some ass and take some names. Nelson was eager to get on with the game, to get his hands on the ball.

"How are you, Charlie One?" Nelson asked.

"Er, just fine, Skipper." I needed to be elsewhere, or I would begin to compulsively confess my faux pas of a few minutes past. I decided on the spur of the moment to take a chance on Major Wunderlich's being too busy to mention my unfortunate choice of words when learning about our new battalion commander, and kept my mouth shut.

Nelson said, "Okay, Charlie One. Just make sure your people keep their heads down out here. It's kinda quiet around here."

"Aye, aye, sir," I replied. I was still not quite comfortable with Nelson as our company commander. I didn't like calling him "Skipper," as Marine company commanders were often called. The title "Skipper" was earned, not automatic. I didn't like Nelson's habit of using my radio call sign, Charlie One, when he was talking to me face to face. It seemed like he couldn't get out of the "command radio voice mode" that had been drilled into all of us during our long months of OCS and Basic School at Quantico.

Still grinning at everything in general, Nelson finally tore his gaze away from the southwestern wall of the Citadel and ducked into the MACV compound. He had obviously seen the NVA flag flying defiantly above the Citadel walls, but he had refrained from commenting upon the view. Charlie Company would now receive our marching orders into the Citadel fortress of Hue. Now we would find out just how long that crimson symbol of the enemy's defiance would continue flying over the Citadel.

The Marines of First Platoon, Charlie Company, First Battalion, Fifth
Marines, at the Phu Loc 6 firebase. This snapshot was taken a couple of
days before the NVA started their mortar and rocket attacks on the combat
base. January 1968. Pfc. Robert Lattimer is on the far left of the front row,
kneeling. SSgt. John Mullan is kneeling, in the center, fifth from the left.
L. Cpl. Ed Estes is standing behind SSgt. Mullan, dressed in a dark green
sweatshirt. Ed's friend and Marine buddy Charles Morgan is standing fifth
from the left. Charlie One radio operator Benny Benwaring is standing
between them. *(author photo)*

1/5's combat base at Phu Loc 6, early January 1968. Tent City, just before
the trenching and burrowing began in earnest. *(author photo)*

The author's OCS graduation picture. Quantico, Virginia. March, 1967. *(author photo)*

Aerial view of the southeast corner of the Citadel fortress of Hue. This photo was taken sometime after the NVA destroyed the main Highway One bridge, which is clearly seen in the lower left-hand corner of the photo. The Imperial Palace, the "inner fortress" of the Citadel, is also clearly seen in the upper right-hand corner. Most of the fighting inside the Citadel's geometrically shaped outer walls took place in the residential district directly below the Imperial Palace, lower right-hand corner of the photo. *(U.S. Marine Corps photo)*

Photograph taken by (then) Major Thompson, depicting 1/5 Marines aboard a Navy Mike 8 boat. I believe that this "Mike 8" boat was actually what I call a "Whiskey" boat, or what the Navy calls an LCU. The very wide gunwales of this boat and the extremely large load also indicate that this was an LCU. It doesn't matter; these are 1/5 Marines advancing by landing craft toward their objective: the Citadel fortress of Hue. *(U.S. Marine Corps photo)*

I believe that this is a Delta Company Marine, near the crest of the Dong Ba Tower, the scene of some of the bloodiest fighting inside the Citadel. The extended wall of the Citadel can be seen clearly in the upper right-hand section of the photo, and it is obviously much lower than the rubble on the tower. *(UPI/Corbis-Bettmann photo)*

Marines of D Company, 1/5. The infamous Dong Ba Porch, or Dong Ba Tower, stands out clearly in the background. This photo was taken after the fighting was over in this area, which is evidenced by the severe battle damage to the tower and the fact that these Marines are standing around in the open. *(U.S. Marine Corps photo)*

The ramp at Hue, June 1967. *(U.S. Naval Historical Center photo)*

An aerial view of the Hue Citadel airstrip looking north. *(U.S. Marine Corps photo)*

An aerial view of the Old Imperial City of Hue as seen from the doorway of a helicopter. *(U.S. Marine Corps photo)*

Chapter Seven

Whiskey Boats on the Perfume River

11–12 February 1968

The rest of the day was a blur. Throughout the remainder of that long and gloomy day, I felt as though we were all sleepwalking through the fringes of hell. Wherever we went that day, we were surrounded by scenes of madness and chaos, populated by other condemned souls equally intent on nothing but survival. Charlie One was on edge, nervous, constantly reminded of the defiant NVA battle flag flying over the Citadel and the fact that we would soon be inside, or trying to get inside, the Citadel, to confront . . . exactly what we would confront, no one knew for sure. All we knew was that it was our duty to cross the river, to enter the Citadel, and to root out the enemy who had taken Hue by force almost two weeks before. To the combat infantryman, two weeks was an eternity. Our enemy was, at the very least, a very determined bunch who were capable of just about anything, in spite of their distinct and obvious disadvantages in numbers and the firepower that they could bring to bear. They would be dug in and just as intent on keeping their ill-gotten holdings. That fact we knew for sure.

Part of the strange feeling of sleepwalking was caused, I was sure, by my bumbling act in the MACV compound. Part of it was knowing that our new battalion commander, from all indications, was a professional logistics officer who probably hadn't a minute's worth of combat command experience. Part of it was the simple act of walking through the suburbs of south Hue and not really believing my own eyes. For the first time since I had arrived in Vietnam, Charlie One was in a city. Not a flimsy, sprawling, insubstantial village to which we had become accustomed, but the closest thing to a roaring metropolis that I had seen since I set foot on Vietnam's soil. The terrain was dominated by paved streets with curbs and sidewalks, with well-established shade trees sheltering the scene. The common structures in this area were two-story houses with glass windows, and a few even possessed TV antennae reaching angularly toward the sky. I wondered, briefly, if they were watching Vietnamese-dubbed reruns of "Father Knows Best." . . . At this point, it wouldn't have surprised me in the least.

After Scott Nelson had received Charlie Company's orders, we moved quickly to comply. We were directed to proceed to the stadium about a click to the southeast, to top off our supply of beans, Band-Aids, and bullets, and then to move into some homes in that area for the night.

The stadium was really hard to believe, the ultimate incongruity. It was a miniature version of the Los Angeles Coliseum, complete with arched entryway, playing field, and enough seating to hold at least ten thousand spectators. At this moment, however, it was obvious that whatever games were being played were not at all sporting and that this gathering was deadly serious. The entire playing field, large enough to host the playing of American football or international soccer, was overwhelmed by stacks of C rations, huge piles of small-arms ammunition, and an incredible array of high explosives. Before the afternoon was over, most of 1/5 had entered the stadium and had partaken of the supplies until we were sufficiently weighted down with a week's supply of the necessary implements of battle.

One item that we were issued caused me some initial concern. Every man in 1/5 was given a standard military gas mask. We had received some raw intelligence indicating that the NVA had a limited capability to engage in chemical warfare, and we weren't going to take any chances.

Late that afternoon, after The Gunny and Scott Nelson were satisfied that we could carry no more, Charlie Company saddled up and moved out of the stadium into the nearby houses in southeast Hue, our rest stop for the night.

There was no question that we would simply take over whatever home we wanted, and although our occupation of several homes was accomplished with the combat Marine's typical lack of military precision, the Vietnamese occupants simply moved aside and let us take over their homes. They seemed to accept our presence as a necessary evil, and they capitulated their homes and hearths without incident or struggle. The Vietnamese homeowners simply disappeared under beds, or squeezed into a single room, or left for parts unknown.

The home Charlie One's CP group slept in that night was fairly unique in that it bragged of indoor plumbing, including running faucets, porcelain sinks, and an actual toilet, of sorts. Actually, the toilet was a hole in the concrete floor of a communal bathroom, which was positioned over a tributary of an ancient underground sewer system. There was one minor inconvenience for all the Americans present. The user of the toilet had nothing to sit on. For the Vietnamese, this was no problem, as we were accustomed to seeing a rural Vietnamese simply squatting beside a path or road and relieving himself or herself whenever and wherever the urge overtook them. Vietnamese men, in particular, were very skilled in urinating down their "pajama" pant legs without getting a drop on their pants. So, a Vietnamese using this very modern bathroom could simply squat over the hole and do his or her thing. The advantage of this particular evacuation point was that there was no concern for dealing with the feces; they dropped nicely into the sewer, never to be heard from again. No flushing was necessary, no heartache of clogged drains. This was not the case for the typical Marine, however. Most men in the Charlie One command post took their turns over the hole, and there were a few near misses. Marines were not accustomed to squatting in spite of our spending a lot of time in the bush. We were still definitely sitters. As a matter of fact, whenever we stopped for any length of time, a lot of time and ingenuity was always expended rigging up a seating area for even the most rudimentary outdoor toilet. Marines only squatted if necessary. To an American it seemed that the Vietnamese people spent half their life squatting.

After the uniqueness of the indoor plumbing had worn off, Charlie One bunked down for the night on whatever floor space we could find. A few of us commandeered a bed with a mattress, and we made good use of it that night.

The next morning, 12 February 1968, Charlie Company moved out of the homes of southeast Hue and moved back to the boat ramp on the south shore of the Perfume River near the MACV compound. Here we would load into Whiskey boats for our journey toward the Citadel of Hue.

Hue's Citadel fortress may be accurately described as a diamond in the rough grasp of the Perfume River. Almost one and one-half miles square, the Citadel is bounded on its entire southern wall by the Perfume River, which then works north but doesn't bend as rapidly as the ninety-degree corner of the fortress. The river wanders northward away from the Citadel walls for nearly two miles, then abruptly turns back southwest and rushes to attach itself to the northern corner of the fortress walls. Then, once again, the river turns back away from the Citadel to find its way northeast to the Gulf of Tonkin. The land mass caught inside the sharp bend of the river but outside the Citadel walls resembles a lazy snail stuck to the eastern wall of the fortress. This land mass, called Bach Dang, is effectively made an island community by the surrounding waters of the Perfume River and an intersecting canal called the Dong Ba canal. Based upon some sporadic stories filtering out of Hue since the night of 31 January, American intelligence then believed that the entire area of Bach Dang was completely controlled and occupied by the NVA. To get to the back door of the Citadel, we would have to go around the NVA, taking the scenic route provided by the Perfume River. Looking at my 1:10,000 map as we approached the boat ramp area, I could only hope that the NVA hanging out in Bach Dang weren't paying too close attention to river traffic that morning.

Despite the organized bedlam that occupied the boat ramp area, Charlie Company managed to get aboard two large landing craft, the Whiskey boats we had seen the previous day. The loading parties had been very busy that morning, because we weren't the only cargo on this voyage. As I realized what the rest of the cargo was, my testicles involuntarily slid up into their protective pockets, instinctively retreating into their safe havens.

The Whiskey boats were filled to the gunwales with supplies. In our case, however, the emphasis had been on high-explosive supplies, such as M-16 and M-60 ammunition, case after case of 81-mm and 60-mm mortar rounds, LAAWs rockets (light anti-armor weapons—the modern, disposable replacement for the bazooka), what appeared to be 90-mm tank rounds and 106-mm recoilless rifle ammo, and even some old 3.5-inch bazooka rocket rounds. We were directed by the shore party to pull up a crate and make ourselves as comfortable as possible. The water portion of our journey was about to get under way. The smoking lamp was definitely not lit. In the Marine Corps, that meant that smoking was not allowed. No one asked, and no one bitched.

There were so many crates lining the bottom of our Whiskey boat that its high gunwales offered very little protection. If a sniper opened up from the banks of the river, we'd be seriously exposed and men would get hurt. With that uplifting thought in mind, I sat down on a crate of 81-mm mortar rounds and silently determined to make the best of an entirely insane situation. As the boat's front ramp began to noisily winch its way closed and its big diesel engines started to rev up, I looked back toward the bank of the river to see, for the first time, our new battalion commander.

Major Thompson was standing by himself, about fifty meters away from the nearest loading party, above and away from them, watching something on the sandy bank of the Perfume River, between the Whiskey boats and the staging areas where the loading parties started preparations for their next assignment. It was obviously him, even at this distance. His utility uniform was very green and looked almost brand-new. His green helmet cover was equally noticeable near a group of combat veterans, whose utilities and helmets were faded and rumpled and soiled by the vagaries of combat. Major Thompson stood out like a huge green thumb in a sea of faded Marine Corps–green utilities. I could even see his gold oak leaves, the insignia for the rank of major in the Marine Corps, glinting in the morning's dampened sunlight. He'd learn soon enough to camouflage his insignia, if he survived long enough.

I was struck by his size and his stance. He was a large man by Marine Corps standards. The average Marine was well under six feet, and often the really short guys were the toughest fighters. Major Thompson was well over six feet, perhaps six three or six four even. He had a broad face and a long, lanky frame.

I couldn't tell from here if what I was seeing on Major Thompson's face was aloof command presence or stunned concern. It didn't matter. My most immediate concern right then was that I was resting my butt on about a million pounds of high explosives. Major Thompson's combat experience factor seemed very insignificant right about then.

The bow ramp clanked into place, and the engines started to pull heavily in reverse, pulling the stern down and the bow up, with finally enough force to overcome the suction of the muddy bank. Charlie Company, packed like sardines inside two Whiskey boats loaded with death and destruction, cast off and turned downstream toward our objective, the ferry ramp just a few hundred meters north of the Citadel's northern corner.

Although the northern tip of the Citadel's walls was only a little over three kilometers away as the crow flies, our river voyage would be nearly six clicks due to our circuitous route. First we headed on a compass bearing of due north, downstream, following the middle of the river. Within a click or so, the river split into two channels, the outside or eastern channel, and the larger inside, or western channel. Our boat skipper opted for the larger channel in an obvious and welcome attempt to keep us as far away from any shore as possible. We had no idea who had control of the shoreline in this area.

The Whiskey boats proceeded at a throttle setting that seemed to be lacking. I couldn't help but wonder, What the hell are they thinking, dawdling like this? We need to get there, like right now; this slowpoke ferry sucks.

No one else in Charlie Company, at least in the Whiskey boat I was in, was saying much of anything. I think we all had our collective breath held, and no one wanted to break the spell. One man unconsciously broke out a cigarette, stuck it in his mouth without thinking, and whipped out his Zippo lighter. He never even got close to lighting it, and no one had to say or do anything to prevent this act of utter stupidity. In the absolute silence, the Marine with the nicotine fit became slowly aware of the tension in the air surrounding him, and he quickly noticed that every man within eyesight was intently focused on him, sending him a vibrant message to wake up and smell the roses. He sheepishly tucked the cigarette inside his helmet, behind his right ear, and tried to look very small. No one gave him any shit. We all knew that this was not a good place to be, but we also knew that we were all in this together.

Five minutes into our voyage I found out that the Whiskey boat's skipper had set the throttle to the maximum speed since we had left the shoreline. But despite the mind-numbing, terrifying pop heard over the rumble of the diesel engines that indicated the first enemy mortar round leaving its tube, aimed at us, the boat gained no additional speed. There was no question that the pedal was to the metal.

We were under mortar attack, rounds were in the air at this exact moment, and we had no holes to jump into. Not a man moved. There was no sense in dropping to the deck, because in this case the deck was the worst place to be. No matter whether this was a 60-mm or an 82-mm enemy mortar, if it struck its target—us—we were all history. My testicles impossibly rose higher in their protective nooks. We sat and waited and held our collective breath. A second round popped out of the enemy mortar tube, and a few seconds later, a third, just as the first round exploded. It shattered the relative quiet of the morning, which had only been broken before by the sound of the boat engines. Waiting for the second round to land and explode right between my feet, I finally realized that the first round had exploded harmlessly about fifty meters behind us in our wake. I still knew there were others in the air, however, falling down, ready to explode and take our lives away. As the second one exploded a hundred meters ahead of us—Oh God, they've got us bracketed—I felt a surging beneath our feet. It dawned on me that the boat skippers had started weaving erratically back and forth. And then the third round exploded between us—God, *between* the two Whiskey boats, oh God, they've got us pinpointed. I finally registered the fact that the .50-caliber machine guns mounted on the stern ramp of the Whiskey boats had been firing steadily at the shoreline, more harassing fire than anything else, and—Was there a fourth round?

Abruptly, the brief clash ended. No more explosions came, and the shattering sounds of battle died away, their fading echoes disappearing into the watery sounds of the Whiskey boats' progress. A few more sporadic .50-caliber rounds belatedly sprayed down suspected mortar launch sites on the river's shoreline, and then engine-muted silence took hold as the Whiskey boats and their passengers proceeded northward. No more mortar rounds were lobbed at us. It became just one more moment of survival, a moment when your entire being goes into slow motion and your sensory inputs go to levels never before experienced. Sights and sounds are extraordinary in their clarity and persistence; your minds scream out to run, run, get the hell out of town; and the body, the highly trained body resists, remains rigidly motionless, and then relaxes slightly as the slow motion speeds back up to normalcy and the breathing steadies once again. Just one more moment of survival in Vietnam, just one more day in the 'Nam.

The Whiskey boats continued their winding pattern, as we followed the winding river back toward the west. The boats maintained their ponderous maximum speed until the ferry ramp was spotted a few minutes later, when they cut their speed in preparation for landing on the ferry ramp, slowed, and then bumped into the shoreline. The craft dropped their front ramps on the ferry ramp and dumped their loads, namely, us. Although at that point in my young life I considered myself a true infantryman, one who would always opt for any mode of transportation other than walking, or humping, as we called it, whenever it was available, this was one trip that I would not look back upon with fondness. I had to physically make an effort not to soil myself as I stepped off the front ramp of the boat and back onto good old terra firma, and my body slowly shed an incredible amount of tension and relaxed for the first time in nearly a half hour.

Charlie Company moved into temporary defensive positions surrounding the ferry ramp and remained in place while the other companies, Delta and Alpha, and the battalion command group were delivered by ensuing waves of Whiskey boats. We didn't mind the wait. We seemed to be alone over here, with the few nearby houses or hooches either being deserted or having their occupants hidden deep within their bomb shelters. And, since our next objective was to enter the Citadel via the back door, no one around here was in any particular hurry.

While we waited for the rest of 1/5 to arrive, I called the squad leaders up for a quick powwow. I reviewed our situation, pinpointing positions and landmarks on my map, and traced the route of march that we would be taking when the rest of the battalion arrived. A narrow, shady road followed the west bank of the river where the ferry ramp integrated river traffic with foot traffic and vehicles of every type. The road went north into the countryside, and south toward the Citadel, now only a few hundred meters away.

When the squad leaders huddled, I said, "All right, listen up. When the rest of the battalion arrives, we'll be moving out. We're not the point element, but we're second in line, and I want to make sure you are all aware of the route in case we get separated or we have to take over point. We take this road southeast, across the canal via this bridge, and then look for a sharp hairpin turn back to the right, or northwest. Take note of the intersection in the road where we either have to go straight ahead, into this snail-like area here called Bach Dang, or we take this hairpin-shaped turn back hard to the right, which will put us on this access road." I was pointing to the road that ran along a strip of land lying between the large canal that surrounded the Citadel complex, the moat that protected the fortress walls, and the walls themselves. "Then, if all went well last night and the First ARVN Division still holds this section of the Citadel, we take the access road about a click to the first moat bridge and gate entrance we come to and go into the Citadel through the back door. Any questions?"

The only question was off the subject and nearly insubordinate, and I chose to ignore it. I dismissed the squad leaders so they could get back with their men. It was just like Estes to ask the stupid question in the first place, and it was just like the squad leaders to laugh quietly with their eyes at the joke-slash-question. Estes had looked up at me from his squatting position and had asked with all seriousness, "Do they expect us to get back in them fucking boats after we're done in here? Like shit, ain't no way I'm getting back in one of them fucking boats, even if I have to swim across that fucking river and hump all the way back to Phu Bai all by myself. No sir, I ain't getting back in one of them Whiskey boats."

Later that morning, the remaining elements of 1/5 were assembled and mounted up. Scott Nelson came over to our position and took me aside for a quiet chat. I could tell from the look on his face that he wasn't comfortable with the news he was about to give me.

Nelson looked at me and said, "The battalion CP group is taking point." There was no use in beating around the bush. His delivery was blunt, as if there was no way to lessen the blow.

Incredulous, I asked, "The battalion CP group is taking point?" I couldn't help my repetitive question, it was compulsive and out before I could shut my mouth. Nelson was clearly not amused.

He said, bluntly, "Yes, Charlie One, the battalion CP group is on point, and Charlie Company will follow them. Alpha and Delta will be behind us. You got the route down? You're on point for Charlie Company, and I don't want you getting lost or taking a wrong turn." I couldn't tell if he was jerking me around or serious, so I decided to take no more risks and simply acknowledged him with an "Aye, aye, sir."

The battalion CP group, along with our new battalion commander, Major Thompson, was comprised of a group of about thirty-five Marines. It seemed that half of them were the proud bearers of the fifteen-foot-tall whip antennae connecting their Prick-25s with the airwaves. They stumbled by in a cloud of dust, so to speak, and headed down the road toward the Citadel of Hue. Perfectly finishing the picture was the cluster of "aiming stakes" that the whip antennae represented, gently swaying in the cool but sweaty air, above the heads of Major Thompson and his staff. The battalion CP group was on point. They were our leaders. It was our duty to follow them, and we did. Keeping our distance and spacing to at least ten meters between men, one of Estes's fire teams moved out on point, followed by Benny and me and then the rest of Charlie One and Charlie Company and the rest of the First Battalion, Fifth Marine Regiment. The battalion CP group was on the point, and 1/5 was on the move.

Chapter Eight

The
Backdoor
Approach

12 February 1968

The First Battalion, Fifth Marine Regiment's opening maneuver into the battle for the Citadel of Hue could have easily resulted in a catastrophe.

The battalion CP group, on point as directed by our new battalion commander and obviously unfamiliar with the responsibilities and subtleties of walking point, proceeded merrily down the road toward the Citadel and promptly missed its first turn. In their defense, I didn't notice it at first either, and it took Estes, who was walking a few Marines behind me, to call it to our attention. We had just walked past a small, insignificant intersection in the road. If we had continued straight ahead, as the battalion CP group had done, we would soon walk into the center of the snail, the area called Bach Dang and a suspected enemy stronghold. The cutback hairpin corner was there, all right, at about the right distance from the bridge over the canal we had just crossed, but it had been very easy to miss.

The hairpin corner led back to our right, north, under an umbrella of low-hanging vines, into a narrow alleyway that widened out after a few

86

meters. This looked like the correct route into our backdoor entry of the Citadel, but the battalion CP group, to a man, had missed it, and Charlie One had almost missed it as well.

I called for a quiet halt and signaled for the men to take up hasty defensive positions on either side of the road. I quickly told Estes he was in charge until Sergeant Mullan came up. Then I grabbed Benny Benwaring and we took off after the battalion CP group, the last few of which were being swallowed up into the increasingly built-up neighborhood of Bach Dang.

As I ran forward, I hollered over my shoulder, "Benny, get on the horn and let the skipper know what's going on. I'm certain the battalion CP group has missed their turn and that they are walking right smack dab into Charlie territory. Son of a bitch!" My thoughts were much more obscene than that lightweight epithet, but being scared shitless while trotting down the road to overtake the battalion CP group with only the combined firepower of my .45-caliber pistol that had never been fired in anger, Benny's M-16, and the probably seldom-used weapons of the CP group Marines, I couldn't command my voice into any further noise.

When we caught up with them, true to their nature, the battalion CP group was huddled in a formation that can only be described as a clusterfuck in the middle of a street intersection. During normal times, this crossroads was probably a significant intersection in a medium-sized business district for the people who lived in the Bach Dang area. A quick glance around the surrounding neighborhood confirmed that there were very few civilians out, and those who were visible weren't very friendly looking. Shit, what a spot for an ambush. What a great time for a total clusterfuck.

Surrounded by the ever-present clutch of whip antennae waving over the heads of the battalion CP group, Major Thompson was studying his map. He appeared to be mentally scratching his head. A couple of staff NCOs in the CP group were kneeling between me and the battalion commander. The kneeling men were the only people in this group with at least the sense to get down (their many years of military service obviously provided them a sixth sense of danger signals that were—from the strained expressions on their faces—firing off at will). Accosting one of them, I quietly let him know by pointing it out on the map, that we were at least five hundred meters past the turnoff and probably in the middle of enemy territory. He looked at me with a knowing look of disgust on his face and reluctantly but determinedly rose and walked toward

Major Thompson and the grove of whip antennae to give them the scoop. Having performed my duty, Benny and I started back to the relative safety of the Marines of Charlie One.

Fortunately, nothing happened at that intersection, and the rest of 1/5's movement into the Citadel went off without a hitch. The 1/5 battalion arrived at the back door of the Citadel, and like a fairy tale castle opening to let the heroes in, the door was opened from the inside by the First ARVN Division and 1/5 slid quietly into the back door of the Citadel.

Although none of us was aware of it then, in the aftermath of the battles that raged in and around Hue, the Viet Cong and NVA had taken total and ruthless control of the snail-shaped area called Bach Dang. Many of the thousands of murders later reported to have been committed during the NVA occupation of Hue were carried out in this neighborhood. Evidently, the few Vietnamese "civilians" seen that afternoon casually observing the 1/5 battalion CP group approach that intersection in the heart of the Bach Dang area were most likely Viet Cong cadre, with the civilians either already dead or cringing in terror behind the walls of the homes and businesses of Bach Dang.

Hindsight, especially in combat, is always twenty-twenty. Using hindsight later on, it seemed likely to me that the 1/5 command group possibly came within inches of, or moments from, a serious brush with the enemy.

All the Marines of 1/5 arrived inside the First ARVN Division complex unharmed, well-supplied, and ready to carry out the next objective of our mission. As I followed the point fire team and stopped for a moment while the rest followed, the walls of the Citadel took on a different hue and shape, beginning to surround me for the first time. I couldn't help feeling a momentary rush of joy. We were inside. We didn't know just exactly what was going on. But at least we were all inside without a scratch. The backdoor approach had worked.

The brief elation of having gotten inside those huge walls without significant difficulty passed quickly, for now the feeling of being surrounded and confined seemed to permeate the air. The Citadel was cloaked with smoky air that only slightly muted a scene of utter, hellish pandemonium.

The Vietnamese soldiers of the First ARVN Division had fiercely resisted the initial NVA attacks, having held their headquarters position in spite of repeated attacks from the Viet Cong and NVA fighters since the long night of 31 January. Their compound had not been held without cost, however. Row after row of wounded men were lying on low cots or pallets inside some large warehouselike buildings missing large chunks of their outside walls. As we arrived through the back door, more wounded Vietnamese soldiers from the First ARVN Division were staggering into the compound through the front gate. Many of their faces and arms and legs were tied up with white and red dressings and bandages, as new squads and platoons prepared to leave the front gate in their repeated efforts at patrolling and beating the enemy back out of RPG (rocket-propelled grenade) range.

One glance out through the barbed wire at the front gate's barrier pinpointed the source of the injuries, evidenced by a pall of heavy, gray smoke rising from an area about a click due south, the direction we were due to travel in soon. Small-arms fire could be heard sporadically from that direction, with brief but persistent exchanges of weapons of slightly different calibers and rates of fire. There was definitely a firefight going on down that street. Number fucking ten.

The wounded Vietnamese soldiers bore their lot much like any group of fighting men who have given the best parts of their lives and, in many cases, their limbs for their country. Most of the wounded men sat or lay quietly, smoking cigarettes and suffering more or less than the others, depending upon what the gods of war had served them for breakfast that morning. Some, unbelievably, slept in the midst of the chaos. A couple of them, inevitably, were screaming with the pain known only by those who have lost large chunks of flesh carved out by the high-speed lead projectiles and jagged hunks of high-explosive shrapnel that rip the battlefield apart with deadly intent. There were always some who screamed, no matter how sedated they were, until the unconsciousness of morphia or death overtook them and released them to their final fate.

As my mind adjusted slowly and reluctantly to this new, yet somehow familiar environment, the rest of Charlie Company filed through the back door. We were guided to our assigned staging area by an ARVN first lieutenant. He stiffly showed us into our quarters for the rest of that day and night, our final assembly point prior to launching our attack in the morning. It was nothing more than an abandoned warehouse, or possibly a barracks completely stripped. It had four huge walls, a tin roof peppered with small and large holes, and a dirt floor. The Vietnamese lieutenant, using halting English, let us know that we could make ourselves at home.

We did. Like all Marines during the many different chapters of our distinguished military history, we had become extremely adaptive to almost any environment. In this case, we were fortunate to have tall walls to hide and sleep behind, and the obvious gaping holes in the corrugated tin roof high above our heads didn't detract too much from our having a roof over our heads for the second night in a row. The dirt floor didn't bother us much either, as it was softer than concrete or wood, both of which were harder to sleep on than dirt. So, with very few complaints and a noticed absence of horseplay, Charlie Company took over the warehouse. We immediately started our final preparations for the attack, which was due to be launched first thing the next morning.

Shortly before dusk The Gunny came and asked Sergeant Mullan and me to join the rest of the platoon commanders and platoon sergeants for a company briefing. First Lieutenant Nelson had received our final operational orders, and it was now time for shit to roll downhill.

Briefings of this type were usually just that: brief. And usually, they were very unsatisfactory. This one was no exception. It took Scott Nelson about ten minutes to explain our situation and to cover what was expected of us. The shit that was currently rolling downhill in our direction was explained as follows:

Division Intelligence estimated that an NVA force of undetermined size, probably a reinforced company or two (in the NVA, a company usually meant approximately one hundred fighting men) had seized control of the Citadel and the Imperial Palace. The 1/5 battalion had been assigned the job of clearing them out.

Scott Nelson pointed out the enemy's estimated location on his 1:10,000 plastic-covered map of Hue, which now had seven multicolored parallel lines drawn in crayon over the seven streets that separate the houses in southeast Hue. The first of these cheerfully colored lines was green, the second orange, and each ensuing line was a different and contrasting color. Nelson explained that since our mission involved street fighting, unit coordination would be critical. He had decided to use "phase lines." Phase lines were imaginary lines frequently established in conventional warfare for coordination and control during an assault. Charlie Company would use phase line green as our initial line of departure, as our best intelligence indicated that if there were in fact a company or two of NVA inside the Citadel (which should have been quite evident from the constant firefights we had been hearing since entering the Citadel), most of them were probably concentrated inside the Imperial Palace walls. The rest of them would most likely be located on or behind phase line orange. The 1/5 battalion should be able to deploy for a frontal assault on phase line green and begin the assault from that position.

Alpha Company would be assigned the battalion's left flank position for the assault, covering the eastern wall of the Citadel and the first adjacent block, and Charlie Company would be responsible for covering the next three blocks, which comprised the majority of the center and the right flank of the battalion's assault force. Charlie Company's forces were totally committed to the initial assault. Charlie One would take the left-most block, Charlie Three would take the center block, and Charlie Two the right block. Charlie One would coordinate with Alpha Company's Marines to make sure that our left flank (and their right flank) was secure during the assault. One platoon from Delta Company, recently released from 2/5's fighting in south Hue and rejoined with 1/5, would be held in reserve and would accompany the battalion CP group as a security force, and would protect our rear. Bravo Company, still detached to 2/5, was continuing the cleanup operations in south Hue and therefore was unavailable for 1/5's operations.

Nelson asked for questions, and when there were none at this point, he continued, "Because the Citadel of Hue is a national landmark, and because it and the Imperial Palace are considered by the South Vietnamese as sacred ground, the decision has been made to carry out our assault without prep fires. Because the enemy force is limited to an NVA force of only a company or two, battalion and division expect that we will be able to reach our objective by the end of the day tomorrow. Our objective is the southern wall of the Citadel, seven blocks south of phase line green. From that position, we should be able to assault and recapture the Imperial Palace with little difficulty. If necessary, you may authorize the use of M-79 rounds and hand grenades, but we should be able to wrap this up with small-arms fire by the end of the day. Although there will be a platoon of M-48 tanks in support, they are under direct orders not to fire their ninety-millimeter cannons under any circumstances. They will, however, be able to make good use of their .30-caliber and .50-caliber machine guns to support you. Time of departure is first light. We should be deployed on phase line green by 0800 hours, and the initial assault will take place at that time. Since we should be done by late afternoon, and since speed and mobility are the order of the day, battalion suggests that we leave our packs behind to lighten our loads. Questions?"

There were no questions. If any others had the same thoughts that were swarming through my mind at that point, they were, like me, too stunned to speak. Squatting next to The Gunny, I heard him mutter, "I don't know what the fuck anyone else thinks, but I'm sure as hell taking my pack!" His muttering was not intended to be overheard by anyone, lest he be considered insubordinate or disrespectful of his superior officer, and Scott Nelson seemed not to hear. I heard him, but it was all I needed to decide to ask only one question: "Skipper, is it okay if we take our packs, just in case? My men can move just as fast with their packs as without, and I don't want to hear any griping about them missing chow at lunch time." Nelson looked at me out of the side of his face and nodded his affirmation of my request. The briefing broke up, and we all returned to our platoons to start briefing our men.

Sergeant Mullan and I walked slowly back to our platoon area without speaking or looking at each other. I can only speak for myself, but I'm sure that Mullan had been taught the same strategy, tactics, and Marine Corps history that I had. So I'm also certain that right then, he was dealing with the same internal struggle that I was.

None of this made any sense at all. During boot camp (and, in my case, during boot camp, OCS, and Basic School), we were continuously exposed to a plethora of "training films" about the glorious victories of the U.S. Marine Corps. In all those movies depicting a situation like this—an impending frontal assault on an enemy that had been given significant time to dig in and fortify their positions—the assault was *always* preceded by prep fires. That meant that mortars, artillery, naval gunfire, and air support would hammer the enemy to "soften" their position, keep the enemy's heads down, and demoralize the enemy soldiers. In some cases, in particular during the amphibious assaults of World War II, these prep fires lasted for many days before the assault began. I remembered sitting in darkened theaters at MCRD San Diego, watching reel after reel of the famous landings of U.S. Marines on Guadalcanal, Iwo Jima, and Okinawa during World War II, and Inchon and other locations during the Korean War. The constant theme of these historical battles was "bomb, blast, and burn."

We certainly understood that these preparatory fires, no matter how devastating, were never enough, and that ultimately the basic Marine would have to go in and, by force of arms, personally kill the enemy that had survived the preparatory fires before these battles could end. But the basic infantry Marine took great comfort in knowing that the U.S. military possessed a vastly superior capability in firepower in comparison with our NVA and Viet Cong enemies, and until this moment, we had all seen ample evidence that we had little reluctance to use it. To be sure, there were many frustrating cases where the rules of engagement in Vietnam restricted the use of this superior firepower, and we knew full well that these rules of engagement were often very arbitrary. In some cases, the rules of engagement were downright stupid. I once witnessed a Huey gunship flying over a Viet Cong squad, who had been caught red-handed and flat-footed out in the open shooting an 82-mm mortar at an American position. Unfortunately, this Huey gunship could not get clearance to shoot for nearly a half hour because they were flying over a "restricted fire zone." The lousy result was that these particular VC got under the camouflage protection of the jungle canopy before the Huey could shoot at them, and the VC most certainly slipped away to come back and shoot at us again another day. But in most cases we could bring our heavy firepower to bear on the enemy with devastating effect. In unfriendly and unfamiliar terrain, such as the rice paddies and jungles of South Vietnam, amid an indigenous population that were supposedly friendly, but who most certainly, out of deadly necessity, screened and protected our avowed enemy force, having superior firepower was one of our only advantages. And now, poised on a frontal assault against an enemy force who were most likely dug in and waiting for us, this advantage was being totally removed.

This part of our operational plan was made more unbelievable considering that we had heard that our sister battalion, 2/5, had been up against the same rules of engagement in their battles with the NVA in south Hue starting a couple of weeks ago, and that they had taken heavy casualties, at least until they started using the heavy stuff. This was certainly not information that had come to us through the appropriate channels, but we all knew what had happened in south Hue via the rumor mill, and I was completely baffled as to why these rules of engagement had been established. I wondered who thought that these rules of engagement would work any better inside the Citadel, where the enemy had many more buildings for fortified positions and we had less room to maneuver, than the rules worked in south Hue.

There wasn't much time to let these questions take hold, and I couldn't let my men know that I was troubled. I didn't dare talk to Sergeant Mullan about it, as we both knew that the Marine Corps demanded absolute discipline, and an immediate, 100 percent effort to carry out our orders, regardless of our opinions. Sergeant Mullan would most certainly have dealt with any misgivings on my part by playing back that old, often used refrain heard in the ranks, "Ours is not to reason why, ours is but to do or die."

Sergeant Mullan went to get the squad leaders, who quickly con-
verged on my position in the growing darkness, ready to receive their
orders. I would like to report here that the briefing was greeted by the
same stoic acceptance of these difficult circumstances, but that was not
to be. During the Vietnam era, the discipline demanded by the Marine
Corps was often met conditionally. A Marine who had survived a few
months in the bush, who had been an eyewitness to the many other stupidities that dominated our daily lives, and who had been friends with
other young men killed or maimed as a result of those stupidities was
often reluctant to carry out orders not well thought out. Many NCOs,
who were the backbone of the enlisted ranks and who often found themselves outside the direct influence of a superior officer (such as when
they were assigned night ambush patrols in fire-team- or squad-sized
units), would often accept those orders and then modify them on the fly,
so to speak, after they left the compound. In Vietnam, there were already
many documented cases of direct insubordination, and the overall discipline of this legendary fighting force had come, in my opinion, very
close to breaking down completely. In some cases, orders were simply
ignored; in others the changes were much more subtle. But I learned
very quickly that I could not simply yell, "Jump," and expect fifty-plus
Marines to start lifting their feet. In Vietnam, a Marine wanted, and
often demanded, to know the reasons why. This briefing was no different. I dutifully passed on the information and operational orders to the
squad leaders of Charlie One and then asked for questions. I'm certain
that there were many more questions in the minds of these young men
than were asked that day, but the ones that were asked were good ones:

"How the fuck do they expect us to execute a frontal assault on a dug-
in enemy without at least *some* prep fires?"

"Don't them assholes at division and battalion know that them tanks
will be sitting ducks rolling down them streets, and they can't even fire
their ninety-mike-mikes?"

"Does the skipper realize that these Marines have been trained to
fight a jungle war, and that we've had about two hours of training on
how to clear a house? Fuck, we're more likely to blow each other away
than the gooks."

That last question got my attention. As usual, it was Estes who put
his finger squarely on the biggest problem that we faced: Unless we had
a chance to practice a frontal assault on a house, we could very easily
screw up and accidentally kill other Marines. I spent a couple of minutes
remembering the extent of the training I had received on house-to-house

fighting. Marines had been exposed to this type of fighting in the past, most notably in Korea during the fighting shortly after the Inchon landings. But most fighting in the recent history of the Marine Corps had been on open terrain, like the South Pacific islands, the open countryside of Korea, and up to this point, in the rice paddies and jungles of South Vietnam.

I was unique in this gathering of Marines, because I had received the benefit of training during enlisted boot camp, the three-week ITR training in Camp Pendleton, and an additional nine months of combat tactics training at OCS and the Basic School in Quantico. With a sinking feeling, I realized that I could count on one hand the combined number of hours that had been spent teaching me and my colleagues about house-to-house fighting.

Worse, one of the main lessons during the limited training was that small-unit coordination was absolutely critical, or the end result would be the deaths of Marines at the hands of friendly fire. That coordination took practice, and we had been given no time or place to practice.

Since there was obviously nowhere else to go in this situation and mutiny was out of the question, all the other questions seemed to pale by comparison. We were in deep shit without prep fires, but we had absolutely no control over that. Even if he had been so inclined, Scott Nelson could not request artillery or air support directly with our supporting units; the chain of command went through battalion, then through regiment, and finally to division, who then ordered the heavy ordinance. Once clearance for heavy support was established, then our supporting forward observers could call in fire missions directly to the providers. But until the chain of command provided the clearance, that simply would not happen. The commander of the tank platoon had his hands tied equally as well, and Scott Nelson was under direct orders to not use the sixty-millimeter mortars assigned to Charlie Company or the 3.5-inch bazooka rocket launchers. We could use M-16s, M-60 machine guns, hand grenades, and our one breech-loaded M-79 (the forty-millimeter grenade launcher lovingly referred to as a "blooper") per squad. That was it. We could only hope that the chain of command would quickly see the error of their ways, as they eventually had in south Hue, and then we would get the support that we would almost certainly need.

The only thing we could do to get prepared for the events of the next morning was to discuss (there was no place to practice) the proper procedures of clearing buildings that were suspected to be occupied by the enemy and to have the squad leaders try to teach their men at least the basics during the remaining hours before morning. We had all been trained to fight an elusive enemy in jungle and rice paddy terrain, with a great deal of emphasis on small-unit patrolling and ambushing techniques. The search and cordon/destroy training we had received supposed that we would be searching and cordoning/destroying flimsy village hooches made of straw and thatch. The houses inside the Citadel were definitely a horse of a different color, and unless we understood that quickly, we would pay for our ignorance.

Vague snatches of memories of the cursory training we had received on house fighting techniques were not at all that comforting: things like remembering to let a couple of seconds tick away after releasing the "spoon" of a grenade before tossing it through a window of a house that might contain the enemy, so as not to give the enemy any time to catch the grenade and toss it right back out at us. Or remembering that a glass window could be a barrier that, if not broken immediately, could result in the embarrassment of the damned grenade bouncing off the glass and blowing the wrong person up. Or remembering that once inside, it would be frightfully easy, unless we called out loudly to each other, to blow away your best friend who, without your knowledge and ahead of you, had gotten into a room you were about to clear. As the evening passed into gloomy night, the leaders of Charlie One struggled with our limited combined knowledge, and we tried our best to provide some last-minute command and communication training that would maximize our efforts and minimize our casualties.

Another sticky issue would be maintaining the security of our flanks. With Alpha Company on our left flank and Charlie Three on our right flank, communications with those groups would be critical. Parallel, intersecting streets would separate those units from the Marines of Charlie One, and one of my most important responsibilities as platoon commander would be to constantly ensure the security of our flanks. We would be confronting an entrenched enemy of unknown size directly in front of us, and we must think only of attacking frontally. It was unthinkable to consider the potential disaster of allowing any enemy units to slip between us and our flanking elements, as we had heard had happened to 2/5 in south Hue. The result was casualties for 2/5, and the battalion had to backtrack several different times. The area between the Citadel wall, which would define the left flank of Alpha Company, and the Imperial Palace wall, which would define the right flank of Charlie Company when we had advanced a couple of blocks past phase line green, was only four city blocks in breadth; if we kept constant contact with our flanks, it would be very difficult for any enemy units to slip between or behind us.

Further, without making sure that our flanks were covered, a frontal assault could become a very exposed and highly dangerous maneuver. Therefore, coordination along the phase lines was absolutely critical.

My final words to the squad leaders as they prepared to retrain their Marines last-minute in the little we had agreed upon regarding the capture of each house in our area of responsibility will haunt me for the rest of my life. I looked at them all, without looking anyone in the eyes in the encroaching gloom, and told them, "Under no circumstances are any of your men to cross phase line green until I give the order to attack."

These words seemed right at the moment. It seemed to be a simple enough situation that confronted us. We had to assault the enemy from the front, and I wanted to make damned sure that Alpha had our left flank secured and Charlie Three had our right flank secured before we attacked forward. So I told them not to cross the street until I gave the word. It's funny how a single word can change men's lives.

The squad leaders acknowledged their orders and moved away to do the best they could to instruct and prepare their men regarding their mission in the morning. I found a corner, wrapped up in my poncho liner, and told Benny to wake me for the early morning watch.

Chapter Nine

Phase Line Green

13 February 1968

Early on the morning of 13 February 1968, the Marines of 1/5 left the relative safety of the First ARVN Division compound and headed southeast toward our designated line of departure, phase line green. Alpha Company was on point, Charlie Company followed closely behind with Charlie One, as usual, on company point. One platoon from Delta Company provided rear security for the battalion CP group.

Dawn had reluctantly and halfheartedly defeated the dismal darkness of the previous night, but the winter sun could not penetrate a thick, low-hanging, gloomy cloud cover with anything other than a minimum of illumination. The only thing complimentary about the weather conditions was that the rain also appeared reluctant to show itself, and we were dry, at least for the time being.

Walking slowly, keeping at least a ten-meter interval between each man, the Marines of 1/5 maintained a staggered column on either side of the street called Dinh Bo Linh after a fifth-century Vietnamese king. Dinh Bo Linh was a two-lane city street parallel to the eastern wall of

98

the Citadel. Dinh Bo Linh would eventually deliver us from the First ARVN Division compound to phase line green.

Alpha Company, as 1/5's point element and responsible for coverage of the eastern Citadel wall and the narrow city block adjacent to the wall, would turn left one block before they reached phase line green. Phase line green was, of course, a street, and its actual name was Mai Thuc Loan. Mai Thuc Loan was named in honor of a Vietnamese general who fought against both the Chinese and the French as they both encroached on Vietnamese soil during the sixteenth century.

Alpha Company would make the appropriate turn to the east and then deploy parallel to phase line green and move through the houses until they reached the point of departure. Charlie Company would move up behind them, deploy in a similar fashion along the three blocks of our responsibility, cover each other's flanks, and move forward until we reached phase line green. Once we were in position on phase line green, we would be given the word to commence a coordinated frontal assault on the NVA who were waiting for us, according to all the available intelligence reports, somewhere south of phase line green.

Because of the ten-meter interval and the deliberately slow and careful pace established by Alpha Company through the quiet, ancient suburbia of Hue inside the Citadel walls, it was very easy to become distracted by the sights. Spacious old estates were the dominant theme along both sides of Dinh Bo Linh, our present route of approach. Dinh Bo Linh was lined by several mansions, surrounded and separated by a mature and somewhat overgrown landscape of trees, shrubs, and spacious grounds, interspersed with reflecting ponds. The mansions were all surrounded by substantial stone walls, four to six feet high, and occupied large chunks of each city block. As we progressed southward, the larger estates gave way to a more normal suburban setting, consisting of many smaller houses in orderly rows facing the east-west-running streets. The only thing consistent about the larger estates and the smaller houses was the distinctly discomforting lack of noise coming from them. It was as though this section of Hue was utterly void of humanity. Inside the Citadel, Hue was a ghost town.

My attention was abruptly wrenched away from the immediate scenery and back in the direction of Alpha Company by the all-too-familiar "whump" of a mortar or rocket explosion, followed by several more of the same, punctuated by a ragged trickle and then a rushing torrent of small-arms fire. Alpha Company, whose point element was several hundred meters ahead of us and who had made their designated left turn several minutes before, had stepped in the shit, no question about it. A healthy firefight was under way, obviously involving Alpha Company.

Without the necessity of commands, the Marines of Charlie Company took cover as best they could along the walls lining Dinh Bo Linh and waited. Finally, after what seemed like hours but was probably only several minutes, the rear element of Alpha Company started to move again, and they turned the corner. Charlie One's point fire team started to move out after them, following about fifty meters behind Alpha's rear element. In my normal position, following just behind the point fire team, I was one of the first Charlie Company Marines to find out what had happened to Alpha Company.

As I began to make the appropriate left turn, Benny and I stopped cold as we were confronted by a fearful sight. Walking slowly and painfully toward us, 1st Lt. F. P. Wilbourne, Alpha Company's executive officer, was carefully making his way on his own, back toward the battalion rear area. Wilbourne had actually been the company commander of Alpha Company for a short time before 1/5 headed toward Hue, but he had been bumped down the ladder of command just a couple of days before by a Capt. J. J. Bowe, and Wilbourne was now the executive officer.

If we hadn't heard the firefight, if we hadn't seen the blood that covered his entire body from head to toe, we would have been tempted to ask him if he had shit his pants, since he was walking, with stiff legs and arms, like someone who had rectally embarrassed himself. But as he approached us it quickly became obvious that Lieutenant Wilbourne had been hit by a shower of shrapnel, and though none of his wounds appeared to be life-threatening, the cumulative effect was that Alpha's XO had become a bloody sieve.

Recognizing me as a Charlie Company platoon commander, Lieutenant Wilbourne stopped his arduous trek momentarily. Although it obviously pained him to do so, he pointed out that several of my men were in an exposed position, still nonchalantly turning the corner of the intersection, and he quietly chewed my butt.

Wilbourne said, "The Alpha CP group just got wasted because we were standing right out in the middle of an intersection, a block *behind* phase line green, clusterfucked around an M-48 tank. The gooks ran out into the street about a block and a half in front of us and fired three RPG rockets, hitting the M-48 directly in the turret with their first shot. Shit, the skipper and the gunny were both blown away, and Alpha has been effectively eliminated on the battalion's left flank. Delta is moving up to take our places, and we'll be falling back to provide rear security. Fuck, the tank commander had his head blown off! Now, you tell your people that if they keep ditty-bopping across the damned streets, they're gonna get themselves blown away, too!"

Having said his piece, he started his painful trek toward the rear of the battalion column once again. As he walked away, he continued to mutter at me that we should get our collective heads out of our asses, get out of the middle of the fucking street, and make goddamned sure to stay alert and keep our heads down.

As I turned away from Wilbourne's unwelcome visage, I noticed that I didn't have to say a damned thing. Most of Charlie One had seen and heard him, and they were taking a distinctly lower stance along the sides of the road and were moving very quickly across the open areas when they had to cross the intersection. Shit. Alpha Company was history before the battle had even begun.

The battalion's assault was delayed for what again seemed like hours as a platoon from Delta Company moved up and relieved Alpha Company, and we got positioned along Tang Bat Ho, another street named for ancient Vietnamese royalty. The street ran parallel to phase line green, one block north of our point of departure. A shallow, muddy ditch ran alongside Tang Bat Ho, and Charlie One hunkered down in the ditch as the rest of Charlie Company got into position and as Delta switched positions with Alpha. As we waited, I resisted letting my attention wander toward the scene of destruction surrounding the now-disabled M-48 tank about fifty meters away and tried to concentrate on other things besides the frantic efforts to save the critically injured and to evacuate the dead members of the Alpha Company CP, but we couldn't avoid knowing exactly what was happening. During the first brief skirmish inside the Citadel, the NVA had struck unexpectedly and viciously, and as a result, several KIAs (killed in action) and many WIAs (wounded in action) had rendered the Alpha CP group totally ineffective as a command unit. Alpha would have to fall back into battalion reserve status and regroup.

As Benny's Prick-25 squawked to life, the orders from Charlie Six tersely broke into my thoughts. "Move out. Maintain contact on both flanks. Move up to the line of departure, and prepare to attack across phase line green."

Charlie One's three squads had lined up three abreast, broken into their fire team units. Slowly and cautiously, we moved into and around each house, taking our time, making sure that we weren't going to accidentally walk past any hidden enemy positions, constantly conscious and fearful of a counterattack from the rear. The houses in this block were much smaller than the estates we had passed on our way; they were very close together and often very difficult to walk around. This was not really a problem, because we had to clear each house anyway, but we still checked the narrow, brushy spaces between the houses to make sure we weren't missing anything.

The shouts of Marines communicating with each other as they practiced for the first time the tactics of house-to-house fighting penetrated the sullen air, muffled by the walls and the damp morning air. These barking commands, obviously made by Americans, reached my ears and gave me some comfort that at least the men of Charlie One were taking this very seriously. They had seen the instant destruction of the Alpha CP group, and they didn't want to be hit unexpectedly.

As was normal when Charlie One was in a frontal assault formation, Benny and I tagged along behind the center squad, Ed Estes's squad, in the middle of the block and kept in touch with the other two squads via their PRC-6 radios, much smaller and much less effective communication devices than the Prick-25. The Prick-6, resembling an overgrown walkie-talkie, quickly proved to be ineffective in penetrating the walls of the houses that the Charlie One Marines were clearing, and it quickly became clear that we would have to rely on runners for a lot of our intraplatoon communications. Each platoon of a Marine company had one Prick-25, for communications with the company CP group and the battalion and support nets for calling in artillery and air support, and we had three or four Prick-6s, which were designed for close-in communications between squads. The Prick-25s worked great; the Prick-6s were completely useless.

Charlie One was organized into three squads, each of roughly thirteen Marines, broken down further into three fire teams and a squad leader. Each squad was further reinforced by a team who lugged and handled the awesome and devastating firepower of the M-60 machine guns. Sometimes they had the added luxury of an M-79 man, who carried the forty-millimeter grenade launcher and somewhere between forty and sixty rounds of accurate and deadly high-explosive firepower. On the morning of 13 February 1968, Charlie One's table of organization was comprised of a total of fifty-one Marines, including the attached M-60 teams, me, Benny Benwaring, and the two Navy corpsmen assigned to travel with us.

The Marine fire team is the basic and fundamental tactical unit of the U.S. Marine Corps, and many hours of every Marine's training after boot camp were focused on the maneuvers of the fire team. The Marines of every fire team were drilled not only on individual movements and covering their buddy's back, but also on the importance of maintaining the integrity of their fire team. Thus it was natural in our current situation that one fire team would be responsible for clearing one house at a time. This tactic worked out very conveniently in the first block, which contained fifteen or sixteen houses, half of them facing north along Tang Bat Ho and half of them facing south along Mai Thuc Loan (phase line green). In this particular block, unlike most other blocks in southeast Hue inside the Citadel, the houses and their respective yards were separated by a narrow alley. The nine fire teams of Charlie One, with Benny and me trailing the center fire team of the center squad, cleared the first seven or eight houses facing Tang Bat Ho. Then, making sure that their flanks were covered on both sides, the men moved slowly and cautiously across the narrow alley, through old, flimsy gates defining the back yards of the houses facing phase line green, and entered the back doors of the eight or so houses along phase line green almost simultaneously.

As Benny and I waited for the fire team ahead of us to clear their assigned house, I checked out the intersecting alley and noticed that although it was very overgrown, it defined a pathway that went all the way to both sides of the block. I could clearly see both of the streets that intersected phase line green and defined Charlie One's left and right flanks. As it was very overgrown, I was not at all disturbed that I couldn't see any Marines across the street on our left flank. An M-48 tank rumbled slowly past the alley on the street to our right and inched toward phase line green. I wondered momentarily how the tank crews were feeling, with their hands tied by not being able to fire their ninety-millimeter cannons and knowing that one of their group had been eliminated from the battle already.

Estes came back out the back door and signaled that this center house was cleared, and Benny and I moved in through the back door. Although these homes were small by American standards, they were very substantial by Vietnamese standards, at least from our limited experience in the paddies and jungles in other parts of I Corps. We stepped up three low steps onto a raised wooden floor and immediately entered a hallway leading from the rear to the front of the house; a stairway led to a second floor. Walking past the stairway into an empty front room, which was lined at the front by multipaned windows framing the front door, we walked through the eerily empty front room. The dim daylight illuminated the front room, and the street, Mai Thuc Loan, phase line green, was dimly visible through the front windows.

As Estes and Benny, just ahead of me, walked through the front room, through the front door, and out into the street, something nagged at me. Something wasn't right here. My feet kept walking. My mind knew that something was terribly wrong, but it couldn't grasp the problem, and my feet kept walking.

As I passed through the front door of that dreary small house out into Mai Thuc Loan and turned my head to the left and then back to the right, I saw my men all standing there along the narrow sidewalk that lined the north side of phase line green. Some of them crouched behind the inadequate trunks of the shade trees lining this side of the street. I couldn't formulate any of the words in my mind. But I knew then, and I will know for the rest of my life, just exactly what was wrong. They had followed my orders to the letter. None of them had *crossed* the street, none of them had *crossed* phase line green, but every damned one of them, every swinging dick of Charlie One, was completely exposed *out in* the street. Charlie One was a collective sitting duck, standing out in the open along the narrow sidewalk in front of the houses. Some of them were crouching behind the trees, but most of them were just standing there, looking at each other, looking at me as I walked out of the front door of the center house.

My mind had no coherent thoughts in that one moment, that one heartbeat that will live forever as a cancer in my soul. I have had uncounted moments since then, during which I've eternally debated what my first words, at that crucial moment, should have been. The raging debate in my soul swings from the extremes of: "Charge!!" to "Shit!!!" to "What the fuck are you idiots doing out in the street? Didn't common sense tell you to stay *inside* the houses until I give you the order to attack?" These debates are all totally useless; they are nothing more than a futile raging, and they will never be anything more than wishful thinking.

Here's what came out of my mouth: "GET THE FUCK OUTTA THE STREET!!"

I wish that the next few seconds had ticked away at normal speed, but with contemptuous certainty, time instantly changed into the slow motion of frustrating nightmares, of trying to run away from unseen but hideous monsters, only to be hindered by glue-covered feet or concrete shoes. I was only in that street that morning for a few seconds, but try-ing to escape the inevitable explosion of the well-prepared ambush of the entrenched NVA thirty feet in front of us, those seconds seemed like hours. Part of me will be there, in that street, for those terrible moments, for the rest of my days.

I have no idea why I didn't just turn around and run back inside the house I had just walked out of. That would have been the most obvious and fastest route to safety. I have no idea why I didn't turn left, or charge straight ahead. I have no idea why I turned to the right, screaming those immortal words at the top of my lungs and running as fast as my legs have ever run before or since, yet taking forever to get to wherever it was that I thought that I was going. I turned to the right, and I was fol-lowing other Marines, my men, as the shit royally hit the fan.

The NVA were dug in and waiting for us on the other side of the street. They occupied the first- and second-floor windows, and many of the NVA were on the roofs. Several automatic weapons raked the street from our left flank, from the tower that protected the eastern entrance to the Citadel. And I ran, and ran, and ran, and I got nowhere fast.

There was no place to hide; I was shit outta luck.

Just before reaching the intersection of Mai Thuc Loan and Dinh Bo Linh, my first nightmare of that fateful day came to a spectacular and horrible conclusion. I was following a man from Charlie One Charlie, the third squad of Charlie One. He was one of its fire team leaders, a lance corporal named Gibson. Running one step in front of me, he was shot through the back by the NVA. The combined force of his running body and the AK-47 round that had slammed into him proved just enough to flatten a corner courtyard gate, which became my escape valve. As Lance Corporal Gibson's bleeding body knocked down the gate, my feet propelled me into the safety of the corner courtyard as I leaped over his crumbling body. I was closely followed by Benny Benwaring, who had gone where his leader had led him, regardless of the insanity of the direction.

The peaceful sanctity of this small corner courtyard had been shat-tered by our abrupt arrival. The scene was a nightmare, something out of Dante's Inferno, with the severely bleeding lance corporal sprawled on top of the wrecked remnants of the gate and several other shocked Marines huddled in the corner, protected by a substantial six-foot-high masonry wall but unable to return fire effectively. Doc English, one of Charlie One's Navy corpsmen, was one of the men in the courtyard, and he immediately began working on the severe wounds that were threatening to take the life of Lance Corporal Gibson. The ferocity of the enemy small-arms fire had not abated; it sounded like an NVA battalion was just on the other side of the street, shooting at us with everything they had. We had really stepped in the shit this time.

I asked Benny Benwaring to get the other squads on the Prick-6, but after a few frustrating attempts that resulted in a very unsatisfactory and unhelpful squelch of static noise, it was clear that if I wanted to find out what was going on, I would have to communicate by runner. Benny was monitoring the company radio net on the Prick-25, and it was very quickly evident that everyone else in the battalion was fully engaged with an entrenched enemy on the other side of phase line green. Charlie Six's instructions were to take care of our casualties, make damned sure of the integrity of our present positions, return fire, and await further instructions.

The leader of this squad, Charlie One Charlie, had begun to assert his leadership; he had made sure that the other Marines in the courtyard had good cover and were returning fire to the best of their ability. Doc English was doing everything he could for the wounded man, and it was killing me not to know what was going on with the rest of my platoon. I decided to go find out for myself.

Instructing Benny to stay with Doc English in case he needed help evacuating the injured man and to monitor the company net, I took off out the back gate of the corner courtyard into the alley. Turning right into the alley that would allow me to get to the other squads, I started running down the narrow, vine-draped alley. As I ran past a well, I tripped on something and nearly fell on my face, but whatever I had tripped on was a small hindrance, and I kept my feet and continued running. Two more heartbeats went by before the booby-trapped grenade exploded, knocking me forward onto my hands and knees, but my feet kept pumping, and I kind of skipped off my hands and knees, bounced back on my feet, and just kept running. The force of the grenade's explosion had hit my legs and lower back, but nothing hurt at the moment. My mind didn't even register that I might be wounded and numb. I just kept running. (I didn't think much about the incident until three weeks later, back in a GP tent in Phu Bai, when I was finally able to take off my utility trousers for the first time, and four small pieces of shrapnel clinked to the floor. I had been running so fast, and the NVA had been so inept at setting up booby traps, that I was out of the effective range of the shrapnel by the time it had exploded. When I saw those pieces of shrapnel fall from my trousers in Phu Bai, I thanked my lucky stars that it had been an NVA who had set up the booby trap, and not a Viet Cong. The latter would have known to remove the time-delay fuse from the detonator of the booby-trapped grenade, creating an instant explosion rather than one that happened a few seconds after the pin had been pulled out by the trip wire.)

Crazily at that moment, running down the alley, I was taken back to my childhood for a few seconds. Once again I was sitting by my four brothers in the living room of the farmhouse on the Coos River in southwestern Oregon, watching the family's eight-millimeter home movies. We were all laughing like crazy as we made my older brother, Steve, go back and forth, forward and reverse, from the back door of my grandmother's house to her outhouse. My father, who had been a fanatic with the old hand-crank eight-millimeter movie projector and who was also a frustrated actor/director, had on many occasions enlisted us boys to be actors in his crackpot, slapstick productions. On this particular occasion, Dad had thought it would be hilarious if Steve would burst out the back door of Grandma's old house, run down the four back steps, along the fifty-foot boardwalk that connected the back of the house with the outhouse, running as fast as possible, with the obvious theme that Steve was running to save his clean britches. In one of those rare and impromptu moments, Steve had slipped on the rain-soaked, ancient wooden slats of the boardwalk while Dad was filming and had fallen on his butt when his feet flew out from under him. But he had amazingly kept his feet pumping, and without losing any ground speed, Steve had bounced off his butt, regained his feet, and completed his urgent journey. All of this had been captured on film, and with the help of the reverse switch on the ancient eight-millimeter projector, my family spent many hilarious evenings forcing Steve to run back and forth, back and forth, while assaulting him verbally with appropriate comments like, "Hey, Steve, why'd you keep running? You probably did it in your pants when you hit the boardwalk, so the emergency was over." You get the drift.

At that moment, running down that shrouded alleyway, I giggled, just briefly, at the similarity of the events, but I quickly smothered that thought because there was nothing funny about any of this. I needed to know what was going on with the other squads, and fast.

Running to the opposite end of the alley, I ran inside the last building on the east corner of the block and found the squad leader of Charlie One Bravo, the squad who had covered the left side of our frontal assault formation. I quickly discerned that our situation was not good. Staff Sergeant Mullan, who had been traveling with Charlie One Bravo on our left flank, was gone. He had been standing out in the street like the rest of Charlie One and had been shot in the head during the initial burst of fire. The squad leader shakily told me that although Sergeant Mullan had been alive when they took him on a quickly improvised stretcher back toward the battalion rear for medevac, it didn't look like he could possibly survive. The side of his head had been severely wounded, probably by an AK-47, and he was unconscious and just barely breathing when he was carried away. Doc Lowdermilk, who had administered first aid, didn't give him much hope of survival.

The blow of losing Sergeant Mullan, who had truly been the leader of this platoon and my mentor while I was going through on-the-job training, was devastating, but there was no time to mourn or even to consider this loss, because we had a much worse situation on our hands. According to the squad leader, there were at least three dead Marines still out in the street, and he thought that Estes's squad had a wounded man down in the street as well. The wounded man was still alive, but stuck out in the street and exposed to enemy gunfire.

Making sure that Charlie One Bravo kept returning fire at the suspected enemy positions and that they kept their heads down as much as possible, I ran back into the alley and retraced my earlier steps following Estes's squad through the back yard and into the back door of the house that had been my initial entry into phase line green.

Bedlam greeted me. Exposed as they were in the front room, several Marines were returning fire toward the enemy across the street. Estes was hunched down in the hallway and was using the stairway for cover. When I came up behind him, he turned toward me with a look of anger and frustration that immediately spelled out the disastrous situation. There truly were three men down in the street right in front of this house, right where I had stood when I had first walked into phase line green and screamed those immortal words. I realized momentarily that if I had turned around and tried to go back inside this house through the front door, there was a very high likelihood that either Benny or I would have been one of the Marines down in the street.

Estes looked at me with a terrible burning fire in his eyes, and he quickly summed up the most serious problem. "Morgan is still alive, Lieutenant. He's hit bad, but we could hear him yelling at us to come get him just a couple of minutes ago. He's totally exposed, but he's hit bad and he can't move. We gotta get him outta there."

Enemy gunfire continued to rake the front room of the house, having long since shattered the windows, and effectively pinned down the Marines in the front room, making the effectiveness of their return fire questionable. From our position in the hallway, I couldn't see Morgan, but I could see two other green-clad bodies a little further out in the street. "How about those other two guys, Estes?"

"They're definitely wasted, Lieutenant. They were knocked down in the initial burst, and they've taken a lot more hits since. Neither of them have moved, and we haven't heard any sounds from them at all. But Morgan is still alive. What the fuck are we going to do?"

I said, "Let's try to give him some cover with smoke grenades, and then ask for a volunteer to go out and get him." Morgan's fire team leader, hunkering down under the window sill in the front room, immediately volunteered to make the effort. After sending two other Marines via the alley to the adjacent squads to tell them to lay down a heavy volume of fire when they saw the smoke pop in the street, we executed the plan.

Two smoke grenades went out the shattered front window, one on either side of Morgan's position, and the fire team leader, a lance corporal named Hallmark, rushed out into the hellfire. The volume of the small-arms fire, both incoming and outgoing, increased immediately, and after three long seconds, Lance Corporal Hallmark staggered back into the front room, blood gushing like a water faucet from his lower left leg. He collapsed in the hallway, screaming and holding his leg, as Doc Lowdermilk pounced on him and started the first aid necessary to stop the flow of blood and save the young man's life. Although the bone was most likely broken and he was in a great deal of pain, the young man had a hard time keeping a grin off his face, because he knew that this wound would put him on the sidelines and get him the hell out of Hue. But the grin vanished immediately when we asked him about Morgan.

Hallmark looked up at me through his pain and said, "Fuck me, Lieutenant, I couldn't tell if he was dead or alive. The shit is really hitting the fan out there, and I lost my grip on him when I got hit. I couldn't drag him over the curb, he's just too goddamned heavy. He might still be alive, but he's unconscious for sure. I think he got hit a couple more times when I tried to get him."

Estes and I helped Doc Lowdermilk carry the young hero out to the back yard and assigned another Marine to help him limp back to the battalion rear for medevac. As I watched them leave out the back gate, my mind was racing a million miles per hour, but none of my thoughts were at all helpful. Morgan was still down in the street, and we didn't know for sure if he was dead or alive. The Marine Corps has long had a proud tradition of making every effort possible to evacuate the dead and wounded from the battlefield, but the cards were stacked against us. Every time we sent more men into the street to try to recover the wounded or dead, even with the cover of smoke, it looked like we were just going to take more casualties, making a terrible situation even worse.

As I turned back toward the house, my vision fixed on L. Cpl. Ed Estes, who was obviously having the same terrible thoughts, but who was now insanely maddened by one other fact: Morgan was not just another Marine, he was his friend. They had been together for over six months, had survived the daisy-chain command-detonated mine outside Hoi An together, and had shared many night ambush patrols and uncountable daytime hours filled with terror and uncertainty. And now Morgan was down in the street and probably still alive. Estes was his squad leader, and he felt completely responsible.

As these thoughts surged through his mind, they were obvious to me as the emotions played across his angry face. Estes was turning slowly in place, walking in a tight circle, frustrated by Morgan's situation, scared to death like the rest of us about the prospects of making another attempt to go get him. As I watched this horrible internal struggle with himself, Estes made a complete 360-degree pivot, as though his right foot was staked to the ground. Our eyes connected for only a moment, and I instantly knew what Estes was going to do. I froze, unable to move, unable to make a sound. Estes completed his pivot, and when he saw the back door to the house, he screamed in fury, "Morgan!!" Unable to believe that Estes was going to run out into that damnable hell, I could only scream his name, "Estes!!!"

L. Cpl. Edward S. Estes knew what he was running to face, but Ed Estes was unable to stop himself. His friend, PFC Charles R. Morgan, was down in the street, and it was up to Estes to help him. Estes ran into the house, down the hallway, through the front room, and out the front door into a terrible hail of enemy gunfire, which was now concentrated on the front door. The smoke in the street was dissipating, and by the time I got inside the back door, finally able to move, Estes was lost to my view for a moment in the smoke. But just for a moment.

Ed Estes didn't even make it to Morgan. He had hardly stepped outside the doorway when an AK-47 round tore through his neck, entering his

Adam's apple. Knowing then that Morgan was dead and that he was also probably dead, Ed Estes turned around and, still trying to run, stumbled back into the house, back through the front room, and collapsed at my feet in the hallway. He had been grasping his neck, but I had clearly seen the entry bullet hole in his Adam's apple. A thick, steady stream of blood was gushing from the hole, leaking heavily through his fingers.

Doc Lowdermilk was also Ed Estes's friend, and now Ed was dying. Doc Lowdermilk jumped on him and rolled him over on his back and onto my lap. Doc pulled Ed's hand away from his neck so that he could assess the damage and do what he could to save his friend's life.

Doc looked over at me with despair in his eyes and said, "We gotta do an emergency tracheotomy; his windpipe's crushed. I need a tube, something to stick into the opening when I cut into his windpipe."

I was stunned, stupid, unable to think or to move. None of the other Marines was any more help. Estes was dying on my lap, making feeble convulsive motions, and I couldn't move.

"Break down your .45, Lieutenant, goddammit. I can use the barrel as a temporary airway."

Still stunned, I was just barely able to pull my never-used pistol out of my Marine Corps–issue holster and break it down without looking at it as I had done so many times at Quantico and Basic School. I handed Doc Lowdermilk the barrel after he cut Estes's throat, and then he inserted the barrel into the bloody opening. Estes had stopped breathing, and Doc Lowdermilk started to push down on his chest to try to jump-start his breathing, when we noticed the terrible pool of blood forming under Estes and leaking from under his body.

Doc Lowdermilk gently turned Estes over, and we all knew at that moment that Estes was beyond any help that we could give him. The NVA bullet had entered his windpipe, and if it had gone straight back out his neck he might have had a chance for survival. But this particular NVA must have been shooting through a second-story window or from the roof of the house across the street, because the trajectory had been downward. The bullet had traveled through Estes's heart and out his lower back, probably shattering his spine for good measure.

Ed Estes, Squad Leader for Charlie One Alpha, was dead.

Stunned as we all were in that dim hallway, we were all forced to start living again when another Marine from Estes's squad was shot through the chest. He had been in the front room sitting up against a side wall, and an NVA gunner had moved into a position where he could shoot down into the front room. We dragged him out of the front room, and I yelled at the rest of the Marines in the front room to get out of there and to take up positions upstairs or on the roof. This particular front room had become way too deadly.

We carried Estes's body out of the house into the back yard and laid him out on an old outdoor table. The firing in the street had diminished to a less frantic and more sporadic level, and I stood there for a while, looking at Estes. I was in shock, and I think I would have remained standing there for a long time, but flies started to buzz around Estes' head, and his face started to take on the ugly greenish cast of the newly deceased. I couldn't bear to look at him any more. I pulled this wasted young man's poncho over his face, picked up his discarded M-16 rifle that had been propped up against the table by one of the other men, and turned my back on Ed Estes forever.

I don't remember too much about the next hour or so. I think time stopped for me. I vaguely remember returning to the house and walking into a back room that the owners had stuffed with the furniture from the front room and sitting down in a rocking chair. I closed my eyes and started rocking.

I remember rocking in that chair and thinking about the small dairy farm where I had grown up in Coos River, Oregon, and my pet cow, Honey, and the peaceful summer afternoons when I would lie on Honey's side and soak up the welcome and infrequent sunshine. Those were the most peaceful and least disturbing moments of my life, and my mind was subconsciously trying to submerge itself in memories of a peaceful moment. I could just not deal with the cruelty and savagery of our situation on phase line green and the death of many good men, in particular the death of Ed Estes. He was a young man who had accepted the responsibility of fighting for his country, of taking care of his men, and who had paid the ultimate penalty for facing up to those responsibilities.

So I sat in that rocking chair, holding Estes's M-16 in my hands between my knees, and rocked away God knows how many minutes. The other Marines from what remained of Estes's squad were reluctant to disturb me, and I probably spent nearly a half hour as a seven-year-old again, finding some peace with a cow named Honey.

Finally, Benny Benwaring brought me back into the present. He had left the corner courtyard and followed my footsteps into that house. Seeing me sitting there, blank-eyed, rocking gently and quietly, he probably figured I had gone off my rocker, so to speak, but he had summoned the courage to shake my arm and force me back into the present.

Benny spoke quietly but insistently: "Lieutenant, the skipper is trying to reach you. We've got orders from battalion to attack across the street."

Part of me came back to life and I somehow reassumed the role and responsibilities of Marine platoon commander, Charlie One Actual. Another part of me stayed in that rocking chair and is still there today, rocking away, thinking about the torn lives and destruction focused on that bloody street. Many of the events I witnessed and participated in on that street that day and the terrible days that followed are so etched in my memory banks that I can hear the sounds, smell the smells, and scream the screams in my mind as though they happened yesterday.

Charlie One was ordered to attack across phase line green three times that day, so the Marines of Charlie One attacked across the deadly avenue three times that day. After the first attack, it quickly became obvious that the main concentration of the NVA's forces were established right across the street from Charlie One, and our battalion commander had now decided that if we could successfully attack and penetrate the enemy's defenses at this point, we could break the back of their resistance and overwhelm them.

Repeated attempts were made to reverse the orders that restricted our heavy support. I pleaded with Scott Nelson to plead with Major Thompson to get us some artillery or air support. At least the major could allow the M-48 tanks to fire their ninety-millimeter cannons into the enemy positions, to soften the positions somewhat, to do something to force our enemy to get his head down, so that we had even a shred of a chance at success in a frontal assault.

My frantic requests for heavy firepower were all turned down flat. At one point, Charlie Six Actual got on the radio with me directly, reminded me of our orders, and told me to pull my men together and to assault the enemy. Running from position to position, Benny Benwaring and I set up the initial attack as best we could, which required one fire team in each squad to attack across the street, while the other fire teams provided covering fire. It didn't work; no one even got halfway across the street. The awful result was several more wounded Marines and another KIA. Now there was yet another dead Marine down in the street.

During the first abortive assault, I noticed that we were taking a high volume of enemy fire from our left flank, from the tower that guarded the east entrance to the Citadel. The NVA apparently occupied the tower in force and had many automatic weapons. From about a block and a half away, a distance of little more than a hundred meters, this firepower was devastating to the Marines who were trying to cross the street in full view of the NVA gunners in their tower positions.

After reporting back to Scott Nelson that we had been unsuccessful in getting a foothold on the other side of the street, he maintained that our orders hadn't changed and that we should get ready to try again. I was getting an awful feeling about the security of our left flank, so Benny and I took off down the alley to its intersection with the street that defined our connection with Delta Company on our left. When I got to the corner of the alley and the street, my heart sank. The M-48 tank that had been the center of the attack on the Alpha Company CP group, having been assigned a new tank commander and put back into action (albeit still under strict orders not to fire its cannon) was now positioned *behind* the intersection of the alley and the street. Furthermore, I couldn't see any Marines from Delta Company in their assigned positions along phase line green.

Benny and I ran across the street and dived behind the tank, as enemy gunners spotted us and started shooting in our direction. I asked for the whereabouts of the Delta Company platoon commander who was responsible for covering our left flank, and I finally found him in a house *behind the alley*. When I confronted him and tried to explain that they were not in position at phase line green, he looked at me like I was crazy and said that his men were in position where they were supposed to be and that they were taking terrible enemy fire from the tower. The Delta Company platoon had stopped their forward movement at the alley, and the platoon commander refused to look closely at his map or even consider that they were a half block back of their assigned positions.

Leaving him in disgust, I returned to the back of the tank, got on the direct telephone that was designed for the trailing infantry to communicate with the tank commander, and ordered him to move up past the alley to the street corner and at least open up with his machine guns. The tank commander, repeating what the Delta platoon commander said, refused to budge. Charlie One's left flank was totally exposed, and it looked like it was going to stay that way.

Running back across the street into the alley, I called Scott Nelson and reported this news. He said he would check it out with battalion and get back to me, and in the meantime, we were to get ready to attack.

After only a couple of minutes, Nelson called me back, forcefully letting me know that I must be mistaken, because the Delta Company platoon commander had assured battalion that he was in the correct position, right on the north side of phase line green. Another frantic request to provide artillery or air support was immediately rejected by Nelson. We were on our own, and we were to attack again within the next ten minutes.

Our second attack involved selecting one squad—the right-most squad (the furthest from our left flank)—to be the assault force, with the remaining two squads setting up covering fire. As ordered, the Marines from Charlie One Charlie, the right-flank squad, attacked across the street, but they were again forced back by a ferocious concentration of enemy fire. The results were predictable: more wounded and yet another dead Marine down in the street.

Benny and I found ourselves back in the corner courtyard after the second assault, trying to assess the damage. Doc English was still there in the courtyard, working frantically on two more wounded Marines who had been hit in the second assault. Doc told me about the Marine down in the street; he could see him through the knocked-down gate from his position, which provided some security from the enemy fire because of the angles, and he knew that this Marine was dead. There were now, by my best count, five dead Charlie One Marines in the street; two more dead, including Estes, who had been evacuated; and many, many wounded. Our fighting strength had been cut in half, and we hadn't been able to budge the enemy an inch.

At this point, as I pleaded yet again with Scott Nelson that our left flank was exposed and that we needed artillery and air support or at least let the goddamned tanks start firing their cannons, SSgt. Robert H. Odum came running into the small corner courtyard from across the street that separated our platoons. He was the platoon sergeant for Charlie Three, the Charlie Company platoon that was assigned the next block on our right flank and that was taking heavy enemy fire from its immediate front. His platoon, however, had yet to be ordered to attack and had not had any Marines knocked down in an exposed position in the street. He was obviously pissed, and although he handled the situation with respect for my rank and the chain of command drilled into all Marines throughout their careers, he was obviously upset with me, that a Marine platoon commander could allow one of his men to stay out in the street without some attempts being made to recover his body.

"Lieutenant, one of your men is down in the street, right out in front of that tank. Maybe you weren't aware, sir?" Sergeant Odum's voice barely covered the sarcasm that was obviously intended to urge me to action.

I replied, "I am well aware of that, Sergeant Odum, and while I appreciate your efforts at running over here to inform me of this fact, I'd appreciate it if you would go back to your men."

Sergeant Odum said, "Sir, with all due respect, we must try to get that man back out of the street." Sergeant Odum was a very good staff NCO, well liked by his platoon commander and his men alike, and he was going to persist.

Rather testily now, I said, "Sergeant Odum, that man is dead. Doc English saw him get hit. He took at least one hit in the head, and he's been shot several times since. He's dead. I've lost several other Marines attempting to get their buddies out of the street, and while I appreciate your concern for that Marine and for the Marine Corps' traditions, I will not lose another Marine trying to get dead bodies out of the street. If I had any hope that he was still alive, *which he is not,* I'd be making the effort to get him right now without your help. Now, go back to your platoon."

Sergeant Odum looked me right in the eye, started taking his pack off, and said, "Well, Lieutenant, if you won't make an effort, I will. If it's not too much trouble, sir, have your men give me some covering fire."

No more words were spoken. He was determined, and there was no way that I was going to stop him. The few remaining Marines from Charlie One Charlie didn't have to be told to start shooting at the enemy positions across the street. Sergeant Odum tightened up his helmet's chin strap, made sure his flak jacket was buttoned all the way to the top, set his M-16 aside temporarily, took out his .45-caliber pistol, pulled back the slide, and seated a round in the chamber. His plan was to go back to the alley and crawl back forward behind the M-48 tank sitting just on the other side of the courtyard wall. Then he would crawl between the tank and the wall, until he got to the street. When he finally got into this position, he would leave his position of cover, rush to the downed Marine, and drag him out of the street in between the wall and the tank.

The Marines in the courtyard increased their covering fire, and Sergeant Odum crawled forward.

I couldn't directly see what happened to Sergeant Odum out in the street, but Doc English could, and since I had a clear view of Doc English's face, I could watch the events in the street by watching the changing expressions on Doc English's face. Doc English saw, from his barely protected position as he worked frantically on a wounded Marine, everything that happened in graphic detail. He could not avoid watching what happened to Sergeant Odum, and I could see it all very clearly, reflected on Doc English's face. When Sergeant Odum made his move, the enemy gunners, no more than fifty feet away from him, saw him immediately and opened up. Doc English's face was already filled with anguish at everything going on all around him—the wounded man in his lap, the dead man in the street, and the heroic and very dangerous effort Sergeant Odum had decided to make to recover the dead Marine. Then the expression on Doc English's face got worse; for a moment his face looked like death itself. I am absolutely positive that this one second in Doc English's life will remain with him forever; the look on his face will remain seared into my brain forever. Sergeant Odum was shot in the face, his lower jaw blown off by an AK-47 round.

I thought from the look on Doc English's face that Sergeant Odum was dead, but he was not. Sergeant Odum did realize then that he would not be able to save the poor dead Marine in the street, though, and he had the presence of mind or enough life-preserving instincts to abandon the dead Marine and crawl back behind the tank and back into the courtyard.

Sergeant Odum couldn't say anything. He tried, looking me right in the eye, but I had no way of knowing if he was saying that I had been right or if he was calling me a cowardly asshole. The AK-47 round had entered his face just below his left eye and had exited his face below his chin. Everything below his upper lip had been blown into mushy strips of flesh and blood. There was no mouth; there were no teeth. There were just shreds of bloody skin.

Sergeant Odum stood up, carefully holstered his pistol, and pulled out a canteen from his utility belt pouch. He calmly poured the contents of his canteen over his shattered lower face, as if he believed that he could simply wash out this nightmare as he would wash out a badly done watercolor portrait and then attempt to paint his lower jaw back in. Doc English quickly finished his bandaging efforts on the other wounded Marine that he had been working on, broke out several more bandages from his medical kit, and crawled across the gate's opening to assist Sergeant Odum. There wasn't much he could do for him except apply the bandages and hope the bleeding would slow down long enough to get him safely medevacced. Without my needing to speak a word, Doc English knew that I wanted him to help Sergeant Odum get to the rear. Sergeant Odum resisted all attempts to have him lie down on a poncho stretcher, however, and the last time I saw him he was walking under his own power, with Doc English and a small entourage of Charlie One Charlie Marines carrying the other wounded men back to the battalion rear for medevac.

That was the last time, with one notable exception, that Charlie Company made any attempts to recover dead Marines from an exposed position in a street during the battle for Hue. There were many heroic efforts made to help wounded men while they were still alive, but after Sergeant Odum walked away from phase line green, all recovery efforts for the dead were made after darkness provided at least the illusion of cover. The only other time that an obviously dead Marine was recovered from the street in daylight hours took place several days later, and it was under highly unusual circumstances. But that story will wait.

As harsh as it sounded, and although it was very contrary to Marine Corps tradition, I gave direct orders to the rest of Charlie One that no further attempts would be made to get any dead Marines out of the street. We would do whatever we could to help save wounded men in exposed positions, but we would take no further risks by trying to retrieve dead bodies during daylight hours. After my brief and unhappy debate with Sergeant Odum on the subject, there were no further arguments.

One more attempt was made to assault across phase line green in the waning hours of that miserable afternoon. Scott Nelson and Major Thompson still did not believe that our left flank was exposed, and they resisted all pleas to provide heavy firepower. The powers that be had established the rules of engagement, and we would go forward across phase line green using the limited firepower of our small-arms weapons, or we would die. And, so, Charlie One died.

Our third attempt to assault across phase line green resulted in getting two Marines completely across the street, but it also resulted in several more wounded and two more KIAs. The two Marines who made it across the street were immediately pinned down behind two separate, low walls. They had made it across the street, but both of them were totally pinned down, unable to move right or left without dying. One of these men, an E-5 sergeant named Bossert, who had taken over as Charlie One's platoon sergeant after we lost Sergeant Mullan, had a PRC-6 radio with him. Since he was out in the street and we had good line of sight from the roof of the house that Estes had died in, we could talk with him. He didn't want to talk above a whisper, because he could hear the NVA talking very close by, and he was afraid that if they knew he was across the street and still alive, they'd find him and blow him away. He could communicate, by hand signals, with the other Marine who had made it across further down the street. Sergeant Bossert was able to tell him to hold on until after dark and then run back across the street to our side when he thought it was safe.

Benny and I had climbed up on the roof of the two-story house along with a couple more Marines from Charlie One Alpha before the third assault, but we couldn't stay on the roof very long before several NVA gunners spotted us and started pouring small-arms fire in our direction. After we had lobbed some M-79 grenades from the blooper, they had quickly figured out where we were and we had to get back down off the roof post haste.

Returning to our right flank once again for the umpteenth time that day, I crawled out behind the M-48 tank that had sat on the corner all afternoon long without once firing its cannon and got the tank commander on the phone. In as demented and angry a voice as I could muster, I told him that if he didn't start shooting his cannon at the enemy across the street, I would blow his tank up with a satchel charge. Either I wasn't very convincing, or he just didn't give a shit. He repeated that his orders were not to fire the cannon, but his machine guns did start shooting faster than they had up to that point.

I finally convinced Scott Nelson that there was no way that we could effectively assault an entrenched enemy across that street without heavy support, and that our left flank was exposed to boot. A few minutes later, he showed up in the corner courtyard.

Without speaking, I led him down the alley to our exposed left flank, and pointed out Delta Company's positions, half a block behind phase line green. He finally agreed that our left flank was exposed. As we moved back down the alley, we made contact with each squad, and by the time we got back to the corner courtyard, our head count was down to twenty-three Marines still able to fight. Eight Charlie One Marines had died that day, 13 February 1968, and twenty more had been seriously wounded and had to be medevacced.

As we huddled in that shattered courtyard, I think Scott Nelson was just starting to believe me, and he started to get just a little pissed off at Major Thompson. He got on his Prick-25, gave a terse report, and after a long wait, he was told to move back away from phase line green after we had recovered the two live Marines who had made it across the street and our dead bodies in the street and to take up defensive positions in the houses on the north side of the alley. The decision had been made to replace Charlie One with Alpha Company (complete with a newly assigned company commander) the next morning, so that they could execute the attack orders that we had not been able to carry out.

Late that night, after we had recovered our lost Marines under the cover of darkness and after I had made sure that both our flanks were secure and our defensive positions were well prepared to repel any counterattack or any attempt to sneak through our lines, I told Benny to wake me for the early morning radio watch. I found a dry bed in a corner of a small house, crawled under the mosquito netting, and dropped immediately into the sleep of the damned.

Chapter Ten

Coping with Disaster: A Dead Dog Day Afternoon

14 February 1968

Early the following morning, Scott Nelson visited the Charlie One CP group, or rather what was left of it. From the look on his face, it was immediately obvious that the news he was about to break was not good.

The numbness that had taken command of my mind and body after Estes had died was still firmly in control. I could hear and understand Nelson's words, and I was cognizant of their meaning, but I couldn't establish eye contact with him, and I'm positive that any responses I made to what he said that morning were, at best, totally conditioned responses.

Nelson said, "Charlie One is no longer an effective fighting unit, so we're going to take the men you have left and split them up to reinforce Charlie Two and Charlie Three. Alpha Company has regrouped, and their new company commander, Second Lieutenant Pat Polk, will be bringing them into your area of responsibility and relieving you within the hour. As soon as they take over your positions, bring your remaining men and join me at the company CP. We're a half block behind the center of Charlie Two's positions, in a courtyard."

I remember that a part of me felt an overwhelming sense of relief that we were being withdrawn from the hell that was phase line green, while another part of me felt a heavy measure of sorrow that Charlie One was dead. But all these emotions were muted. I felt as though I had been immersed in a vat of novocain. A disoriented feeling of unreality had taken hold of me, and my exterior self was completely numb and distinctly separated from my interior emotions.

About an hour later, Alpha Company's Marines moved into our positions, eyes wide open in anticipation of the fighting that was ahead of them. Alpha Company had already been bloodied and had lost their company commander and much of the company CP group before the fighting had really started (was that really only yesterday?). Now they had the further shock of seeing what we looked like when they took over our positions. We must have looked like hell.

Just prior to Alpha Company's arrival, I had ordered a head count and found out that there were twenty-three Marines remaining in Charlie One. Fifty-one of us had arrived at phase line green yesterday morning, and after one day of fighting, twenty-three remained.

After we joined up with the Charlie Company CP group, Charlie One was officially disbanded. Eleven of the Charlie One survivors, including Doc English and Benny Benwaring, were directed to join up with Charlie Two. The remaining ten were assigned to Charlie Three. Doc Lowdermilk was reassigned to the company CP group and was made the Charlie Company corpsman. As the twenty-third survivor of Charlie One's long and deadly day on phase line green, I reported to Scott Nelson at the Charlie Company CP. Charlie One was now officially deactivated; more appropriately, Charlie One was dead.

I was assigned to be the Charlie Company weapons platoon commander, a position that, on paper, was always part of the table of organization of a Marine rifle company. However, during this period of the Vietnam War, this leadership position was seldom actually staffed with a lieutenant because of the constant shortages of junior officers that plagued Marine units in early 1968. In fact, Charlie Company was fortunate in that we had three second lieutenants assigned as platoon commanders; it was not at all unusual to see staff NCOs assigned, at least temporarily, as platoon commanders. Since Charlie Company had been stranded in the Lang Co area when the Tet Offensive had exploded and we had seen very little combat during the previous two weeks and had taken no losses during that period, we were as close to fully staffed as we had ever been.

Because the machine gun teams had long since been attached to the rifle platoons, my only immediate responsibilities as the new weapons platoon commander were to "command" the sixty-millimeter mortar teams. I actually knew very little about the workings of a sixty-millimeter mortar team, and The Gunny seemed to already have everything well under control. Common sense therefore dictated that my duties as the Charlie Company weapons platoon commander eroded down to breaking open crates of sixty-millimeter mortar rounds and keeping the mortar teams supplied with ammo.

Scott Nelson eyeballed me a lot that morning. I think he was worried about me. The exterior numbness that had taken hold of me didn't allow me to think about much of anything except Estes and the other Charlie One Marines who had lost their lives on phase line green. I simply could not shake off the feelings of frustration, futility, and loss, and I continued to play the terrible scenes over and over again in my mind: *Our left flank is totally exposed; we have no heavy weapons in support; we are facing an entrenched enemy of superior size; and we are ordered three times to assault into this meat grinder. Morgan and many others down in the street; Sergeant Mullan gone; Sergeant Odum with his face blown off; Estes dying in my lap.* I guess I just didn't give a damn what Nelson thought about me at that point. He could eyeball me all he wanted; I was just simply numb. And then, in the middle of that long afternoon, Scott Nelson had come and asked me for some help.

His request had led me to this place, hiding behind this wall, having weird conversations with a dead dog, and thinking about the terrible fate of Charlie One. With my Prick-25 sometimes tuned into the battalion frequency, sometimes the Charlie Company frequency just to stay in touch, and sometimes the Alpha Company frequency to monitor the progress of their assault, I had a play-by-play radio dialogue of the fighting. With and without the aid of the Prick-25, I could hear the screaming of the wounded and dying. From my grandstand seat behind that low wall, I was within a hundred meters of most of the fighting. It was plenty close to hear the agony of a young Marine's last few seconds of life or the terror of another who had been knocked down in the street by machine gun fire from the tower and who was now a stationary and doomed target for the NVA gunners in the second stories of their houses across the street.

No one ever called me over that radio that afternoon; I was superfluous; I was forgotten. It was just as well, because if anyone had asked my advice at that point, I'm certain that I would have been immediately charged with cowardice in the face of the enemy. I would have advised them all to withdraw, to leave this city in the hands of the enemy who obviously wanted it so badly, and to tell the goddamned politicians who had gotten us into this mess and had then tied our hands behind our backs so securely to go fuck themselves. The rules of engagement that they had used as rope the day before were still in effect. We were even violating them by dropping the sixty-mike-mikes on the enemy positions, but I guess Scott Nelson had asked himself what would be the worst thing they could do to him for allowing the sixty-millimeter mortar crews to earn their pay. A question we all asked ourselves at one time or another during our tours in Vietnam was, What the hell can they do to me, draft me and send me to Vietnam? I guess he had decided the hell with it, at least we could keep down the heads of the NVA across the street during Alpha Company's assault, and to hell with the consequences. The sixty-mike-mikes were one asset that we didn't have to request through battalion, who would most certainly at that point have denied our request.

This insanity, these damnable rules of engagement that prevented American fighting men from using the only tactical assets that gave us an advantage during firefights—that of our vastly superior firepower represented by air strikes, artillery, and naval gunfire—these orders continued to remain in force and hinder, wound, and kill 1/5 Marines until the fourth day of fighting inside the Citadel of Hue. In fact, after the initial rules of engagement were rescinded and 1/5's frantic requests for heavy support were finally approved on the fourth day, it took another three days of heavy fighting, including many artillery missions; round after round of 90-mm cannon from the tanks and 106-mm recoilless rifles from the Ontos; many sorties of napalm, 250-pound, and 500-pound high-explosive bombs from F-4s; and even some naval gunfire, combined with the small arms and M-79 grenades of *two* Marine rifle companies (Alpha and Bravo) before the first block directly across phase line green opposite Charlie One's original area of operations on that first day was finally secured. In the process, all the two-story buildings lining the southern, enemy side of phase line green were flattened. So much for trying to protect this valuable real estate.

During the long afternoon of fighting on the second day, though, Alpha Company somehow managed to establish a tenuous toehold on the enemy side of phase line green. Although Alpha Company was also hindered by the same rules of engagement that Charlie One had been hindered by the day before, the Marines bravely charged into the face of the prepared enemy soldier's positions three separate times. As with Charlie One's experiences from the previous day, and although Alpha Company had three times more Marines to thrust into the battle than Charlie One, Alpha was thrown back the first two times with a terrible loss of life and many wounded who had to be evacuated. Dead Marine bodies once again littered the pavement on phase line green.

Alpha Company was now being led by 2nd Lt. Pat Polk, who had been a platoon commander with Charlie Company when I joined the company at Hoi An. I quickly learned that Pat really had his act together and, I am sure, had the complete respect of his men. Pat had sort of taken me under his wing when I had first joined Charlie Company, and he had helped me learn a lot in those critical early days. But Pat was not a superman, and he was handicapped by the same limiting rules of engagement that had killed Charlie One the day before.

Meanwhile, Delta Company had made no progress whatsoever in trying to take over the dominating tower at the east end of phase line green. The NVA occupying the tower had terrific fields of fire down the street, and since they were no more than two hundred meters from the furthest Alpha Company position, their cross fire was devastating to the Marines who charged across the street into the NVA positions on the south side of Mai Thuc Loan. Twice Alpha charged, and twice they were turned back, getting absolutely nowhere, at a terrible loss of life.

As I numbly monitored the radio nets, I continued my conversation with the dead dog. "I told them bastards, dog. They gotta take out the NVA on the tower, and that's going to take heavy weapons. They're just going to have to start bringing in air strikes and arty. They're going to get Alpha Company wiped out just like they got Charlie One wiped out. Dog, have you ever seen such a stupid clusterfuck as this one? Shit."

I was tempted many times to just turn off the Prick-25, but it wouldn't have done much good. I could still hear the shooting clearly without the help of the radio, and I could hear the results of the stupidity—the screams and the agony of the last moments of the dead and the curses of those who lay dying in the street. And, like someone who can't leave a sore tooth alone, a deeply perverse part of me wanted to listen to this tragedy unfold. So, I sat safely behind the wall and listened and talked to the dead dog.

As mentioned, late that afternoon, Alpha Company finally succeeded in getting a squad across phase line green, establishing a tenuous toehold in the corner house for the first time. Listening to the events of that long afternoon, I'm convinced that this squad would have also been wiped out except for the unbelievable bravery, or perhaps the utter frustration, of an Alpha Company sixty-millimeter mortarman.

This particular Alpha Company mortarman had also been monitoring the Alpha Company radio frequency, waiting for a fire mission that had never come, and he had probably momentarily lost his mind. Alpha Company's third assault across phase line green had concentrated a squad of Marines in the corner courtyard where Staff Sergeant Odum had lost his face and Doc English had lost his youth. Alpha had rushed across the street en masse into the corner house. Only one of them had been hit during the rush, and he had fortunately not been hit so bad as to fall down in the street, having made it across the street with the rest of his squad. Unfortunately, the squad had immediately come under fire as the NVA on the second floor of the house shot at them down the stair way, and two more Alpha Company Marines were seriously wounded before the NVA on the second floor were killed by the Alpha Company Marines. At the same time, the Alpha squad leader was hit by a machine gun that raked the first floor from the back yard of the house next door, and two more Marines were hit by fire from yet another machine gun shooting at them from directly behind the house. The Alpha Company squad, the first to establish any kind of position on the south side of the street, was being systematically destroyed by the deadly cross fire of a well-prepared ambush.

The frantic cries of the squad's radio operator were trying to sear my mind and destroy my soul. Only my state of numbness saved me from insanity. I sat and listened, looked over at the dog, and said, "I told them so, dog. I told them dumb bastards that we should just get out of Dodge and leave this damnable Citadel to the gooks. Now look where it's gotten Alpha Company. Those guys are in big trouble, dog."

The frustrated Alpha Company mortarman was obviously *not* sufficiently anesthetized, because he just simply lost his cool. Of course, I had no way of knowing that this subplot to the drama was starting to unfold, but based upon the eyewitness accounts of the Alpha Company Marines who survived that deadly cross fire, this is what happened:

The Alpha Company mortarman, hearing the crazed calls for help from the pinned-down squad's radio operator, just took off running for phase line green, and with no thoughts for his own safety, ran across Mai Thuc Loan through a hail of fire from the tower before anyone could stop him. He made it into the death trap that was the corner house. The mortarman immediately took control of the situation, yelling at one of the most coherent Marines to tell him where the enemy positions were, and in what strength.

At least one of the Alpha Company Marines was coherent enough to give the mortarman a situation report of sorts. He reported that all the NVA on the second floor were dead, or at least the Marines were no longer taking fire from upstairs, but there were two machine guns raking the house in a deadly cross fire. One machine gun nest, out the side door and about fifty feet away, was manned by at least five NVA soldiers, and the other machine gun had two or three enemy soldiers. This lance corporal mortarman, who had no business being there in the first place, calmly gathered up as many M-26 grenades from the dead and wounded Marines cringing in that corner house as he could carry and, without looking back or saying anything, charged out the side door and assaulted the main machine gun nest. The mortarman ran right up to within a few feet of it, tossing two M-26 grenades into the enemy position as he dived forward and hit the dirt. Both grenades hit their marks, and the first enemy machine gun nest was wiped out and silent for the first time in nearly a half hour. The mortarman didn't even stop to catch his breath. Scrambling back into the corner house, he grabbed some more grenades and charged out the back door into the teeth of the second enemy position's fire. He took the second machine gun position out in the same way as the first. The sudden silence on that corner, my first indication that something remarkable had happened, was almost deafening.

When the Alpha Company mortarman returned into the corner house, he noticed for the first time that he had been wounded four times from machine gun fire. All the wounds were minor, but he was definitely going to be awarded multiple Purple Hearts.

Using the twenty-twenty vision of hindsight, I am certain that the Alpha Company mortarman's heroic act was the turning point of the battle for Hue's Citadel fortress because it gave 1/5 its first "beachhead" across phase line green. I am also certain that if that mortarman had not done what he did, many more lives would have been lost on that damnable street.

Several weeks later, Scott Nelson asked me to write up some recommendations for medals and awards for Marines who had distinguished themselves during the battle for Hue. I immediately thought of this young Marine, the Alpha Company mortarman, who had risked his life for his fellow Marines even though his job was to stay in the relative safety of the rear area and lob sixty-mike-mikes on the enemy. In my opinion, this man's heroism had turned the tide of battle and had saved many other lives. I spent a few hours interviewing a few Marines from Alpha Company who had survived the battle inside the Citadel, including his fellow members of the mortar crews and one Marine who had been pinned down in that corner house that afternoon. I was given his name and the facts necessary to recommend him for the Congressional Medal of Honor. I felt very strongly that his efforts met all the criteria to be awarded his nation's highest award for valor.

About three months later, I heard from Scott Nelson, now the Alpha Company commander, that this young hero had received the Silver Star and that my request for the Medal of Honor had been denied. The main reasons stated for this downgrading were that the mortarman had not died during his acts of heroism and that the request "had not been well written." It is to my everlasting shame that I accept full responsibility for this travesty. I am even more ashamed, however, that today I don't remember this young man's name. Of all the heroic acts that I witnessed and heard about during my tour in Vietnam, in my opinion this was by far the most heroic and the most significant. The Alpha Company mortarman hopefully knows just how crazy and heroic his efforts were on that day, and if he is anything like most of our American fighting men, he probably doesn't really care too much about not getting the Medal of Honor. He is probably very proud of his Silver Star, so my poor efforts went unnoticed. Were I to meet him today, I would thank him to the best of my ability, and I would tell him that what he did that day did not go unnoticed and that his acts of heroism will always be remembered. The Alpha Company mortarman was a true American combat hero.

As I think the reader might understand, I became very cynical about awards after that. The only award that I received during my tour in Vietnam that I have any pride in whatsoever was the Presidential Unit Citation awarded to the First Battalion, Fifth Marine Regiment for our part in the battle for Hue during the Tet Offensive of 1968.

Perhaps the Alpha Company mortarman had not been considered a model Marine, and therefore his chain of command had not gone to bat for him. Most of the enlisted men, the combat Marines who did all the dirty work in this, the dirtiest of wars, had experienced that same problem at one time or another. What some of the upper echelon considered being a model Marine, the grunts considered just plain bullshit. It became really difficult for the lifers to give distinguished awards to these "crazies," these "misfits." And yet these "misfits" and "crazies" were the ones the higher-ups counted on to walk point or to assault machine gun positions.

As the pale afternoon sun faded on 14 February 1968—the second day inside the Citadel of Hue—the dead dog and I continued to monitor Alpha Company's radio net. Two more squads from Alpha Company had rushed across phase line green and reinforced the beleaguered squad who had just barely escaped death, thanks to the lone mortarman. The dead and wounded, including the heroic young mortarman, were helped back across the street under cover of the darkening sky, and the seriously wounded were carried back to the First ARVN Division compound to wait for a medevac chopper. The reinforcing Alpha Company squads took firm control of the two-story house on the corner and held their position through the long night with no further incidents.

The dead dog had been a perfect companion throughout that long afternoon, as he had never given me any problems or even made one smart-ass remark, although I am sure that much of what I said to him that afternoon deserved serious rebuttal.

Cringing behind the low wall that afternoon, I had at one point decided to take yet another chance with a C ration meal, in spite of the mute warning from the spoon in the dead dog's mouth. I opened my pack to see what delectable delights awaited me in the form of yet another C ration experience. We had been fully resupplied with six C ration meals each during our brief stay in Phu Bai, and as I had only eaten a couple of times since then, there should have been several choices. There were, but one of the best choices, a large can of Beans and Weenies, had been rendered inedible by the NVA snipers. This disgusting discovery solved the mystery of why I had been knocked off my feet at the end of my sprint to the wall earlier that afternoon. Upon further investigation, I found that there was a bullet hole through the right side of my pack. The can of Beans and Weenies was a mess of crumpled tin, with beans and weenies interspersed throughout the interior of my pack. A large, shredded hole on the left side of my pack clearly identified my pack's exit wound. I immediately lost my appetite.

I knew now that the fit of giggles that had seized me during the slow-motion sprint to the wall had probably saved my life, bending me over at the precise moment that the NVA sniper had squeezed his trigger.

The impact of the bullet, while wiping out the Beans and Weenies, had provided enough force to knock me off balance. Fortunately the bullet had missed the Prick-25 by at least two inches and my body by at least four, but it had destroyed my favorite C ration meal and my appetite for the rest of that day. It had also given me one more thing to complain about to the dead dog, who stoically ignored my indignant complaints.

Just after full darkness, I said a fond farewell to my canine companion, muttering some futile advice to stay away from Ham and Mutherfuckers, and crawled away from my hidden position in the darkness.

Chapter Eleven

Life Is Renewed
in the
City of Death

14–15 February 1968

Just as the pitch-black gloom of night took hold, I returned to the Charlie Company command post area. As the Charlie Company weapons platoon commander, or sixty-mike-mike assistant, I had no frontline responsibilities that night. After a quick consultation with Scott Nelson, I joined up with a few of the Charlie Company CP group, including Doc Lowdermilk, one of the Charlie Company radio operators, and a couple of Charlie Company mortarmen, and together we sought out shelter and sleeping quarters for the night.

We quickly discovered, to our amazement, that many civilian Vietnamese residents of the Citadel of Hue, whose homes were behind our lines, were still in residence. We hadn't seen any of them, but they were still there. Our small group picked out a small house in the center of the block at random, and we pounded on the front door. Expecting a house this close to the fighting to be deserted, we were surprised when we were promptly and politely greeted at the front door by a middle-aged Vietnamese gentleman. Unfortunately the man spoke no English, and the

Vietnamese that I had learned during my six-week "high-intensity" language school at Quantico proved to be totally inadequate for anything other than a barely understood greeting. Fortunately, Doc Lowdermilk knew some French, which turned out to be the Vietnamese man's second language, and we were finally able to communicate to some degree.

The man was of average height for a Vietnamese, standing about five foot six and, from his dress and manners, appeared to be from the affluent class of Vietnamese. He was probably a teacher in the nearby university. His western-style clothing was comprised of conservative dark slacks and a white shirt and was completed with a dark-colored French beret. He welcomed us into his home with no hesitation. Since he probably understood quite clearly just how close his home was to the fighting, he readily welcomed this small but well-armed group of Marines to share his home for the night.

Initially, we thought that he was alone, but as we entered the dimly lit house, he spoke a few soft, staccato words in Vietnamese, and the rest of his family slowly and hesitantly appeared from their hide-hole under the family bed at the back of the one-room structure. His wife was young, probably no more than thirty, and his three children looked to be between four and ten years old. We only saw their heads, and they didn't linger outside the inadequate protection of the large bed; they just acknowledged our existence with a slightly hopeful aspect to their fearful expressions and disappeared under the bed once again.

Using Doc Lowdermilk's rusty French, we confirmed that the owner of this small house was welcoming us to spend the night. When we made obvious movements to bunk down on the floor in the corners of his cozy little home, he beckoned us to take full advantage of the large, communal family bed, indicating that he had no intention of allowing his family out from under the bed throughout the night, and that we were more than welcome to it.

Before retiring under the bed for the night, the head of the household smiled at us, excused himself for a moment, rummaged around in a dark corner closet, and came out with a large, colorful metal box of French cookies, the kind that were made with lots of butter and sugar, reminding me of the Lorna Doones that I had loved so much as a child. The five of us took one look at these exquisite pastries and started to gorge ourselves with cookies. A sort of temporary insanity overcame all of us, and before any semblance of reason came back to us, we realized that we had wiped out the entire box of cookies, an obviously hoarded delicacy that this poor man's family undoubtedly carefully indulged in, probably one cookie at a time, on special occasions. We couldn't help it; we had eaten nothing like it since having left the States, and our constant subsistence on C rations had created a dietary standard that was barely tolerable. The sight of those cookies had overwhelmed all five of us, and all judgment and manners had flown out the window. During our display of American gluttony, the Vietnamese gentleman said nothing; he just accepted his empty metal box back with an astonished look on his face. No jury of our peers would have convicted us of theft; our plea of temporary insanity would have stood the test of justice.

Temporary insanity or not, I couldn't help but feel very guilty, so I looked at the other Marines with the sheepish looks on their crumb-covered faces and said, "Shit, guys, we've wiped this guy out of cookies. Any of you have anything worthwhile to give him in return?" Although I was one of the guilty gorging culprits, I had nothing in my pack but C rations, messy ones at that, to offer as reparations, and offering to compensate him with C rations would have been an insult of the highest magnitude. I knew that in spite of the many regulations forbidding it, the chances were excellent that at least one Marine had a bottle of liquor in his pack, preferably unopened, to offer as at least partial compensation. It turned out that there were three such bottles, and we decided upon an unopened bottle of Jack Daniels since its owner had a second, only partially consumed bottle of booze rat-holed away in his pack. Armed with the Jack Daniels, we offered the Vietnamese gentleman our apologies and the bottle of America's finest sippin' whiskey, in hopes that he would forgive our out-of-control appetites and our poor manners.

Our gesture was received very graciously, and our host's eyes lighted up once again as he accepted our offer and then hid the bottle of Jack in the corner closet that the cookies had, until recently, been stashed in. Having secured the Jack Daniels, he walked to an ornate, open-front cabinet standing against the wall on the west side of the small house. Reaching up to one of the higher shelves, he very carefully lifted an ordinary American mason jar that was sealed with a metal screw-lid and contained a very strange and suspicious-looking substance. The quart jar was about 85 percent full of what looked like nuts, banana, coconut, and other fruits; the top 15 percent was a clear liquid.

Our host very carefully, almost reverently, set the jar down on the only table in the house, retrieved several small, dainty cups from the open cabinet, and with what can only be described as great pleasure, opened the jar and poured a small amount of the clear liquid off the top and into the cups. One of the mortarmen in our small group understood first, blurting out, "Shit, Lieutenant, this is homemade hooch. Booze. I'll be goddamned!"

The young Marine, eager for any form of mental anesthetic available, started to hoist his cup with the obvious intention of chugging the hooch, but the Vietnamese gentleman, our host who had the most, stopped him just in time, preventing him from making a very bad mistake. Restraining the young Marine, he held up his own small cup and, through hand gestures and unmistakable body language, indicated that careful sipping would be in order here. We all accepted his advice, took our first sips, and were immediately very grateful for his warning. Whatever that stuff was, it was as near to two-hundred-proof alcohol as you could possibly get. It went down our gullets like liquid fire, although after the initial kick, it was very smooth and had a touch of sweetness I had never before experienced in drinking alcohol, probably because of the fruit used to ferment it. Looking around at the small group, I noticed that I was not the only one whose eyes had filled with involuntary tears caused by the liquid fire. It didn't matter. It was the perfect ending to the second-worst day of my life.

The celebration lasted only a few moments, and then the reality of our situation came quickly back into focus and once again took control. Our host bade us farewell and good luck with hand gestures and a smattering of French and quietly joined his family under the bed. Setting up a rotating watch, we doused the lantern light and let sleep shut out the terror of the day.

Around midnight that night we were rudely awakened by a commotion at our front door. Several Marines were pounding on the door, looking for Doc Lowdermilk.

One of the Marines, a Charlie Company mortarman, said, "Doc, we need your help. This Vietnamese lady a few houses down has just gone into labor, and she needs a hand. Get your shit together and get on down here, Doc."

Doc Lowdermilk didn't hesitate for a moment; he had seen so much death during the past couple of days that any opportunity to help bring a life into the world was obviously welcome, regardless of the circumstances. And although he had never been involved with childbirth in his young life, he was a medical professional and was going to do his best to help out, no matter what.

Doc Lowdermilk grabbed his corpsman's medical kit and left with the other Marines, and the rest of us quickly returned to our dreamless sleep. Just before dawn the next morning, Doc Lowdermilk returned with a slight grin on his face and woke us all up with the news of the arrival of a new baby boy. For just a few hours, Doc Lowdermilk had been allowed the opportunity to forget all the death and destruction to focus on the most constructive of all of life's events, the delivery of a new life.

Although there was about a half hour before full daylight and Doc could have caught a few minutes of much-needed sleep, he was much too wound up from his experience. The rest of us woke up easily to hear his story; it gave all of us a brief but much-needed respite from the stress and terror of the previous two days to hear Doc's story and to watch the gentle smile on his face as he recounted the moment of birth.

After just a very few moments of peaceful contemplation of the blessed event, the increasing daylight forced us from our reverie. We mounted up and said a brief good-bye and thank you to our host for his hospitality and left the small home behind, facing another day, not knowing what would happen to us, and not knowing at that moment just how lucky this small Vietnamese family was to be alive.

We had heard some rumors of atrocities at the hands of the occupying NVA in and around Hue during the past several days, but many weeks would go by before we knew the extent of the terror that the NVA had generated during the several weeks that they controlled Hue. After-action reports released by MACV indicated that as many as three thousand Vietnamese civilians were murdered and buried in mass graves by the Viet Cong and NVA during their occupation of Hue. Any Vietnamese civilian who was even suspected by the NVA or the agents of the National Liberation Front, the political control organization of the Viet Cong, of possessing sympathy for the South Vietnamese government or their American allies was executed on the spot. Their bodies were hastily buried in unmarked mass graves over a wide area in and around Hue. Those who survived had necessarily professed to being longtime supporters of the Viet Cong and North Vietnamese goals.

Although it was often very difficult for American soldiers to empathize with the position of the average Vietnamese citizen, who was caught between the proverbial rock and a hard place, learning about the mass murders in Hue helped to create at least a small amount of understanding of their plight. Because of our experiences in the Hoi An area, the Marines of Charlie Company had developed an active hatred of the Vietnamese villagers who lived near where some Marines had been torn apart by command-detonated mines. This hatred was born from the Marines' knowledge that the Vietnamese villagers must have known exactly who was responsible for these acts of terror. The villagers may have even been aware of the presence of the Viet Cong terrorists before the acts were perpetrated, but they always denied knowing anything. Despite the hatred that seemed to always be seething just below the surface of the young Marines, an understanding of the average Vietnamese civilian's untenable position was brought to a focus, at least briefly, by the murders of the people of Hue. We began to understand that these people either had to help the enemy or at least look the other way, or they were dead.

On the other hand, our host during the previous evening could have been quite possibly a Viet Cong operative himself, incognito among his young family and chuckling to himself at the blindness of his enemy, at our utter inability to tell the difference between friend and foe. I prefer to think otherwise, and I remember him still as one of the lucky ones who somehow escaped the deadly attentions of the invaders. He was one of the few Vietnamese civilians we met who was openly hospitable or voluntarily friendly toward American grunts.

The Charlie Company mortarmen and Doc Lowdermilk returned to their assigned duties, and I started opening sixty-millimeter mortar crates once again, having nothing else to do. The two Charlie Company sixty-mike-mikes, our only form of artillery at the moment, were by now well dug in and surrounded by sandbag berms in a small courtyard about a block and a half behind phase line green. Small-arms fire had started up again in the area of Alpha Company's penetration of the enemy's positions across phase line green, and the fighting increased steadily as the day progressed. At the moment, however, the sixty-mike-mikes were silent, as the Alpha Company Marines were just too close to the enemy and we were fearful of hurting our own people.

About an hour after first light, 2nd Lt. Travis Curd, Charlie Company's artillery forward observer, and his corporal radio operator, both of whom were attached to us from the 11th Marine Regiment (the artillery regiment of the First Marine Division), joined The Gunny and me as we tried to eat a cold C ration breakfast. I had known Travis Curd for several weeks now. He had traveled with Charlie Company since we left Phu Loc 6 back in early January, and he had been stranded with us at the Lang Co Bridge. A basic comradeship, if not a friendship, had grown between us. He really had his act together as an FO, and he was a pretty nice guy besides. He had let his mustache grow well beyond Marine Corps regulations and had trained it into a Fu Manchu look, but since we were rarely in a rear area and most often quite distant from the scrutiny of any "spit and polish" types, he got away with it.

On this particular morning, Travis's Fu Manchu looked more droopy than usual, and his eyes were dark with fatigue. He didn't say a word as he pulled up a sixty-mike-mike crate, sat down heavily, and tossed his pack onto the damp ground with a look of disgust.

"Hell, Lieutenant, that Fu Manchu looks like shit. Hell, *you* look like shit. What the hell have you been up to?" The Gunny was never one to mince his words with anyone, even those who were theoretically above him in the chain of command.

Travis shot The Gunny a look of pained disgust and said, "Hell, Gunny, I feel like a big pile of waterboo shit. That goddamned company commander of yours damn near got us killed last night. We're lucky to be alive right now. Shit, I didn't sign up to be a goddamned grunt! I'm supposed to be an FO, and just because battalion won't let me do my goddamned job, doesn't mean that I should have to be turned into a goddamned grunt!" Travis's haunted eyes emphasized the harrowing experiences that he and his radio operator had obviously just survived.

Travis went on to explain to us that Scott Nelson had given him the job of setting up a listening post on Charlie Company's right flank the previous night. Now, Travis was not opposed to taking command of a small group of well-armed Marines to man this listening post, and he understood that our right flank *was* totally exposed and that the listening post *was* absolutely necessary to ensure the integrity of the company's right flank. He had assumed, however, that when Nelson gave him the assignment, he would send a squad of Charlie Three's Marines with him, or at least a fire team.

Travis shot us a look of abject disgust and said, "Shit, Nelson said that he couldn't afford to send any of the Charlie Three Marines with us, 'cuz they're needed on phase line green in case of a counterattack, that he wants me and my radio operator, all by ourselves, to take over the second floor of that house out on the right flank and stay there and let him know if we hear anything. Shit, there was nothing between us and the fucking Imperial Palace walls, nothing but a few trees, so the gooks would have to cross all that open ground to get around us, but

Jesus Christ was it dark! An entire battalion of NVA, armed to the teeth and dragging 82-mike-mike mortars along for good measure could have walked right by us and we would have never known about it. I reminded Nelson that neither Corporal Talbot nor I had any weapons except our .45s, but he didn't blink an eye, and the next thing we know, we're both holding M-16s and several bandoleers of ammo, and The Gunny here is handing us several M-26 grenades apiece. Shit, it looks like we're both grunts now."

"So, it looks like you survived the night. Did you hear anything?" I couldn't help but grin a little at Travis's tale of woe and to give him just a little shit about his experiences of the previous night, and I noticed that The Gunny had just an inkling of a grin on his otherwise impassive face. I added, "Hell, maybe we have a whole battalion of gooks behind us right now. . . ."

"Hell, no, we didn't hear a thing, didn't see a thing, and didn't either one of us sleep a wink. Christ, we were out there totally on our own, you think we could sleep for even a minute?" asked Travis, and then he answered his own question, "Hell, no. Shit, my eye sockets are sore from being stretched, my eyes were so wide open all night. I was afraid to blink, for Christ's sake. I gotta tell you the truth, Charlie One, I've never been so scared in my entire life!"

The story of Lieutenant Curd's and Corporal Talbot's harrowing night rapidly spread via the rumor mill throughout Charlie Company. It became an oft-recounted part of Charlie Company's lore and was here-after referred to as "The Night of the Lost Outpost" by the Marines of Charlie Company. In those rare moments of relaxation during and after the battle that raged inside the Citadel of Hue, many Marines who survived ultimately heard that story, and they were afforded at least a small amount of comic relief by its telling. It really was funny, but only because nothing bad had happened that night.

That was one of the strangest aspects of the battle for the Citadel, the fact that nothing much ever happened after dark. With one very significant exception, when the sun went down, the shooting stopped. It was as though, by mutual understanding, both the NVA and the Marines decided that the terrible house-to-house fighting would be just too terrorizing after dark. The fighters would undoubtedly die from terror if the element of darkness was added to the equation of fighting a well-armed enemy at close quarters. We were always fearful of an enemy counterattack at night, and we never reduced our alert level below 50 percent at the point of contact, but the NVA stayed in their positions. They very seldom even fired small arms as harassment and only occasionally fired a rocket or a mortar round after darkness fell. I didn't question this much while it was happening; I just took advantage of it and got at least five hours of sleep every night, except one. But thinking back on it, I am absolutely certain that if the NVA *had* counterattacked just once in the middle of the night, they would have successfully penetrated our front lines. The resulting chaos from a nighttime counterattack would have been terrible and may have even forced the battalion to withdraw back to the First ARVN Division compound to regroup. And then we would have had to do it all over again. . . . It was too terrible to consider for even a moment, and thankfully, it never happened.

As usual, the dark humor of Travis's telling of "The Story of the Lost Outpost" was not allowed to linger for long, and our razzing of Travis was rudely interrupted by Scott Nelson, who joined our motley crew. Nelson addressed The Gunny and me and gave us our next orders.

Nelson squatted down next to us and said, "We're finally getting some fixed wing support, although it's going to be limited to the tower. Delta is getting the shit shot out of them by the NVA in the tower, and Alpha isn't going to be able to make much more progress until Delta can take and hold the tower. So, battalion has finally come to the realization that heavy support is needed. A flight of Phantoms will be arriving from Da Nang in a few minutes, and they're loaded with snake-eyes and napalm. Gunny, your mortar crews are too exposed, we're just too damned close to the tower, and one of your guys might get hit by stray shrapnel. When the F-4s start dropping their ordnance, I want you to make damned sure that these guys have their heads down behind the sandbag walls. Charlie One, take all the spare men from the company CP group, including your hang-dog hero buddies here." Nelson was obviously referring to Travis and Corporal Talbot, but his expression was nothing but playful and sympathetic. "And go back a few hundred meters to the rear and take cover. The Phantoms are gonna drop a shitload of napalm and both 250-pound and 500-pound bombs on that damned tower, and I don't want anyone getting hurt because they're watching the show from a front-row seat. Got it?"

I didn't have to be told twice. I had been a front-row spectator at enough air strikes to understand the danger. The Marines on phase line green were safe enough inside the houses, but those of us who were out in the open were exposed to stray shrapnel, which was wicked as hell and could be thrown a long way from its impact point.

So, along with about a dozen men who were, at least for the moment, considered expendable from the fighting, I retreated two blocks toward the First ARVN Division compound. We took seats on a low brick wall to wait for the show.

One of the most amazing forms of entertainment during the Vietnam War (at least for anyone not at or near the target of this particular form of entertainment) were the close air support strikes provided by Marine, Navy, and Air Force pilots flying a wide range of attack aircraft. Any air strike directed at enemy forces was very satisfying to any bush Marine regardless of the type of aircraft being featured as the main attraction, and they all beat the hell out of any fireworks show I had ever seen. But the shows provided by the F-4s—the Phantoms—were, without a doubt, the absolute best.

There was just something nasty-looking about Phantoms. They were mean-looking, with swept-back gull wings similar to their World War II predecessor, the F4U-1A Corsair, the aircraft made famous by Pappy Boyington and his Black Sheep squadron. An F-4 Phantom's wings were gull-like, although much shorter and sharper than the prop-driven Corsairs, but that's where the similarity between these aircraft stopped, abruptly. The Corsair was a single-engine prop plane, and the F-4 was powered by two immensely powerful jet engines. When those suckers kicked into afterburners, the power they emanated was awesome.

I had seen many Phantoms from a distance while going through training stateside, and I had always been fascinated by them. But I didn't really develop a distinct appreciation for their raw power until shortly after landing in Da Nang at the beginning of my tour in Vietnam. Stateside pilots must have had to fly with major restrictions near their airfields, because I had never seen a Phantom in an afterburner mode until that unforgettable afternoon in Da Nang. The pilots in country were under no such restrictions. They routinely kicked in their afterburners during takeoff, cranking up as much speed as possible to leave the earth with their heavy loads of destructive power and to make it as difficult as possible for the neighborhood VC to hit them with ground fire, if they were so inclined to try such a foolhardy thing. I remember being nearly hypnotized that day as I watched flight after flight of F-4s tear down the runway in Da Nang with their afterburners kicked in, and I was deafened by the roaring chaos of their powerful engines throwing them skyward. I remember thinking to myself that no one in his right mind would knowingly resist their awesome firepower. But I knew by now that our enemy did resist them, every day and every night, and I knew by now that our enemy was clearly not in his right mind.

And now the F-4s were coming to Hue, finally, to try to blow the NVA out of the tower. Sitting on that wall, waiting for the show, I knew with an absolute certainty that the NVA in the tower were doomed, and that we would have control of this critical piece of high ground very soon, or that it would no longer be high ground.

I was wrong on both counts.

Oh, the F-4s came, and the F-4s dropped stick after stick of napalm, 250-pound snake-eye bombs, and 500-pound high-drag, high-explosive bombs on the tower. And nearly every bomb dropped was a perfectly placed direct hit. The awesome firestorms from the detonating napalm canisters engulfed the tower, burning every square inch of the tower's surface; the high-explosive bombs pounded the tower and eventually reduced its height by at least ten feet. But the NVA did not run away; few of them died; and every single bombing run made in the F-4 pilots' valiant attempts to destroy our enemy entrenched in the tower was greeted by a high volume of small-arms fire from the enemy.

The NVA AK-47s and .30-caliber machine guns ripped upward, directing their light green and white tracer rounds at the invading Phantoms. The enemy's constant and defiant small-arms fire was only momentarily interrupted exactly when the napalm burst into a whooshing roar of flame and smoke and exactly when the high explosives burst their gut-wrenching concussive power on the tower. Immediately after, the NVA gunners stuck their crazy heads back up and started shooting again at the flame-spewing dual exhausts of the departing Phantom's jets. The Phantoms made pass after disciplined pass, dropping no more than two bombs at a time, but the determined NVA gunners survived all of them and always had the last word in the deadly duel. One Phantom even took a couple of hits up one of his tailpipes and had to limp back to Da Nang without dropping all his ordnance on the tower.

The NVA in the tower were absolutely crazy! It turned out that Delta Company would need two more days, several attacks, and the heroics of some even crazier Delta Company Marines to finally take the tower the first time. Shortly after that, the NVA counterattacked, and Delta had to withdraw in a hurry, dragging their wounded back with them. Delta would attack and take the tower four separate times, only to have the NVA take it back again. Finally, on the fifth day of the fighting, Delta would finally seize and hold the tower, after having taken terrible losses.

Obviously, the NVA understood that this tower was the high ground in this battle and that whoever held the tower could easily keep their enemy pinned down. The NVA were not going to give up the tower just because of the annoying Phantoms!

While we were sitting on the wall watching this surreal duel between the NVA Davids and the Phantom Goliaths from what we thought was a safe distance, a battalion mule driver pulled up on his mechanical mule (a small but rugged vehicle that looked like nothing more than a platform with four tires and a steering wheel). He stopped about thirty feet away from us, letting his engine idle for a few minutes and taking advantage of our vantage point to watch the show. The cargo platform of the mule was empty, so the driver had probably just dropped off some more ammo or other supplies at the Charlie Company CP and was heading back to the First ARVN Division compound where the Air America choppers and the occasional Marine helicopter were starting to bring in supplies. He had seen our group perched on the low brick wall and had stopped to take a short break and watch the show. Fishing out a cigarette, he lit up with his Zippo and sat back in his seat while his mule, the four-wheeled pack animal of the Marine Corps, idled with a low-popping rumble.

The next Phantom emerged from the low cloud cover and dropped two snake-eye bombs, the 250-pound high-explosive bombs that had earned their names from the four distinctive fins that popped out after they were released and that stabilized their final flight. When you looked at them from close to the impact point, the fins looked similar to a snake's eyes. Also, if you were close enough to see the view that reminded you of a snake's eyes, you had just rolled "snake-eyes." Craps. You're out of luck. You're probably dead.

Snake-eye bombs sort of wobble during their descent and always looked like they were out of control. But they were actually very accurate, and both of these two hit dead on their target. The crazy NVA in the tower started shooting at the Phantom again. Since I was paying close attention to the deadly duel, I didn't really hear the whooping sound of the huge chunk of shrapnel that took out the mule driver until a couple of seconds later. I mean I heard it, but I didn't register it. It was just a strange, not very loud sound, so until it hit the mule driver, drove him through the back of his "L"-shaped seat, knocked it flat, and drove him right off the back of the ten-foot-long mule and flat onto the street on his back, I didn't pay attention to the noise. The *whump* of the twelve-inch-long, two-inch-thick chunk of shrapnel hitting the mule driver and the loud grunt that the driver made as his breath was violently forced from his body did get our attention. We jumped off the wall and ran over to see if there was anything we could do.

As we approached him, we realized that the poor mule driver was probably dead, but it didn't matter, we had to do what we could to help him. Doc Lowdermilk, whose life-saving instincts had torn his attention away from the Phantom/NVA duel before any of the rest of us, got there first. The mule driver was out cold, but incredibly, there was no blood or obvious wound. This Marine had taken the battle for Hue seriously; he had zipped and buttoned his flak jacket completely. The chunk of shrapnel apparently had struck the mule driver at the exact moment when it had rotated into a flat position in relationship to his body.

I saw the huge chunk of shrapnel sitting innocently on the street a few feet away from the mule driver and went to fetch it. Grabbing it without thinking, I got several superficially burned fingers for my trouble. Five hundred meters of cold air hadn't cooled this giant piece of death in the couple of seconds it had taken to fly from the detonation point on the tower to the unfortunate mule driver's relaxed position.

Amazingly, the mule driver quickly regained consciousness and started breathing again, but although he was alive, he was not a happy camper. When he saw the chunk of shrapnel sitting there, he slowly realized that if the piece of shrapnel had hit him straight on, rather than flat, it would have done a hell of a lot more damage and could have gone right through his body, flak jacket or no flak jacket. He realized that he was really lucky to be alive, but he was having a hard time taking a normal, let alone deep, breath.

I assigned another wall-sitting Marine to take the mule driver and his flat-seated mule back to the First ARVN Division compound, and we climbed back up on our bleacher-seat wall and watched the rest of the show. After what we had all just witnessed, we probably should have gotten down behind the wall, but I think we all realized that this had been a fluke, and the odds of it happening again were very low. But I know that every one of us had registered in the front of our brains that whooping sound that the wicked chunk of shrapnel had made, as we had all previously registered the sound of an enemy 82-mm mortar round hitting its tube, and we would have all dived, unashamedly, behind the wall if we heard anything that remotely resembled that sound again.

About a half hour later, the Marine who drove the mule back to the ARVN compound returned on foot with terrible news. The mule driver had died before a chopper could pick him up. He had started convulsing just as they pulled into the ARVN compound, and he had been declared dead a few minutes later. The unlucky mule driver had obviously sustained major internal injuries and hadn't been the lucky guy we had all thought he was after all. For some strange reason, that ended the entertainment aspect of the Phantom strikes on the tower. We sat there for a while longer, watching the crazy NVA idiots getting shot at and shit on, watching them shoot at the Phantoms, but somehow it just wasn't any fun anymore.

Chapter Twelve

The Return
of Heavy
Firepower

15 February 1968

The rest of that third day, 15 February 1968, went by with little forward progress for the Marines of 1/5 inside the Citadel. Alpha Company had their hands full trying to consolidate their positions across phase line green, and 1/5's battalion command group made the sensible decision not to require Charlie Company to attack frontally across phase line green. The battalion decision-makers understood that when Alpha Company finally controlled their block, they would be in an excellent position to support a Charlie Company frontal assault with flanking fire, or we could support them while Alpha attacked the entrenched NVA in front of us from their flank. Either maneuver would be much more effective than the bloody frontal assaults ordered on the first and second days.

Delta Company had started their deadly attack/counterattack chess game with the crazy NVA who had persevered in spite of the F-4 Phantom air strikes and who were still firmly in control of the tower that so effectively dominated phase line green and hampered our progress. The Marines of Charlie Two and Charlie Three took potshots at targets of opportunity directly across the street and tried to keep their heads down to avoid the constant answering enemy small-arms fire. I continued to help The Gunny with odd jobs and opened more sixty-mike-mike crates. The Charlie Company sixty-millimeter mortar crews continued to fire harassment and interdiction missions on the NVA across phase line green, and we continuously monitored the house-to-house fighting of Alpha Company and the tower assaults by Delta Company using one of the company's Prick-25s.

Eventually night crept over the Citadel again, and the third day of fighting was behind us. As before, when daylight faded into night, the fighting diminished and then stopped. I checked in again with 1st Lt. Scott Nelson, and since he had nothing for me to do, I found another house in the rear area, commandeered a real bed in a small corner bedroom, and at about 2300 hours crawled in and quickly found unconscious peace in a deep, dark sleep.

Shortly after midnight, my sleep was shattered, and I was rudely forced into consciousness by several explosions. These explosions were very loud, which meant that they were probably very close.

The house I was holed up in was just one block behind phase line green, and my initial reaction was a numbing terror caused by the abject certainty that these explosions signaled the start of an all-out counterattack by the NVA. But I quickly shook those unwelcome thoughts off, because the explosions were just too big to have been caused by the NVA. I had never been near an enemy 120-mm or 140-mm rocket attack, so the largest "artillery" weapon that any Viet Cong or NVA unit had directed toward me was the 82-mm mortar. These explosions were much larger than 82-mm mortars. Perhaps they were sappers with satchel charges? Maybe, but they sounded more familiar than that.

Shaking off sleep, I pulled my helmet and flak jacket back on and decided to venture into the house's back yard to see if I could find out what was going on. It didn't take long, and when I found out what had shattered my sleep, I received the news as a mixed blessing.

Finally, 1/5 was getting heavy support. After three days inside the Citadel, and with the notable exception of the fearful but futile F-4 Phantom air strikes on the tower, it appeared that the First Marine Division had finally decided that we needed heavy artillery. The five explosions had been caused by naval gunfire, probably five-inch guns. I should have been happy because we were finally getting the heavy artillery support we had been screaming for, but like many things in

Vietnam, this was another two-edged sword. All five of these naval gun-fire high-explosive rounds had detonated inside a block occupied by Charlie Company Marines. One of the damned things had hit just a few feet from the back wall of the house I was sleeping in! Shit, we finally get heavy support, and we damned near get blown away by friendly fire!

Scott Nelson joined me and several now fully awake Charlie Three Marines and sort of shook his head in disgust. He gave me one of his patented grins, pulled at his nearly nonexistent mustache, and said, "Well, Charlie One, you asked for it, and you got it! Here's your artillery support!"

Nelson and I talked for a while longer. It seemed that there were rumors floating around battalion that some NVA had infiltrated through our lines and that there might be a few snipers holed up behind us, but Nelson shrugged this "intelligence" off as simple nervousness from Marines of the battalion CP group, and he didn't appear to believe any of it. I didn't want to believe it either, and I tried to simply ignore the possibility. About that time we heard over the battalion net that they had suspended the naval gunfire until the next day, so Nelson took off, and I returned to my commandeered bed. I was asleep again within seconds of hitting the feathers.

I awoke at first light, pulled on my helmet and flak jacket, and emerged into another dull, overcast day. It looked like it was going to be just another dreary day in paradise, but the sounds of the nearby deto-nations of large-caliber artillery a few hundred meters south of us meant that this was at least a new kind of day, a day wherein we could finally expect to get the heavy firepower support that we had become accus-tomed to before we entered the Citadel. The whining incoming sounds and high-explosive detonations of American artillery support being directed at our entrenched NVA enemy made me feel a whole lot better.

Obviously, Travis Curd and his forward observer radio operator had been working overtime, and they had effectively adjusted the errant fir-ing of the five-inch guns. They had directed the five-inch guns and their 105-mm and 155-mm artillery cousins onto enemy positions well on the other side of phase line green, so I probably didn't have to worry about being blown apart by friendly fire any longer.

I checked in with Scott Nelson, who directed me to work with The Gunny and the sixty-millimeter mortar crews again. I was starting to feel self-conscious and just a little silly doing this menial labor, but Scott Nel-son had better things to do than worry about me. So I joined The Gunny without comment and started opening sixty-mike-mike crates once again.

About midmorning, PFC Robert Lattimer, one of those who had survived the death of Charlie One and who had been reassigned to Charlie Three on the morning of the second day, came running into the Charlie Company CP area with a couple of other Marines and breathlessly reported that yet another mule driver had driven into the jaws of death. First Lieutenant Nelson was fetched, and when he arrived, Lattimer made his report.

Lattimer said, "Skipper, this dumb-ass mule driver must have zigged when he should have zagged, because he just drove right smack into the NVA positions. Before we knew it, he just came screaming up this street at full speed, driving right toward the enemy positions, and the NVA waited until he was at point-blank range and then opened up on him and blew him away." Although Lattimer was usually pretty unflappable, now he was pretty agitated. He was obviously disturbed by something more than the death of another mule driver.

Nelson knew that Lattimer was a good point man and that he had been coolheaded under fire in several previous situations, so he quietly probed him to continue. "Look, Lattimer, are you sure he's dead? If so, there's not much we can do about it until after dark, when we can retrieve the body and get him back to a chopper."

Lattimer looked at Scott Nelson and let us know what was under his skin. "You don't understand, Skipper, the mule driver is dead, we're damned sure about that, but the fucking mule is still alive. I mean, sir, that the stinking thing is still running. The mule driver got it a couple of times in the head and a few more times in the chest, and he's just sitting there in his seat, deader than dog shit. But his mule refuses to die! It's getting to all of us up there; we know there's nothing we can do for the mule driver, but hearing the fucking mule putt-putting away is making it impossible to put him out of our minds. The guys have debated trying to blow away the engine, but the angle is bad, and we'd probably really fuck up the mule driver's body in the process. The NVA shot that damned mule up pretty good, but it just refuses to die."

Lattimer, his young black face serious and pale in the midmorning gloom, looked his company commander in the eye and quietly but emphatically explained that the men wanted to try to get the mule driver out of the mule and off the street, so that they could then blow away the damned mule without feeling shitty about shooting their fellow Marine, even if he was dead. The nearby thuds of the supporting artillery, the ebb and flow of the small-arms fire of Alpha Company's struggle for their block, and Delta Company's assaults on the tower faded away. The morning became very quiet as each of us in that small group finally understood the horror being experienced by the Marines on that corner of phase line green. As horrible as it had been to have to ignore the bodies of our fallen comrades in the street during that long first day, as much as we knew that any attempts to rescue dead Marines was seriously risking even further death, we could live with it, because we didn't have to think about them. We were sure they were dead, we didn't have to look at them, and we knew we would fetch them and send them home under the cover of darkness. But in this situation, these men could not ignore their Marine brother, because the stinking mule kept running, and the popping engine noise was a constant reminder that the mule driver was out there. The way things were, the situation would drive the men to the brink of insanity unless something was done. The mule would, undoubtedly, eventually run out of gas, but no one had a clue just how long that would take. It seemed as though this was a mule from hell, and it just might keep on running until all these men went out of their minds.

There was only one choice. The men wanted to make an effort to get the dead mule driver off the mule and out of the street, and then they could try to blow away the mule. Lattimer and his men were willing to take the chance, and they were volunteering to try. In a world of poor choices, these men had made a choice between the surety of slowly encroaching insanity and the risk of death for a few seconds. They would rather face almost certain death for a few seconds than have to listen to the maddening noise of the mule until nightfall, still several hours away, or until the mule ran out of gas.

Scott Nelson considered the equation and then looked over at me and said, "Go up there and check it out, Charlie One. See if you can figure out a way to get the mule driver out of the street without getting anyone else hurt." With that, Nelson took off for the rear, probably headed for another consultation with the battalion CP group. I hoped he would make the point to whomever was in charge of the mule drivers that they should know where the hell they were going before they made their supply runs.

As we cautiously worked our way back toward phase line green, Lattimer quietly explained that they had already considered all the angles and that they wanted to try smoke. He looked at me and said, "We figure that we'll throw several smoke grenades at the mule, and at the same time, some of the other squads can throw more smoke grenades into the street as a diversion, and then, at some signal, we'll have the other squads and Charlie Two open up with a base of fire. Me and Gomer will have worked our way into the closest covered position to the mule, and we'll just go get the dude. We figure it will take ten seconds, max." Lattimer explained this all to me as though he were discussing an evening on the town: they would hit the coffee shop for a burger or two, take in a good movie, and go have a couple of beers. He and I both knew that despite the diversion of the smoke and the supporting base of fire, he and Gomer (a private who got his nickname from constantly wearing his helmet backward and who was another Charlie One survivor) would be running into a swarm of enemy gunfire from a range of no more than fifty feet. Their chances of pulling this off unscathed were remote, but there was simply no other choice. As we approached the corner of the street from the back yard of the house that faced it, I could hear the mule engine popping away. It was already starting to get to me as well, and I'd only been there a couple of minutes.

As we approached phase line green, I stopped Lattimer for a minute and said, "All right, Lattimer, you've obviously thought this through completely. Thanks for volunteering. I'll shoot a red star cluster, which will be the signal for the smoke rounds and the supporting fire, and you and Gomer better hit the bricks the second you think the smoke has you covered. I'll go let the platoon commanders from Charlie Three and Charlie Two know what's going down and what the plan is. We should be ready to rock and roll in about fifteen minutes. See you back here in a few minutes."

I couldn't look at him any more, couldn't think about the odds anymore, so I took off toward the right flank and got the plan ready. Moving back away from phase line green to the street behind it, I headed west toward the next intersecting street and eventually found 2nd Lt. John Aamodt, Charlie Three's platoon commander, and then 2nd Lt. Rich Lowder, Charlie Two's platoon commander, who were covering phase line green and Charlie Company's right flank. I let them know what was going down and what was expected of them.

Fifteen minutes later, I was back on the left flank, a few feet behind Lattimer and Gomer, who had shed their weapons and all other unnecessary gear. They had tightened their flak jackets and helmets and were ready to rock and roll for better or for worse.

I pulled a red star cluster hand rocket out of my pack and, aiming it in the general direction of the enemy, detonated it. The swoosh of the rocket was always expected but somehow always startling. The almost immediate red sparkling burst of the rocket at an altitude of about a hundred feet over the NVA positions across the street was seen by all the Marines on phase line green. This effectively signaled the simultaneous throwing of several smoke grenades into the street in several locations. Red, yellow, green, white, and purple clouds of smoke quickly obscured the street and covered the mule with their insufficient protection, while the other squads opened up on the enemy across the street.

The NVA across the street immediately responded with a fierce volume of gunfire, and the steady, rapid firing of many AK-47s answered the M-60 and M-16s covering their buddies. Lattimer and Gomer didn't look back for even a moment; they just ran into the smoke and disappeared.

Time perversely ground down once again into a damnably torturous slow motion. The ten seconds that they were out in the street, amid the hot hell of small-arms fire, seemed like ten hours. No way could Lattimer and Gomer survive the volume of fire being directed at the mule. The gooks would probably shoot an RPG-7 at the mule, and then it would be all over but the shouting. They were probably all three dead. Now we would have three Marines down in the street, and the stupid mule would probably still keep on chugging away. My heart seemed to stop beating, and I involuntarily held my breath.

And then the smoke finally parted, and Lattimer and Gomer, both their faces stretched into grimaces of pain, ecstasy, fear, triumph, and pure adrenaline exhilaration, ran out of the swirling clouds of smoke and death and dropped their burden in a position of relative safety. The mule driver was on his way home.

Neither Lattimer nor Gomer had gotten a scratch. Neither of them said anything. They didn't want to celebrate the retrieval of the mule driver; they just wanted to go blow the mule away. They grabbed their M-16s, put their M-26 grenades back on their flak jackets, reslung their extra 5.56 ammo belts, threw their packs back on, and took off. They were just tired of hearing the damned mule, and they were going to put an end to it!

Just as he was leaving, Lattimer looked over his shoulder and briefly caught my eye. He gave me a casual sidelong grin as though what he had just done was as ordinary and about as dangerous as taking out the trash. Then he turned away, grabbed Gomer by the arm, and said, "C'mon Gomer. Let's go put that fucking mule out of its misery."

A few moments later, the Marines occupying the corner house opened up with a hellacious volume of fire with their M-16s and an M-60 machine gun, with a few M-79 40-mm grenades thrown in for good measure, and shortly thereafter the popping noise of the mule's engine coughed, seized, and died. The silence that followed, although constantly disturbed by the fierce fighting of Alpha and Delta Companies just a few hundred meters away, was a blessing. The mule driver's body was loaded onto a makeshift poncho stretcher and carried back to the First ARVN Division compound, there to await a chopper to start his final journey home.

If my senses and thought processes had even approached normality during those few minutes, I'm certain that I would have been amazed and dumbfounded by what I had witnessed. The undaunted heroism of Lattimer and Gomer as they charged into the withering enemy fire to retrieve the body of a fallen comrade with only the vaporous protection of the smoke was extraordinary. However, I was still in a sort of stupor; the automaton was still in control of my outward movements. My inward thoughts were not allowed to be perceived by others or spoken by my external self. I remained silent as I stood for a few more moments in that back yard, and then I shrugged, turned away, and returned to the Charlie Company mortar crews. Most likely, they were running out of ready-to-launch mortar rounds, and they needed my help.

About 1600 hours that afternoon, after continued heavy fighting between Alpha and Delta Companies and the NVA defenders, and the continued sporadic small-arms duels between the NVA and Charlie Company Marines across phase line green, a group of Marines from Charlie Three stumbled into the Charlie Company CP area, carrying their platoon commander, 2nd Lt. John R. Aamodt, on a door. Aamodt had been shot through the upper leg by an AK-47 round, and the bullet had shattered the bone. Charlie Three Actual was out of the action and headed to a medevac.

From the look on his face, it was difficult to tell just exactly how Second Lieutenant Aamodt felt about his circumstances. Although he was obviously in great pain, he couldn't keep a smile from his lips. He had his ticket home. If he could just survive being carried to the First ARVN Division compound, the medevac chopper ride, the U.S. military medical care, and the long ride to the World on a big bird, he was going home. His wound was severe, but it would eventually heal up, and he would most likely not be required to visit South Vietnam ever again. The hell of the past few days was nearly over for him. He was going home.

As I watched Doc Lowdermilk work on him, I started to slowly realize that Lieutenant Aamodt's ticket home was my ticket back to phase line green. Charlie Three was a fighting unit, in contact with the enemy, and they now needed a leader. I was the only other commissioned officer available. I was now going to be the new Charlie Three Actual.

None of this mattered. I was numb, and the automaton was in full control. I would go wherever Scott Nelson told me to go, do whatever he told me to do. The automaton would obey any lawful command from my superior officer. I continued to break open mortar crates, waiting for the inevitable orders that would move me back to the hell of phase line green.

"Sergeant Grant, you're the new Charlie Three Actual. Get back up there with your men, keep the NVA's heads down, and await further orders." Scott Nelson had not even looked in my direction. He had given the job to Sergeant Grant, a tall, young E-5 sergeant who had been the Charlie Three platoon guide when we entered the Citadel and who had taken over as the Charlie Three platoon sergeant when Staff Sergeant Odum had been shot in the face on the first day. Sergeant Grant was now Charlie Three Actual. Sergeant Grant acknowledged his orders, and after making sure that his former platoon commander was in good hands, he headed back toward phase line green. I continued to open ammo crates.

Sergeant Grant wasn't gone very long. A few minutes after he left, a large volume of small-arms fire, punctuated by several explosions, erupted on phase line green from the direction he had headed. Soon thereafter another small group of Charlie Three Marines, with Sergeant Grant walking slowly and uncertainly in their midst, stumbled into the Charlie Company CP.

Sergeant Grant and another Marine were covered from head to toe with white plaster dust. They looked as though they had jumped into a swimming pool filled with white flour flecked with red dye. Leaking blood from small wounds inflicted on several places on his body, his eyes glazed over from shock, Sergeant Grant was obviously in no condition to continue in the role of Charlie Three Actual.

Scott Nelson heard the commotion and joined the group of Charlie Three Marines. Taking one look at the ghost-white Marines, he asked what the hell had happened.

A Marine who had been helping evacuate Sergeant Grant explained that the sergeant had taken two other Marines into the front room of a house fronting phase line green, against the advice of several Marines who had been there since the first day. These Marines recognized that although the front room had large windows that would provide a good view of the enemy positions across the street, it was also very exposed to the very same enemy positions.

"Shit, Skipper, we told him to stay out of there, but he didn't listen. He said he wanted to get into a good vantage point. He took Smitty and Jones in there with him. Shit, they weren't in there more than thirty seconds before the gooks opened up with RPGs. Them fucking rockets flew right in the front window and detonated against the back wall. Smitty's blown away; some of the others will bring him back in a little while. Sergeant Grant is hit, and both him and Jones probably need to be medevacced, 'cuz I think they're in shock." This young Marine, a lance corporal, tried very hard to keep the disgust out of his voice, but wasn't very successful in doing so.

Sergeant Grant was a good NCO, had always obeyed orders, and had run a good platoon. Until he had been assigned as their platoon commander, however, he had remained with the platoon CP group, and he hadn't really taken an active hand in the fighting. When he got his orders to take over as platoon commander of Charlie Three, he wanted so badly to be effective that he had exposed himself and his men to the enemy's gunfire and rockets to get a better perspective. The result was one of the shortest combat assignments in Marine Corps history.

Scott Nelson considered Sergeant Grant and just glanced in my direction. The automaton took over; I got to my feet, swung my pack on, and threw Estes's M-16 over my right shoulder. Nelson didn't have to say anything. I knew where I was headed, and the automaton was ready to take me there.

As I passed Nelson to join the other Marines from Charlie Three and started toward phase line green, Scott Nelson touched my arm and said, "Keep in touch, Charlie Three. And keep your head down!"

Chapter Thirteen

Snipers' Lair

16 February 1968

The automaton took the new Charlie Three Actual forward with the small group of Charlie Three Marines, and shortly thereafter we arrived at a house facing phase line green in the middle of the block. Here I was, once again, facing the treacherous and deadly barrier, this street called Mai Thuc Loan by the Vietnamese and phase line green by the Marines. It was a little past noon on 16 February 1968, the fourth day of fighting for Hue's Citadel fortress.

Although Charlie Two and Charlie Three had not yet been ordered to assault across phase line green, the attrition of four days of fighting the NVA at point-blank range in their dug-in positions across the street had taken its toll. So, despite having been reinforced by the remnants of Charlie One two days before, Charlie Three was seriously below the manpower strength called for by the Table of Organization of the U.S. Marine Corps for an infantry platoon.

Normally, a Marine rifle platoon was comprised of three squads of fourteen men each. Squad strength was further broken down into three four-man fire teams, with an additional Marine assigned to carry and shoot the M-79 grenade launcher, and a squad leader. Added to these forty-two men were the platoon guide, the platoon sergeant, the platoon commander, and two radio operators, giving a total of forty-seven men, not including our two Navy corpsmen. Finally, added to these were three four-man machine gun teams, rounding out a full force of nearly sixty Marines to a platoon. On the morning that we first attacked across phase line green, Charlie One had been at its highest manpower level since I had assumed command in November 1967, with a total of fifty-one men. The combined strength of the three platoons of Charlie Company and the additional men from the mortar crews and the company CP group stood at nearly two hundred Marines when we entered the Citadel. Now, four days later, Charlie Company was comprised of two forty-man platoons and the CP group; we were at about 50 percent of our normal strength. Still, we were better off than Alpha and Delta Companies, who had taken even more casualties in their battles to take control of the first block across phase line green and the infamous tower.

Early on the morning of 16 February, Bravo Company was taken out of reserve status and committed to the battle. They were ordered to move across phase line green to assist Alpha Company in securing Alpha's control of the block, and by the end of that day, the combined force of two companies of Marines had forced the NVA to escape south across phase line orange, or Nguyen Bieu, the next parallel street south of phase line green. Once that block had been completely secured, one of the Delta Company platoons not currently engaged in the attack on the tower was able to cross the street and flank the NVA defenders. By nightfall on the sixteenth, Delta Company had established at least a tenuous foothold across phase line green as well. However, in Delta's case, since they were still battling fiercely with a determined, stubborn enemy force in the tower, they could not rest easy. The NVA in the tower had the advantage of the high ground, and so they could easily keep Delta's heads down. This made it very difficult for Delta Company's Marines to maneuver any further until the tower was under the firm control of 1/5 Marines.

Late on the afternoon of the sixteenth, Scott Nelson found me and told me that Alpha and Bravo Company Marines would lay down flanking fires so that Charlie Company could assault across phase line green. The dreaded but expected order affected me very little; the automaton continued to control my actions. I don't think that at that moment I expected to live much longer, anyway, so now was as good a time as ever.

With Charlie Two on our right flank and Alpha and Bravo Company Marines providing flanking fire on our left front, with the recent prep artillery fires having softened the enemy up, and with the Delta Company Marines keeping the NVA busy on the tower, we had a much more reasonable chance of success at crossing phase line green. We prepared to carry out the assault.

When I had assumed command of Charlie Three, I had acquired a new radio operator, who was introduced to me simply as Chief. Like many Native Americans who served in the Marine Corps, this sturdy young man bore his inevitable nickname stoically, never complaining about the unintended ethnic slur. In fact, true to his heritage (or at least to my then limited understanding of his heritage), he was a man of few words, unless he was transmitting and receiving messages via his Prick-25. He simply acknowledged his new leader by calling Charlie Six to let them know that I had arrived and had assumed command, and awaited my communications pleasure. I would grow attached to Chief over the next few weeks, much as I had grown attached to Benny Benwaring before him. A combat commander relied heavily on communications, and a platoon radio operator was a very critical resource for a platoon commander. Radio operators, because of the necessary antennae (or, as they were often referred to in the dark humor of combat Marines, "aiming stakes") that made them easy to be located, identified, and fired upon by the enemy, suffered a casualty rate similar to that of point men and platoon commanders. Radio operators were an unusual breed of fighting men, and those who experienced combat in the Vietnam War, with their extra twenty-five-pound burden and constant exposure to enemy gunfire, were, in my mind, extraordinary human beings. Chief fit into this category extremely well, and I quickly grew to rely upon him.

I had Chief call up the squad leaders for a briefing before the assault, and we huddled together for a few minutes in the dreary afternoon drizzle in the back yard of the house that had served as the Charlie Three CP. I told the squad leaders that we would be assaulting across phase line green soon and asked for their input. We decided that the two squads covering the left two-thirds of our blockwide area, Charlie Three Alpha and Charlie Three Bravo, would join the Alpha and Bravo Company Marines in laying down a base of supporting fires. The third squad, Charlie Three Charlie, would assault across the street. The assault team would enter the second house in from the intersection on our right frontage, clear it, and then move back left, or east, toward the tower, clearing each house as they moved. If they experienced resistance, we'd move another squad across the street, and they could leapfrog each other, until eventually we'd clear all the houses that faced phase line green on its south side. This way, the initial assault team would be as far as possible away from the tower, but also not be exposed to NVA positions across from Charlie Two. The squad leaders returned to their men and conducted their preparations for the assault, and I let Scott Nelson know, via Chief's Prick-25, that we were ready to assault across phase line green.

After giving the squad leaders enough time to get their men ready, I pulled another red star cluster signal rocket out of my pack and shot it off, signaling the assault. The supporting Marines from Alpha and Bravo Companies, Charlie Two, Charlie Three Alpha, and Charlie Three Bravo opened up with a terrific rate of small-arms and M-79 fire. The Charlie Company and 1/5 battalion forward observers called in an increasing amount of artillery and mortar fire on NVA positions further south of phase line orange, and the third squad, Charlie Three Charlie, emerged from their positions of safety and ran across the street, fully expecting death at any moment.

Chief and I had taken up a position behind the middle squad, Charlie Three Bravo, and we monitored the assaulting squad's progress via the platoon radio net. They all made it across the street quickly, and no one was hit crossing the street.

After a few suspenseful minutes, the assaulting squad leader called us over the platoon radio net.

"Charlie Three, this is Charlie Three Charlie, over."

"Three Charlie, this is Three Actual. What's your situation, over?"

"Three Actual, this is Three Charlie. Looks like they've retreated. We have total control of both of the houses on the right-hand corner and have taken no enemy fire. We're going to take the next house toward you and check in again. Out."

A few moments later, we heard the shouts of Marines entering another house, a few bursts of M-16 fire, but no return AK-47 or .30-caliber firing. We all took our first deep breaths since the assaulting squad began their attack.

Within the next hour, both platoons of Charlie Two and Charlie Three crossed phase line green and we finally had control of all the north-facing structures that had, until very recently, provided the NVA with defensive positions along phase line green. We then moved cautiously, in covering fire-team movements, out the back doors of these houses, through their yards, and into the yards of the next houses. We entered and occupied the houses facing phase line orange with no enemy resistance or friendly casualties. It appeared as though once Alpha and Bravo Companies had completely consolidated their block, their area of responsibility, the NVA realized that their right flank was exposed, and they had deserted the territory between phase line green and phase line orange. With the significant exception of the tower, which was still being fiercely contested, 1/5 had full control of four city blocks. We were one-seventh of the way home!

The mathematics of 1/5's attrition rate in this battle were still not very good, as we had lost nearly 50 percent of our fighting strength to take one-seventh of our assigned territory. I think that every 1/5 Marine still fighting on that morning inside the Citadel carried those mathematics around in the pit of his stomach. But at least we had finally moved toward our objective, the south wall of the Citadel, still six blocks away. Since having finally been given the heavy air and artillery support, and since the M-48 tanks had been allowed to start using their heavy weapons, Marine Corps tactics and firepower superiority began to take effect and the enemy was forced to withdraw. Maybe we could win this battle after all. . . .

Reality shattered the late afternoon, as the NVA suddenly opened up with an intense volume of fire from just across phase line orange, and both Charlie Two and Charlie Three took casualties. Charlie Company Marines returned fire, keeping their heads down as much as possible, and the dead and wounded were carried back to the Charlie Company CP for evacuation. For just a few moments, the automaton allowed a sinking feeling to settle in, and I was allowed to feel the despair of the tactical situation. We were going to have to cross another street, facing a well-armed, entrenched, and determined enemy of experienced fighters. At least we would get heavy support. That was the only bright side to the equation, although it provided little comfort.

As darkness settled in and ended the fourth day of fighting, the automaton took back full control of me, and I stopped worrying. There wasn't a damned thing I could do about the situation, anyway.

Early the next morning, 17 February, I spent a few minutes checking out the houses that had, for four days, served our enemy well by providing them with ready-built fortified defensive positions facing phase line green. I finally began to understand why we had experienced such difficulty getting across the street.

Most of these houses were one-story homes, but a couple were two-story affairs, providing excellent and advantageous firing positions for the waiting NVA. From these positions, the NVA could shoot right down on us, point-blank, as we tried to run across the street. This was obvious, and we understood the situation clearly, so we had directed our return fire at the windows and doorways of the houses across the street, which were the likely enemy firing positions. What we had not realized was that the NVA were also shooting at us from well-concealed, dug-in positions *between* the houses, at street level.

The enemy's Tet Offensive had kicked off on the night of 31 January, and the NVA had taken almost total control of the Citadel overnight. The 1/5 battalion had not entered the Citadel until 12 February. This gave the NVA two weeks to prepare, and they had taken full advantage of this time.

The houses that faced phase line green had been built very close to each other, presenting an almost solid frontage of structures for the entire length of four city blocks. They resembled today's condominium complex structures, with individual units nearly touching each other. Although the homes along phase line green were actually all individual structures, the gaps between them were small, only a few feet at most. However, ancient shrubbery, which grew to the height of the eaves in many places, gave the illusion of a solid frontage. The NVA had made good use of this excellent cover and concealment.

During the two weeks that they had had to prepare, the NVA had cleverly chosen Mai Thuc Loan as their primary defensive position for several reasons. First, it was obvious to them that our only choice for a relatively easy entry point into the Citadel would be through the only gate that the NVA didn't control, through the First ARVN Division compound. Thus, they could plan, with a high amount of assurance, that we would have to attack from there, from the north. Second, the full length of Mai Thuc Loan was completely dominated by the tower (the Dong Ba Porch, as the Vietnamese called it) that guarded the eastern gate into the Citadel, and which the NVA totally controlled. It was probably a total coincidence that 1/5 planners designated Mai Thuc Loan as our initial phase line, our initial line of departure for the attack, but it worked out extremely well for the defending NVA. The near-solid frontage of homes that lined the south side of Mai Thuc Loan provided excellent defensive positions for the NVA defenders. The layout of the street also provided the opportunity to prepare well-camouflaged, almost invisible positions between the houses at the base of the thick, ancient foliage growing between the houses. For four days, we had been directing our fires at the windows and doors, and although we had most certainly been taking enemy fire from those positions, we had also been taking deadly enemy fire from ground level, from the fighting holes dug in under the bushes between many houses.

The NVA had cleverly and energetically prepared these positions well in advance of our arrival, and from the looks of those that I inspected, the NVA gunners who had occupied them had scored very well with nearly total impunity. There were no evident blood trails in the hidden foxholes that I inspected that morning, as there were in many houses we had passed through.

I called Scott Nelson on the company radio net, and he came across phase line green a few minutes later and took a look at what we had found. When he realized the implications of what we had discovered, he looked at me with a pasty, pale complexion, tugged once again at his nearly invisible mustache, and said, "Well, no shit. Pass the word about this around, Charlie Three. I gotta get back to battalion and let them know. Start directing your fires to include likely dug-in positions between the houses as well as the obvious enemy positions in the houses." With that and a hasty, somewhat sheepish grin, Nelson took off back toward the 1/5 command post, which was still several blocks behind us.

Charlie Company spent the rest of that day making sure that the blocks we had finally gained were completely secure. Every house was checked and rechecked, including the dusty, dirty attics, because we were fearful that an attempt might be made to hide a few NVA snipers, who could cause terrible chaos and confusion if they got behind our lines, especially at night.

We knew from our brief skirmishes the previous evening that the NVA were waiting for us on the other side of phase line orange, Nguyen Bieu, and that we would eventually have to assault across the open exposure of yet another phase line. But for the time being we concentrated on making sure that we had systematically checked every possible hiding place. The Marines of 1/5 understood that Delta Company would have to take and hold the Dong Ba Porch tower before it became safe to cross phase line orange. We also understood that until we had the high ground, especially in light of our dwindling strength, we could not be expected to pull off another frontal assault.

Shortly after noon, we got some good news. Second Lieutenant Bruce Morton's Ontos platoon had finally made it across the river, and they had joined up with 1/5. Although his unit was seriously under strength, Bruce still had two Ontos vehicles (fast, maneuverable, and powerful armored beasts) to throw into the fight, and we welcomed them.

Bruce Morton, a native of the Cape Cod area of Massachusetts, had been my next-door neighbor in Quantico, Virginia, while we were going through Basic Infantry Officer's School after OCS. Although he was one class ahead of me in Basic School, Bruce and I became good friends. We were both married, which was the exception rather than the rule with our peers during Basic School, and so it was natural that our wives and dogs became very friendly during the long, lonely (for them) summer weeks of 1967.

I lost touch with Bruce when he finished Basic School and went "OCS" (Over the Choppy Seas), but I was happy to run into him again at the Phu Loc 6 firebase. Bruce and his Marines, the men who manned the unusual Ontos armored vehicles, had already achieved hero status with the 1/5 Marines during the weeks that preceded the Tet Offensive, because the mobility and awesome firepower of their Ontos had saved many Marine lives.

The Ontos platoon had been visiting a Highway One bridge defensive position one night in early January when it had been hit hard by an enemy attack. The bridge's defenders were an understrength squad of Marines and some South Vietnamese Popular Forces soldiers (the PFs were South Vietnam's civilian militia and were considered by their American allies as unquestionably the worst and most unreliable South Vietnamese fighting men with whom we ever had to team up). The squad would have certainly been overrun and wiped out if it had not been for the presence of Bruce Morton's Ontos platoon. The enemy attack, unexpected and very fierce, was stopped cold in the defensive perimeter's concertina wire when both Ontos vehicles had loaded up beehive rounds in several of their 106-mm recoilless rifles. They had set the beehive rounds, containing something like ten thousand tiny flechettes each, to detonate as soon as they left the muzzle of the awesome "reckless rifles." The shotgun effect of the beehive rounds had wiped out the enemy attack.

More recently, when Phu Loc 6 was under heavy attack and the 1/5 battalion commander, Lt. Col. R. P. Whalen, unsuccessfully tried to lead a force of CP group Marines to flank the attackers and had been seriously wounded and pinned down in the attempt, the Ontos platoon had again distinguished themselves. On this occasion, 2nd Lt. Bruce Morton formed another group of Marines from the battalion CP group and his Ontos Marines to try to rescue the pinned-down Marines. Morton successfully maneuvered his volunteer command into a position to suppress the enemy fire on the beleaguered Marines, managed to medevac the dead and wounded without taking any more serious casualties, and brought the rest safely back inside the firebase compound.

Bruce Morton had his act together as a combat leader, so it was really good to see him. It was also good to see that at least some reinforcements could get inside the Citadel, although we still had received no new infantry troops to offset the losses we had taken.

Bruce had come up across phase line green to our positions facing phase line orange to observe the situation and to see where he could best direct the fires of the Ontos and the M-48 tanks, which had been loosely combined as a supporting armored force for the infantry Marines. After I explained what we had been dealing with and what we knew about the enemy's positions, he came with me to the houses facing phase line orange to get a better look.

After due consideration, Bruce gave me a smile and said, "Well, since we can team up with the tanks, maybe we can help you guys out. Have there been any RPG attacks recently?"

Understanding just how vulnerable the Ontos were to an RPG rocket attack, I couldn't be too comforting. "Yeah, Bruce. Yesterday, my predecessor was blown away by two RPG-7s that came right through the front window of that house over there. Also, in case you haven't noticed, the tanks haven't been much help. They're just too damned slow, and they have to drive right down the street and get into the intersection before they can shoot their nineties. One of them took an RPG right in the turret on the morning of the first day, and the tank commander's head was blown off; that RPG put a hole right through the turret."

"Yeah, I saw it. That M-48's still in service, but I was wondering what the hell they've been waiting for. Maybe we can figure out a way to cover each other, so we can do you guys some good. Well, thanks for the tour. See ya."

With that, Bruce headed back across phase line green and rejoined his Ontos Marines back at the 1/5 command post.

This was very encouraging news, because the Ontos carried an awesome amount of firepower. These small, speedy armored vehicles had six 106-mm recoilless rifles mounted on them, three to a side. In addition, they had a 7.62-mm machine gun that could be fired by the Ontos commander. Furthermore, in comparison with the lumbering M-48 tank, they were very fast and could drive over clear terrain faster than forty-five miles per hour.

Their disadvantages were several. First, although they were classified as an armored vehicle, their armor wasn't very thick and could be pierced easily by an armor-piercing small-arms round. One well-aimed RPG rocket could easily knock out an Ontos, and if the rocket hit anywhere on the main body of the Ontos, the Ontos team members, buttoned up inside, were doomed to an instant and violent death. An Ontos carried nearly seventy 106-mm high-explosive rounds, and the gasoline and ammo, if ignited, would turn the Ontos into an instant death trap. The second disadvantage of the Ontos was that visibility from inside the vehicle was severely limited, and at forty-five miles per hour, the Ontos commander was seeing a vibrating blur. Third, their 106-mm recoilless rifles could not be reloaded from inside the vehicle; rather, the loader had to open the rear doors, get out, and individually load each of the weapons from their breeches. Fourth, the "back-blast" from the open breeches of the recoilless rifles was lethal to within about thirty meters *behind* them, so friendly troops had to be very careful around them. Finally, the six 106-mm "reckless rifles" were mounted in a fixed position on the top of the vehicle, three on each side, in an inverted, inward-pointing "L" configuration, and their trajectory could not be adjusted very much. An Ontos could mostly hit only what it was squarely facing.

Those of us who had been fighting inside the Citadel for the past few days didn't give a damn about the disadvantages; the firepower of six 106-mm recoilless rifles was more than enough to blow down any house, especially at point-blank range. If the Ontos could use their speed and machine gun fire to get into position, quickly fire all six rounds (all six recoilless rifles could be shot either simultaneously or individually), and then get the hell back to safety, we thought they would be very effective.

It turned out that when teamed up with an M-48 tank, Bruce Morton's Ontos made a huge difference thereafter in the house-to-house fighting inside the Citadel of Hue. About an hour after Bruce left our positions, the first nasty one-two punch was directed toward the NVA across phase line orange, with devastating effect. We heard the obvious rumble of an approaching M-48 tank, its diesel engine screaming in an effort to move at top speed, about thirty miles per hour, toward the intersection of phase line orange and Dinh Bo Linh, the street running perpendicular to the phase lines and dividing the two platoons of Charlie Company. The M-48's .50-caliber machine gun and 7.62-mm machine guns were blazing in an effort to keep any heroic NVA RPG gunners from getting into an open position to shoot at the tank as it lumbered forward to get into position. In quick succession, the tank blew off two high-explosive 90-mm cannon rounds into the two houses on the other side of phase line orange and which framed the south side of the intersection. The vehicle then immediately threw its transmission into reverse and started its retreat to a safe location, machine guns still blazing. As the M-48 lumbered backward, we heard the distinctive noise of the smaller Ontos engine screaming at top speed, as the Ontos raced down Dinh Bo Linh, passed the tank, slammed on its brakes just short of the intersection, pivoted itself sharply until it was facing the house on the southeast corner of the intersection, and blew off all six 106-mm rounds simultaneously. As quickly as was humanly possible, the Ontos shifted into reverse and, machine gun blazing, retreated to safer ground to reload.

The NVA were caught totally unprepared, and although there was a small amount of answering enemy small-arms fire, the tank and Ontos crews were unharmed. The house that had been devastated by the Ontos caught fire, and the wooden rubble eventually burned to the ground.

This deadly tactic proved to be a major asset for the Marines throughout the rest of the battle inside the Citadel, and it significantly added to our momentum. Although the NVA defenders eventually adjusted to this tactic and attempted to blow away the tanks and Ontos with their RPG-7s, they were often caught out of position. Because of the speed of the Ontos and the combined firepower of the two armored beasts, the Marines nearly always came out ahead. To a man, the Marines of Charlie Company were very happy to have the Ontos join us inside the Citadel.

The Ontos/tank teams periodically and randomly made runs to the different intersections along phase line orange for the rest of that day. They pounded the enemy positions, accompanied by many choruses of "Get some!" sung by the infantry Marines holed up in the houses facing phase line orange. This was much more like it. This was beginning to resemble the tactics used during recent Marine Corps history: blast, burn, and bomb, and when the enemy positions were softened up, the infantry could then assault with a reasonable expectation of success. Charlie Company maintained our positions along the two-block frontage facing phase line orange that night, and we all slept just a little bit better.

The next morning, 18 February, our belated but welcome heavy support continued to chip away at the stubborn NVA across phase line orange, and Delta Company continued to hammer at the fanatical NVA who were still defending the tower. Tank/Ontos teams made several high-explosive runs at the tower, which had alternately been overrun by Delta and then counterattacked and overrun by NVA reinforcements, in the continuing deadly chess match. Until Delta could finally take and hold the tower, 1/5 was stuck, so we stayed put and kept ourselves busy by continuing to call in mortar and artillery strikes on enemy positions and continuing the harassing small-arms fire on the enemy positions we had pinpointed on the other side of the street.

Finally, early on the afternoon of the eighteenth, we received the good news that Delta Company had finally taken control of the tower, and the inevitable NVA counterattack had been repulsed. We had the high ground!

Chief handed me the handset of the Prick-25, and I listened to Scott Nelson update us on Delta's success. I acknowledged his request for Charlie Two Actual (Rich Lowder) and me to make our way back to the Charlie Company CP area for another briefing.

Chief and I headed back toward phase line green, and as I angled toward Ngi Hieu (the street on our east, or left flank, which intersected the phase lines), my field of vision of the street opened up and uncannily took the form of a large movie house screen between the houses. On that huge, panoramic movie screen, I saw something, live and in living color, that has and will remain stuck in my memory cells, like unwanted superglue, forever.

A dead NVA soldier lay face down in the street. I had noticed this body a couple of times before, but I hadn't paid too much attention to it. This was one of the few NVA bodies that had not been recovered by the usually body-conscious NVA. As our front lines had advanced and the NVA had been forced to retreat, the body was simply too exposed to Marine gunfire to risk retrieval. The dead NVA body had been there for a couple of days, face down, legs and arms splayed out, resembling a grotesque cartoon character that had fallen from the sky and stuck to the street.

Precisely when the movie screen had presented itself to my vision, an M-48 tank from a tank/Ontos team, having just delivered another deadly one-two punch against the NVA on our left front, lumbered in reverse gear back toward our rear area and safety. The tank commander opened his lid, raised himself out of its protective turret, and turned to face the rear of the tank, in the direction they were headed. Although there was considerable room on the street for the tank, and although the dead NVA was just barely on the street surface, the tank commander put his hand over his mouth, a gesture that I immediately recognized as his voicing a command over his internal tank radio net. The tank driver immediately obeyed his tank commander; he swerved violently and ran over the dead NVA body.

As much as the human being inside of me wanted to, I couldn't look away. The scene wrenched into perverse slow motion, and my eyes recorded the frames, in graphic Technicolor detail. The tank's right tread ran over the dead NVA soldier's body at about thirty miles per hour, and the dead NVA's arms and legs involuntarily thrust upward, toward the heavens, as though beseeching the gods against this utter humiliation. The spastic upward thrust of arms and legs looked, for all the world, as though the dead NVA soldier was embracing the tank tread, but since the dead NVA soldier's body was lying face down, the embrace was impossible. After only a few frames of my mind's camera had clicked by, the tank passed completely over the dead NVA body and continued on its hurried way, and the dead NVA body flattened itself on the street once again. A few seconds later, the Ontos, trailing the tank to the rear area for reloading, followed precisely in the wake of the tank and also ran over the dead NVA body, although not quite as squarely. In the diesel-fumed wake of the tank and Ontos, the dead NVA body did not complain; it just lay there, even flatter than it had been a few moments before.

The automaton, who was then completely in control of my actions, kept my feet moving forward, one foot at a time, step by step. I kept going, and eventually the wide-screen view of the street was obstructed by another house, and my vision ratcheted out of slow motion and regained the normality of life. But the entire scene was burned irrevocably into the permanent celluloid of my memory cells, and there it remains to this day.

The separation of my two personalities, the automaton and the human being, became very pronounced again, and as I continued to walk toward the Charlie Company CP, thanks to the continued work of the automaton, my mind raged with a futile debate about what I had just witnessed. The automaton argued that it was nothing, just a dead body, a dead gook body at that. That gook had probably shot at me before he had been killed; he had probably tried to kill me. Maybe he had even been the one who had killed Estes or who had blown Sergeant Odum's face off. This is what happens in war. Don't worry about it; just keep putting one foot in front of the other until you get to where you have to go. The human being inside me was horrified at the witnessing of the brutality of this deliberate act of violation, but I was at a loss to do anything but attempt to compartmentalize the scene into some dim corner of my mind that would be capable of forgetfulness.

The automaton fully in control, Chief and I proceeded to the Charlie Company CP. The house that Scott Nelson had declared to be the Charlie Company CP was the large, two-story house that I had holed up in on the third night. When Chief and I arrived, Nelson told Chief to take a break, that he would let him know when he was needed. Chief muttered a quiet, "Aye, aye, sir," found a corner to sit in, and immediately broke open his pack to pull out a C rat or two.

Nelson, looking me over with his concerned but still grinning countenance, asked me how it was going and made some small talk for a few minutes. Rich Lowder hadn't joined us yet, so he wanted to wait for Rich before he started his briefing. I knew, at least the human being part of my personality knew, that we would be hearing that another frontal assault, this time across phase line orange, was going to be ordered soon. The automaton did not allow me to show any emotion or concern.

Nelson said, "I have a surprise for you, Charlie Three. I want you to see this." With that, Nelson led the way to a staircase and took me upstairs.

This particular house stood on the south side of phase line green and hadn't suffered much damage. It was large, containing several bedrooms, two stories, and as I was soon to find out, a very roomy attic. Nelson guided me to the second floor and continued down a short hallway to another, shorter staircase that ended in a small door at the top of a half dozen stairs. This was the entrance to the attic, which covered at least half of the house. Grinning his sheepish grin, Nelson gestured for me to crawl up into the attic.

There were a couple of Marines in the attic, and it looked like they had been there for quite some time. Many C ration cans and other litter surrounded them. But I didn't recognize these guys, and they didn't look like everyday Marines. Finally, I noticed what set them apart. On close inspection I discovered that it was their weapons that were obviously different.

During this stage of the Vietnam War, all Marine infantrymen carried the distinctive M-16 rifles. Although we had all carried and qualified with the older, more reliable M-14, which was a wooden-stocked, heavy 7.62-mm semi-automatic weapon, someone in the Department of Defense had decreed that the new M-16, which looked like a Mattel toy, was more suited to the type of combat that we were engaged in. The M-16, which shot a smaller, but more deadly 5.56-mm round, was lighter, faster firing, and smaller. After a few bugs were ironed out, Marines quickly came to rely upon the much-lighter M-16, although a combat Marine in the Vietnam War knew absolutely that he must clean his weapon three or more times a day to be able to rely on its functionality. Unlike the M-16, you could drop an M-14 in the mud, plug the muzzle with debris, pick it up, and shoot off an entire magazine with no problems. Try that with an M-16 and you were much more likely to have a jam or, even worse, blow your own face up with an exploded round in the breech. But the M-16 weighed about half as much as the M-14, and once we learned the lessons of constant cleaning, the Marines of 1/5 had accepted the trade-offs and had adapted to the M-16.

The Marines in the attics had weapons that, on first glance, looked like M-14s. As I approached their positions about a dozen feet inside the small door, the gloomy light from several holes in the roof gave me enough illumination to see who these guys were. These men were Marine snipers.

Their weapons only resembled M-14s because they were about the same size and had the traditional gun-metal gray metallic parts and dark but highly polished wooden stocks. But there the similarities disappeared. On closer inspection, the weapons were bolt-action, with no magazines, and they both had sniper scopes mounted on them. Behind the two Marine snipers, their Marine Corps–green plastic carrying cases were carefully stowed out of their way. Both men were sitting on stacks of C ration cases, using them as stools, so that they could comfortably sit and point their weapons out a couple of holes broken out of the red clay roof tiles. From this position, just over a half block behind phase line orange, peering out of almost invisible holes in the roof, the snipers had very advantageous firing positions against the NVA across the street.

Scott Nelson grabbed the closest Marine sniper's shoulder and asked him to let me take a look. The young Marine, with just a ghost of a smile on his face, pulled his sniper rifle out of its shooting port, stood up, and moved out of my way. As I started to move my face into position to look out of the hole, Scott Nelson grabbed me and quietly explained what he wanted me to do.

"Look through the sniper scope, Charlie Three. This is the surprise I was telling you about." As the Marine sniper held out his weapon, I was somewhat confused by all this (I had not done badly on the rifle range, but I was by no means rated an "expert"). There were four possible results from an attempt to qualify on the rifle range. The highest-scoring shooters earned the coveted "expert" badge; those shooting decently but not quite as well were given a "sharpshooter" badge, which looked like a German cross of sorts; and those who barely qualified were awarded the dubious distinction of being "marksmen." The marksman badge itself was so unremarkable, it was often referred to as a "toilet seat." The only thing worse than having to wear a "toilet seat" was not having qualified at all. I had earned the "sharpshooter" badge at Camp Pendleton during boot camp, so I couldn't imagine that Scott Nelson was reassigning me as a sniper. However, I accepted the weapon from the Marine sniper, sat down on the C rat crates, carefully pointed the muzzle of the weapon out of the hole, and got into a firing position so that I could look through the scope.

The other Marine sniper, sitting calmly on my left side began to quietly direct my vision, and I quickly discovered and focused in on Nelson's surprise. The sniper said, "Look across the street, Lieutenant, across phase line orange, in the middle of the block, about halfway to the next phase line. You will see two large structures, three stories in height, with a courtyard between them. Look in the center of the courtyard."

Following the sniper's directions and adjusting the focus on the scope, I found the surprise. There were four dead NVA bodies, lying very closely together, sprawled in random heaps, their weapons dropped or flung to the ground during the moments of their instant death. One dead NVA body lay on top of another's lower legs. All four of them had been dropped within a ten-foot diameter.

As my vision became rooted to this scene, the second sniper continued his dialog, as though he was narrating a documentary film; there was no emotion in his voice, no indication of horror, or glory, or anything. He was merely reporting the facts.

He stayed in his firing position as he said, "We came up from battalion early this morning, after having caught an Air America chopper in from Phu Bai. One/five sent us up here to Charlie Company, and Lieutenant Nelson thought that we could do some good up here in the attic. We popped the first gook at about 0930, and the second one a few minutes later. They were just ditty-bopping back and forth between those two houses. I guess they thought that they had plenty of cover, because they're about fifty meters behind phase line orange, and several houses protect them from the guys on the street. The range can't be more than a hundred meters. Easy shot."

The second sniper continued the dialog, "The second dude came out a few minutes later, only this guy was moving fast. He tried to get his buddy, and we blew him away with one shot. He's the one who's draped over his buddy's feet; the guy he's laying on was the first one."

My mind was trying to take this all in, but it was difficult. Up until this moment, the NVA had represented a sort of mythical enemy, like their Viet Cong brethren. They had moved fast, hit hard, and eluded us seemingly at will. We had taken terrible casualties that first day on phase line green. We had taken many casualties as Marines exposed themselves to help their dead and badly wounded buddies lying exposed in the streets. I suppose we had killed or wounded a few NVA with our counter fires, and certainly many of them in the tower had been hit. But with the exception of the now-squashed NVA body in the street, I had yet to see any dead NVA bodies. And now here were four of them. From this view of the grisly scene, it looked like they were just as human as we were after all. Three of them apparently had been killed in futile attempts to retrieve the dead bodies of their comrades.

"We had to wait for over an hour for the third one, but one thing they teach you in sniper school is patience. The third one is the guy on the left. It took us two shots, because we had to wait for an hour, and he kinda surprised us 'cuz he came outta the building on the left. I hit him with the first shot, and he went down, but he started to crawl back toward cover, and Riley had to take him out completely. We had to wait almost two hours for the fourth guy, but I hit him and blew him away with one round. He was moving fast, but it was an easy shot. Piece of cake."

Just as their story was starting to sink in, and just as I started to feel some strange kind of a moral victory about some measure of revenge for Morgan and Estes and the other Marines who had died very similarly, reality struck home once again, with explosive force.

The distinctive whooshing noise of an enemy RPG rocket terminated with a brutally loud explosion and shattered my thoughts. The NVA had finally begun to zero in on our Marine sniper position, and although they had not pinpointed them yet, they had come damned close. The RPG-7 had hit the wall of the house we were in no more than thirty feet to my right front. Just when the rocket detonated, my vision, still rooted to the four dead NVA bodies, ground insanely into slow motion. Although the automaton inside me struggled with something else, something that just wanted to get the hell out of here, to leave immediately and go elsewhere, anywhere, my body refused to move. A fiery kaleidoscope of red-hot shrapnel disturbed the sniper scope's field of vision, looking very much like the Fourth of July sparklers I had loved to light and fling around in the dark as a child, leaving burnt-in, glowing trails on my vision.

Very quickly, the slow-motion camera was shut down by the automaton, and the survival instinct kicked in. I pulled the sniper rifle out of the hole in the roof and, with only a glance at the young sniper, communicated my "job well done" mentally and hastily withdrew from the attic. This attic was about to become very hot, and I had to get back to Scott Nelson for the inevitable preparations for another bloody assault. We were still only one-seventh of the way toward our objective, and phase line orange was waiting for us.

Chapter Fourteen

The Night Movement

18 February 1968

As I stumbled back down the stairs away from the Marine snipers' lair, conflicting visions and emotions played through my mind like the unpleasant, dissonant counterpoint of a demented symphony. The human being inside me was swamped with frantic thought, threatening at any moment to capsize what was left of my sanity, but the automaton was fully in control of my outward movements, and he faithfully and steadily took the rest of me to find Scott Nelson for the next briefing.

Vivid mental images of the bodies of the four dead NVA soldiers heaped ignominiously in a pile were dominating my thoughts. These grisly images gave rise to vicious thoughts of gleeful vengeance for the deaths of Morgan and Estes and all the others who had lost their lives in the streets of Hue. The pile of dead NVA had been fittingly terminated; the dark robes of justice had visited them and had ended their lives in a very appropriate manner. They had run out into the open, into the kill zone, trying to recover their buddies' bodies.

At the same time, as these thoughts were swarming around my brain, the scene of the pile of dead NVA played out over and over again in another part of my mind. The moving picture frames of my newly etched memories always ratcheted forward, and my vengeful reverie was again and again shattered by the detonation of the RPG-7 rocket that had exploded uncomfortably close by. As the automaton took me down the stairs, the scene played through my mind. Every time it replayed, the fiery, kaleidoscopic paths of the red-hot shrapnel from the RPGs left afterimages on my eyes and on my mind's eyes and refused to dissipate. And then, out of a dim corner of my mind, Staff Sergeant Mullan's confident yet sarcastic voice reminded me of the one lesson worth learning about Vietnam. "Mother" Mullan's voice said to me, "No shit, Charlie One; you get caught looking too closely at the 'Nam, and you'll step in shit every time!" It was the memory of Sergeant Mullan's wisdom that forced the human being inside me to finally shut out the image of the pile of dead NVA bodies and to shut out all thoughts of righteous vengeance. Finally, the automaton allowed the human being inside me to mutter my acknowledgment of the hard awareness of our situation, "What the hell am I thinking about, starting some kind of stupid celebration just because of a few dead NVA. We've got six more streets to cross!"

With that, the human being inside me shut down the visions of the dead NVA bodies, tucking the mental film away in a distant corner of my memories, there to be archived until another day, and the automaton took me to find Scott Nelson.

I found him back at the sixty-millimeter mortar pits. When I saw him, I knew something was up, because his face had lost the constant grin that had become, at least for me, his trademark.

Nelson looked at me and said, "We just lost Charlie Two. He's going to be okay, but I had to medevac him. He and a couple of his men were coming back for this briefing, and when they ran across the intersecting street, the NVA opened up on them with RPG and AK-47 fire. He took some shrapnel in the neck, but he was on his feet and walking around. It looked like he got hit pretty close to his jugular vein, and I was afraid that his wound might get infected, so I sent him back. Staff Sergeant Lunsford is acting Charlie Two Actual. He'll be here in a few minutes." Nelson delivered this bad news with a calm demeanor, which didn't for a moment betray the feelings that I knew had to be raging through him.

2nd Lt. Rich Lowder, the injured platoon commander, had been with us since just before 1/5 left the Hoi An area, and he had become a very close friend and stabilizing influence to all of us. (He was the man who barely escaped death at our hands when we imagined him to be getting more than his fair share of C rations at the Lang Co railroad station in early February.) His troops loved him because he was a very competent tactical leader and strategist, and he did everything he could to take good care of their nonmilitary needs as well. Besides those admirable qualities, his absolutely unflappable nature made him seem fearless. Every one of the Marines of Charlie Two would follow Rich Lowder anywhere.

Rich had experienced several close calls since arriving in South Vietnam; he had already received one Purple Heart before entering the Citadel. Now he had his second Purple Heart medal. His neck area seemed to be a favorite target of the enemy. His first wound was also in the neck, received when a command-detonated Chicom (Chinese communist) antipersonnel mine, the Chicom equivalent of our deadly claymore mine, had exploded no more than fifty feet in front of where he had been walking, up on the Hai Van Pass. Fortunately for everyone in Charlie Two that morning, the Chicom claymore had not functioned properly, and only a small portion of the potentially lethal fragments had been flung in their direction. But one of them had hit Rich Lowder in the neck and had torn a chunk of flesh out of him. He had been medevacced to Da Nang via helicopter, but he had rejoined us after only a couple of days in Da Nang.

And now, once again, Rich Lowder was headed toward a medevac helicopter, and Charlie Two was being led by its platoon sergeant. Not counting Travis Curd, our artillery FO, Charlie Company was down to two commissioned officers—Scott Nelson and me.

I wasn't worried, however, about the leadership of Charlie Two, because Staff Sergeant Lunsford (not his real name) was an experienced staff NCO and had been "in country" for several months. He was another "Mother" Mullan, although Lunsford was a more typical Marine in stature. Whereas Sergeant Mullan was tall and well built, Sergeant Lunsford's largest physical feature was his bushy mustache. His shaggy mustache always seemed to me like a caricature, a mustache that a sidewalk artist would draw as an overdone feature on an otherwise unremarkable countenance. He was short, barely over five feet six, one of the many thin, wiry types in the Marine Corps. He had been good company for Rich Lowder, as he was also a man of few words.

While we were waiting for Sergeant Lunsford to join us, Scott Nelson guided me back into the two-story house that the snipers were holed up in, and came right to the point. Nelson grabbed my right shoulder with his left paw, gave it a little squeeze, and said, "I want to do a night movement, Charlie Three. I'm asking for volunteers, a reinforced squad, to move across phase line orange tonight, under cover of darkness, and to occupy that large building, the schoolhouse, in the middle of the block. I think we can take the NVA by surprise. What do you think?"

The automaton did not move, blink, or react in any way. The human being inside of me was screaming, trying to run away, anywhere, away from this moment and from this place. *What in the hell is he thinking of? Is he* insane? *We have been getting the living shit kicked out of us for nearly a week, we are at or below 50 percent strength, and we are just finally starting to get our act together in the* daylight, *and this* idiot *wants to do a* night movement? All these thoughts and many, many more crammed themselves into the mind of the captive human being inside the automaton, who continued to look Scott Nelson in the eye and who impossibly succeeded in not betraying even a single bit of the turmoil that burned just below the surface. One thing that I knew for sure was that I *loathed* any kind of night movement.

Memories, long compartmentalized and now clamoring for recognition, shattering memories of our previous attempts to execute night movements—memories of the near-paralyzing fears that accompanied every second of those long nights—now swarmed to the surface:

Taking command of a reaction squad, going through the wire of Charlie Company's Hoi An compound to rescue a Charlie Three squad that had been shattered by a command detonated mine . . .

Calling in my first medevac chopper to remove the bits and pieces of the several Marines who had been the designated casualties on that particular night . . .

Leading Charlie One through downtown Hoi An during a "zero dark thirty" movement required by some screwed-up thinking at 1/5's Operations Shop, and nearly shitting my jungle fatigues when my point man shot off a hand-held flare unexpectedly, only avoiding the humiliation of unplanned defecation by the involuntary selection of pissing in my trousers, the lesser of two evils . . .

Leading Charlie One through the CAP Unit outpost west of the Hoi An Charlie Company compound on a night when both the Marine and Vietnamese sentries fell asleep at their posts, and then subsequently attempting to work our way through the protective concertina wire that

guarded the bridge entrance to the CAP compound. When Charlie One's
point man that night snagged the trip wire of a ground flare, and our
dazzled vision showed us the four claymore mines staring us in the face
. . . once again, I nearly shit my drawers. . . .

No, you had to be absolutely nuts to want to move at night in the 'Nam.
And this idiot wanted to pull a night movement, right across phase line
orange, right into the NVA defensive positions, right where the NVA had
blown away that poor mule driver just a few hours before.

I have no idea how long I waited before the automaton allowed me to
react to this new development; it could have been several minutes,
because all of these memories played across my mind in utter detail. I
hope it was only a few seconds. Finally, and still without betraying any
discomfiture, the automaton spoke: "Are you ordering me to take Charlie
Three on a night movement across phase line orange? If so, I'll do it." But
before Nelson could respond, the automaton was forced by the human
being inside me to add, "But if you're asking my opinion about such a
maneuver, I think it's crazy. We're just now starting to get our act
together in this hellhole, just now starting to figure out how to fight
house-to-house. The area that you want us to go into is crawling with the
enemy who are sure as hell waiting for us in fortified or well-dug-in positions. If you're asking my opinion, sir, I think it's a suicide mission."

Scott Nelson received this unwanted editorial stoically, and my only
indication that he was the least bit disturbed was that his patented grin
was gone. He released his grip on my shoulder, involuntarily stepped
back a pace, and then said, "If I was going to *order* someone to do this
job, I'd go myself, and *I'd* walk point myself. I'm asking for a volunteer
to lead a reinforced squad of volunteers."

The automaton looked at Scott Nelson for a long moment, and finally
I replied, "I cannot volunteer for a mission that I believe is foolhardy
and that I believe will result in certain death for everyone involved."
There was no emotion contained within these words, but they were spoken with conviction. I knew that if Nelson had simply assigned me with
the mission, that the automaton would have taken me across phase line
orange in the dead of night. I knew that if the automaton had taken me
across phase line orange that night, that I would have assigned someone else to walk point, and probably a fire team would have been in front
of me. And I knew undoubtedly that Nelson would have been signing my
death warrant and that of all the volunteers.

Scott Nelson considered my words for a few seconds and, with no further conversation or discussion, dismissed me. He looked at me with a forced grin on his face and said, "Go on back to your men, Charlie Three. Keep your head down."

A few minutes after I left and headed back for the relative comfort of the remaining daylight, Sergeant Lunsford, the new Charlie Two Actual, finally reached the Charlie Company CP area. Sergeant Lunsford had the same or a similar conversation with Scott Nelson, and the required volunteers were produced. I will never know the details of that conversation or if Scott Nelson had let Sergeant Lunsford know that I had been the first to receive this wonderful opportunity and had politely declined. I only know that Sergeant Lunsford and about fifteen other Marines volunteered to make the night movement, and that the night movement was the single most successful and decisive maneuver in the battle for the Citadel.

There was no possible way that this crazy venture should have succeeded. Charlie Company had been engaged in constant firefights with the NVA dug in on the other side of phase line orange for two days, so we knew that they were there, waiting for us.

The penetration point that was selected for the daring night movement was about fifteen feet to the right, or west, of the corner, a position occupied by a significant force of NVA, the same enemy gunners who had blown away the mule driver. Marine tanks and Ontos crews had been pounding this corner position and had taken return gunfire from the NVA during each armored attack. The night movement mission required the small volunteer force to cross the open ground of phase line orange, find the breach in the wall that had been blown by the M-48 tanks and Ontos, and sneak or shoot their way through the NVA defenders. The volunteers would then occupy the three-story schoolhouse most certainly occupied by a significant force of NVA, as evidenced by the pile of NVA bodies in the courtyard. (The target schoolhouse was the building that defined the left, or east, boundary of the open courtyard that had proved to be the fertile killing ground for the Marine sniper team.) Once inside the schoolhouse, the Marines would hole up until daylight and then hold out until the rest of Charlie Company could cross the street and reinforce them. It was a bold and baldly reckless chess move and, in my opinion, would very likely end in disaster.

This was the one night that I spent inside the Citadel when I didn't get any sleep at all. Oh, no, there were no internal recriminations that night, no self-loathing for behavior unbecoming a combat Marine officer, for having "chickened out"; those thoughts didn't start until several weeks later, after the automaton had slightly loosened its grip on the human being inside me. Those recriminations, however, have continued inside my soul almost every day of my life, for over twenty-five years.

But the self-loathing was not what bothered me that night; I was still mentally very numb from the devastating events on the first day on phase line green. No, I couldn't sleep, because I had helped Sergeant Lunsford and his volunteers get ready, helped check them for noise abatement and ammo loads, and had looked into the faces of every man in that volunteer force. I knew from their faces that every one of them knew where he was heading and that every one of them had accepted his fate. I knew also that they were all doomed.

The sad look on Sergeant Lunsford's face at 0200 hours the following morning, 19 February, as he followed his lead fire team into the gloomy night and disappeared toward phase line orange, was resigned. His eyes were filled with pure sardonic humor, as if to say that he too was a captive of his own automaton. He was like a young boy, riding on a rickety old roller coaster that scared him to death, but he was too addicted to the adrenaline rush it gave him to ever get off. One more ticket, one more ride.

A few minutes after 0200, Sergeant Lunsford and his volunteers crept quietly across phase line orange, crawled through the shattered opening in the wall on the corner, sneaked breathlessly across the open ground to the schoolhouse, and quietly occupied and cleared all three floors of the schoolhouse within fifteen minutes of their departure. Not a single shot was fired. The NVA had abandoned their positions in the schoolhouse before Lunsford and his volunteers had arrived. The company radio net's static was abruptly interrupted by a whispered, abbreviated situation report that summed up the impossible, "Objective secured. Out."

Then, just before first light the next morning, the Marine volunteers occupying the schoolhouse opened up with a shattering volume of M-16 fire and wiped out about twenty NVA soldiers who were crossing some open ground about fifty meters south of the schoolhouse. Most of them were killed outright by the Marines' concentrated firepower at nearly point-blank range, and the killing zone quickly became another pile of dead NVA bodies. A couple of wounded NVA managed to escape the killing ground, and they most assuredly let their leaders know that they no longer controlled the block, because it quickly became evident that the NVA had pulled back across the next street. Sergeant Lunsford's volunteer force had the high ground, and the rest of Charlie Company moved across phase line orange with no further casualties.

Scott Nelson's idiotic idea had turned out to be the genius move of a master strategist; more importantly, it had saved many Marine lives. I don't know if he had gotten some indication that the NVA had left their murderous corner positions at night, and I didn't really care that I had been so wrong. Sergeant Lunsford and all of his volunteers deserved recognition for undaunted bravery in the face of certain death.

Chapter Fifteen

Coke-Bottle Glasses

20 February 1968

After a week of constant, bloody, and vicious house-to-house combat inside the Citadel of Hue, on the morning of 20 February, 1/5 had established full control of two-sevenths of our assigned area of operations. The incredibly harrowing and equally brilliant night movement across phase line orange turned out to be the linchpin that quickly resulted in 1/5's capture of four more city blocks. Now, 1/5 controlled the eight city blocks contained inside of phase line green on the north, the Citadel wall on the east, phase line black (our next obstacle) on the south, and the Imperial Palace moat and wall on the west. Since the NVA had finally abandoned all efforts to recapture and hold the Dong Ba Porch, the infamous tower that so effectively dominated phase line green, 1/5's eastern flank was now secure. Although there were many fighting holes built into the eastern wall, the NVA would have had to significantly expose themselves for many long seconds to try to get into those positions, and after the NVA finally lost the tower, they never really tried to use the wall as high ground against us again. Now, 1/5's Marines could attack across phase line black, or Dang Dung as the Vietnamese had called it, with little concern about our left, or eastern, flank being exposed. There were no more towers dominating the wall on our left flank.

There was, however, a very distinct terrain problem on our right. The NVA inside the Imperial Palace, with the advantage of excellent cover and high ground from their positions atop the parapets of the twenty-five-foot walls of that "fortress within a fortress," could shoot small arms and rockets with impunity directly down on the Charlie Two Marines who were holding 1/5's right flank. And, since the Imperial Palace was considered "hallowed ground" and was still protected by the South Vietnamese and American "no fire zone" restrictions (meaning that we could not shoot at any target on the Imperial Palace wall with anything larger than an M-79 round no matter what they shot at us with), Charlie Two had the very difficult task of securing our right flank while not being able to defend themselves from enemy fire from the Imperial Palace with anything larger than small-arms fire.

Late on the afternoon of 20 February, a squad from Charlie Two finally made it across phase line black, Dang Dung, and into a small house on our right flank. Unfortunately, it quickly became apparent that they could not maintain this foothold for long. The small house was blatantly exposed to small-arms and RPG fire from the NVA on the Imperial Palace wall, and the attacking Charlie Two Marines immediately came under a horrendous volume of enemy fire from a deadly cross fire. The NVA were shooting at them from positions in and around the houses directly in front of them, and from the Imperial Palace walls.

As they were the only Marine unit to make it intact across phase line black, this squad was very exposed, and since there was very little daylight left to work with, Scott Nelson made the decision to pull them back across phase line black. Staff Sergeant Lunsford, the acting Charlie Two Actual and the leader of the heroes of the night movement, radioed me over the company net and asked if we could spare a few men to beef up his forces to lay down supporting fires for their retreat back across the street. So Chief and I led a couple of fire teams across Dinh Bo Linh, the perpendicular street that separated the Charlie Two and Charlie Three AOs, and we joined up with the Charlie Two CP.

After a quick consultation, I deployed my men with the understrength Charlie Two squads facing phase line black and then rejoined Sergeant Lunsford in his hastily occupied command post, the second house in from Doan Thi Diem. Doan Thi Diem was another perpendicular street that defined our right flank and separated us from the moat surrounding the Imperial Palace. The house that had become Charlie Two's CP faced phase line black and afforded us an excellent view of the street.

The living room of this house had two large windows, the glass panes having long since been broken out by the occupying Marines. The windows afforded us with good fields of fire and reasonably good observation of the street in front of us. The thick mortar walls of the house provided us with good cover from the NVA gunners on the Imperial Palace walls. Fronting the house were a shallow porch and a small front yard, which was surrounded by a low block wall. The wall was subsequently fronted by a sidewalk. A narrow area of struggling, ancient lawn with a row of old, shaggy trees spaced a couple dozen feet apart separated the sidewalk from the street. Phase line black could have been a residential street from any middle-class neighborhood in America. The street had plenty of room for two-way traffic and for parked cars on either side of the street. The street itself was about forty feet wide. The houses that faced each other across the street were perhaps eighty feet apart. At this point, like most streets inside the Citadel, this one was void of vehicles. The terrain on the far side of the street was a mirror reflection of that on our side of the street: starting with a low curb, a three-foot-wide strip of grass hosting well-spaced, but thickly branched and vegetated trees, a sidewalk, a wall with an open gate, a small front yard, and then the single-story house that the beleaguered Charlie Two squad was now hunkering down in. In order to make it back to safety, the young men from this pinned-down squad would have to run across about eighty feet of relatively open ground.

Orders were given, another star-cluster rocket was fired, and the Marines of Charlie Two and Charlie Three opened up with a tremendous volume of small-arms fire against the known NVA positions. Their fire was supported by a tank/Ontos team that roared down Dinh Bo Linh on Charlie Two's left flank, continuing to pound the NVA on the other side of phase line black with their heavy weapons. The NVA just opposite us opened up, and their friends on top of the Imperial Palace walls also increased their frantic rate of fire. In the middle of this utter and deadly chaos, the Charlie Two squad started running, in twos and threes, back across phase line black.

Again, time and motion slowed agonizingly. Afterward, it seemed as though many minutes had passed before all the Charlie Two Marines made it back to the north side of phase line black and safety. In reality, it was probably all over in less than ninety seconds. Fortunately, none of the nine Marines was struck down in the middle of the street; unfortunately, two of them were wounded, one horribly.

The first three Marines ran out of the house, sprinted through the yard and across the sidewalk, ducked under the low-hanging trees, and raced across the open street through a ferocious volume of enemy fire striking all around them. The Marine in the middle was hit and then immediately hit again, but somehow he kept running. His buddies, hearing his screams, grabbed his arms and continued the mad dash across the open ground, across the street, under the trees on our side of the street, across the sidewalk, through the yard, and rushed in the front door. All three of them crashed into a heap on the floor. Our house came under heavy enemy small-arms fire, but we were relatively safe because of the protection of the thick mortar walls and the increasingly difficult angle for the NVA gunners. The Charlie Two corpsmen jumped on the three Marines heaped on the floor, sorted them out, and started working frantically on the wounded man, a young black Marine who had started screaming as he ran in the front room, "God damn, God damn, they shot off my dick, them mutherfuckers shot off my dick. Oh, sweet Jesus, they shot off my dick!"

There were still six more Marines on the other side of the street, and a large part of me wanted to watch those men running across the street, but this Marine's screams captured my attention. As I turned to my left, the cameras of my mind still ratcheting obstinately in slow motion, he came into my view. As he started to frantically rip away his bloody trousers, he continued to scream that the mutherfuckers had shot off his dick, and the more he ripped away his own clothing, the more distraught he became. The camera of my vision zoomed in on his groin area, and it was obvious that this Marine had lost most, if not all of his manhood; there was only a huge amount of blood staining the lap of his trousers and some pubic hair, where there should have been a penis and testicles. His screaming became louder and louder as his frantic search for his penis and testicles continued, and he began to understand with unwanted clarity his awful fate. One of the Charlie Two corpsmen, unable to do much more than apply a wad of thick bandages in an attempt to stop the bleeding, had the presence of mind to immediately shoot the young Marine up with a morphine capsule, which had an almost immediate effect on the shattered young man. His screaming never lost its intensity, but the volume tapered off rapidly, and in a few moments the screams became a frantic, slurred mumbling.

The volume of shooting in the street, which had diminished slightly when the first three Marines had reached the safety of the house, increased again, recapturing my attention. I turned back to allow my mind's cameras to refocus on the frantic attempts of the Charlie Two Marines to get back across the street. A second group of three Marines had started their run for safety across the bloody gauntlet of phase line black.

Incredibly, two of these three made it across the street without a scratch; the third, well, it is still hard for me to believe what happened to the third Marine.

The third Marine had been with Charlie Two since Hoi An days. I had seen him a couple of times before, and I had once known his name. He was either a lance corporal or a PFC. From the first moment that I saw him running across phase line black that day, I remembered with the clarity of instant recall what had made him famous (or, rather, infamous) to the other Marines of Charlie Two. He wore Coke-bottle glasses. The Marines of Charlie Two called him Coke-Bottle Glasses.

I am certain to this day that this young man was legally blind and that he should never have been permitted to join the Marine Corps, let alone any branch of the service. It was common knowledge by then that the expanding Vietnam War and the directly related increasing demand for new recruits had a deleterious effect on the legendary high physical standards that the Marine Corps is famous for. But even given this understandable relaxing of the standards, none of us who knew Coke-Bottle Glasses could ever figure out how in the hell he had ever gotten into the system.

Shortly after the Tet Offensive broke out, Coke-Bottle Glasses had been accidentally left behind during a night ambush patrol above the Lang Co Bridge. His squad leader had ordered his men to pull out of their positions at about 0400, well before first light, and they were nearly halfway back to the bridge when Coke-Bottle Glasses was reported missing. They backtracked and found him, scared half to death, squatting down in a defensive firing position, slowly turning around in circles, obviously unable to see anything, not even seeing his buddies returning to fetch him. He couldn't see a damned thing in the early morning gloom, and yet he was wearing his thick-lens glasses that night! Why his squad leader had not reported this before was beyond any of us who watched him, as he ran for his life, back across phase line black.

Here they came, the three of them. Coke-Bottle Glasses was in the middle, running out of the house, across the front yard, through the gate in the wall, and across the sidewalk, into the teeth of the gauntlet. The other two Marines, using their God-given normal vision, ducked low, negotiated the low-hanging trees, quickly ran across the street, and made it to the safety of our house without being hit. Coke-Bottle Glasses, however, did not realize that the branches of the tree that he vaguely saw were low-hanging, and he failed to duck. A thick branch caught him full in the face, and although his glasses survived the collision with the leafy branch, it caused his heavy glasses to turn sideways on his face. One moment he had some vision, the next moment one lens of his glasses covered his mouth, and the other covered the middle of his forehead. Coke-Bottle Glasses, momentarily stunned, was effectively blind, sitting on his ass in the middle of an enemy kill zone.

Valiantly, Coke-Bottle Glasses got up and, knowing from his hearing (which was not in the least impaired) that he was in the middle of a very hot kill zone and not yet understanding why he was blind, started to run in the direction that he thought he should go in. Amazingly, he made it across the street without getting hit. Unfortunately, he did not see the low curb on the north side of the street, and he tripped over it. Coke-Bottle Glasses crashed into the low concrete wall, and once again fell down, this time on the sidewalk, but still completely exposed to the enemy's deadly gunfire.

By this time, the third and final group of three Charlie Two Marines had started their mad dash for safety, so at that moment some of the NVA gunners probably shifted their fire toward them. Perhaps the gunners thought that they had shot the crazy Marine who had been careening across the street for what seemed like several minutes. Coke-Bottle Glasses once again picked himself up and groped his way through the front gate. Then he stumbled across the front yard as the third group raced past him. Finally, beyond all odds, Coke-Bottle Glasses tripped once again on the front steps, but his momentum carried him crashing through the door into the front room of the house.

Coke-Bottle Glasses had made it to safety. Although he was shaken and winded from the exertion of a hundred-foot dash about as straight and fast as the path of those little steel balls in a pinball machine, he finally realized why he had hit so many obstacles. Breathing heavily, looking at no one in particular, Coke-Bottle Glasses retrieved his battered, but otherwise unharmed glasses from their skewed position on his face. With the unconscious grace of a longtime glasses-wearer, he repositioned them properly on the bridge of his nose and anchored them to his ears. All of us in that room were speechless for at least a couple of minutes, watching this unbelievable finale to an incredibly insane, but extremely lucky performance.

One of the three Marines in the final group, who had blown by Coke-Bottle Glasses as he had bounced from tree to wall to porch, had also been hit a couple of times. Although his buddies had helped him make it the final few steps, it turned out that his wounds, although painful, were superficial, and he didn't even require medevac.

Just before Coke-Bottle Glasses had started his zany dash, Sergeant Lunsford had gone back toward phase line orange with a small group of men who were assigned the task of carrying the young black Marine back to the First ARVN Division compound, and he was momentarily gone from his command post. And although I technically had no business involving myself in his platoon's business, I simply could not believe what I had just witnessed. By all the odds, Coke-Bottle Glasses should be dead, lying in a pool of blood in the middle of phase line black. All eight other Marines who had run across the street, two of whom had been badly wounded, had probably only been in the street for ten or twelve seconds, total. Coke-Bottle Glasses had been in the kill zone for well over a minute, maybe as long as two minutes, and had been continuously exposed to enemy gunfire during that entire time. He had also fallen down in the street not once, but twice, and here he was, standing unscathed save for a few bruises and bumps, rearranging his glasses as though this was no big deal, as if this had happened to him every day. Perhaps it had.

At that moment, my only thoughts were for the Marines who would have had to risk their lives going after him in the middle of the street if Coke-Bottle Glasses had been hit and wounded, but not killed outright. My decision was made for me. I walked over in front of Coke-Bottle Glasses and said, "Let me see those glasses, Marine." Good Marine that he was, Coke-Bottle Glasses didn't bat an eye (at least I *think* he didn't bat an eye, because truly his eyes were very difficult to see through the extra-thick lenses). At least he could see that I was his superior officer, and he obeyed me without hesitation. He came limply to attention, removed his glasses, and handed them to me, his vague, watery eyes full of trust. And although I was positive that this young man was very attached to those glasses, he didn't flinch at all when I dropped them on the hardwood floor between us. I placed my right, size-ten combat boot directly over his glasses and stepped down firmly and deliberately. Then, with all my weight on my right foot, I rotated my boot slowly back and forth, thus ensuring that both lenses of Coke-Bottle's glasses were crushed into very small pieces. Coke-Bottle Glasses was now truly blind, but he knew perfectly well what had just happened.

I asked him just one question: "Do you have another pair of glasses with you, Marine?"

Coke-Bottle Glasses squinted up at me and answered my direct question without equivocation.

"No, sir."

Turning to his squad leader, one of the young heroes who had survived the run across the street, I said, "Corporal, this Marine has hopelessly broken his glasses, and he doesn't have a replacement pair. It is obvious to me that he can't see without them. For the good of everyone in this city, I believe that he should be medevacced immediately and sent to Phu Bai, or better yet, to Da Nang, so that he can get another pair of glasses. Any questions?"

There were, of course, no questions. Coke-Bottle Glasses, one of the luckiest men alive, was taken in hand and guided by the Marines who were taking the last wounded man back to the First ARVN Division compound.

Late that evening some Marines from Charlie Two shot a few 3.5-inch white phosphorus bazooka rounds into the house that the stranded Charlie Two squad had gotten pinned down in, and it burned to the ground before midnight. Although we could never occupy that particular house, the enemy was also denied that defensive position.

As the flames burned low in the midnight gloom, the Marines of Charlie Company hunkered down in their defensive positions along the north edge of phase line black. I found another corner, crawled into an abandoned bed, and subsided into a deep and dreamless sleep.

Early the next morning, 21 February 1968, our eighth morning inside the Citadel, I met with Scott Nelson and got our marching orders for the day. They were simple. Phase line black was in front of us; we had to cross it and destroy the enemy forces on the other side so that we could continue toward our final objective, the south wall of the Citadel.

At this point Charlie Company's manpower was down to five understrength squads. Charlie Three, my platoon, was the most fortunate, still having three squads of either eight or nine men; Charlie Two was down to two squads of ten men each. With only about fifty fighting men left, Charlie Company was just barely effective as a fighting force. Charlie

Company's responsibility along phase line black had been reduced to the one-block frontage on the right flank of 1/5. Alpha and Bravo Companies were given the two center blocks, and Delta was still holding down the left flank, covering the narrow eastern block and the wall.

In planning this next assault, 1/5 had decided that Charlie Company would attack first, with the other companies putting down a base of fire, trying to keep the NVA soldiers' heads down across the street from them. If we were successful in establishing a firm toehold across phase line black, Alpha Company would send a platoon across behind us—in our wake, so to speak—who would then pass through our "beachhead" and attack the NVA's exposed flank.

Scott Nelson's briefing was succinct and to the point. He said, "I think we should try to take the house on the left corner of our AO, Charlie Three. It's the farthest away from the NVA on the Imperial Palace wall, and the guys from Alpha can give us a good base of fire." Scott Nelson's terse order summed up the obvious. We all understood that whichever house we targeted would be difficult to take, since we had to cross the exposed kill zone to get inside the house, and it was very likely that the attacking Marine element would be running right into a waiting NVA position. The house on the left corner was as good as any other.

I returned to my platoon and briefed the squad leaders, and together we picked the point fire team, the four men who would have to run across phase line black first. Scott Nelson headed back to the battalion CP to coordinate our heavy support and the supporting fires from Alpha. Nelson was going to ask for a tank/Ontos team to make a double hit on the house opposite the one we were going to take out, right at the moment of the assault, to keep the NVA on our left front pinned down while the point fire team made their dash across the street.

L. Cpl. Charles Davis and his three men were selected as the lucky point fire team. Although Lance Corporal Davis had been in the thick of the fighting inside the Citadel, you couldn't tell that from just looking at him. He was a veteran of over seven months in the 'Nam, but since he was a very quiet young man, it would have been very easy to mistake him for a raw recruit.

Lance Corporal Davis was an otherwise unremarkable Marine, much like most of the rest, who simply went quietly and professionally about his assigned duties and complained very little about his lot in life. His fire team was also frequently picked to walk point. Once again, Davis's team was chosen.

The plan we had agreed upon was that Davis and his three men would start out spaced a few yards apart, having worked their way into four different positions of cover on the northeast corner of phase line black. As soon as the red star cluster rocket signal was fired, they would all run across the street at the same time, converging on the target house, and quickly try to clear the first of two floors. If they could clear the first floor, they would immediately move upstairs and clear the second floor as well. Once they had control of the house on the corner, Chief and I would cross phase line black in their wake, followed closely by another fire team, and we would then consolidate our position.

After that was accomplished, the rest of Charlie Company would follow us. Subsequent fire teams would then attack the next house, clear it, and then allow another fire team to leapfrog through that position. The teams would continue to leapfrog units forward toward our right flank until we had cleared all the houses on the south side of phase line black in our AO, except, of course, the last house, which was now just a pile of charcoal.

The signal for the assault's supporting fires was the arrival of the tank/Ontos team, who acted on their cue perfectly, nearly demolishing the house catercorner across phase line black in front of Alpha Company. Many of Alpha Company's Marines opened up with an intense and sustained volume of small-arms fires, and the rest of the Marines of Charlie Company, spread out along phase line black on our right side, joined in ferociously. The steady thunking of sixty-millimeter mortar fire from the Charlie and Alpha Company mortarmen joined the crashing chorus, which hopefully meant that the NVA in front of us had to hit the dirt to avoid being blown away.

I fired off a red star cluster signal rocket as the tank/Ontos team reversed away from phase line black, and Lance Corporal Davis and the three Marines from his fire team unhesitatingly emerged from their positions of safety and ran into and across the street.

Chief and I could easily see the action on the corner, and we held our breath, expecting one or more of Davis's men to be hit and knocked down in the open ground. Amazingly, however, they all made it across safely and disappeared quickly into the front door of the target house. In spite of the almost constant din of the supporting fires, I heard Chief's next words, and my veins turned to ice. As I said, Chief was a man of few words, so when he spoke, I listened.

"Ontos coming!"

I wondered what in the hell another Ontos was doing up here. We were supposed to get a tank/Ontos team, but they had been here already and done their thing. No one had said anything about another Ontos. I heard the screaming, high-revolution engine straining toward phase line black, and I knew that something wasn't right.

And then I saw it. It was another Ontos, all right, only this one had gotten its orders screwed up. It screamed up and slammed to a stop at the intersection, pointed *right at* the house that Davis and his fire team had just entered. There was no time for slow-motion cameras; before I could even scream out the one word that I did, the Ontos had fired off all six of its 106-mm recoilless rounds of high-explosive death and destruction and had quickly reversed its course and started screeching back away from phase line black.

"Nnnooooooooooooo!!!" That was it; one word, the most futile and negative word in the English language. That was all I could say. Davis and his men were surely dead, slaughtered by friendly fire.

Dust and cordite smoke enshrouded the house, and for a few moments the supporting fires tapered off and died out. The Marines on both sides of us had seen what had happened, although none of us wanted to believe it. Davis's fire team had all made it across the damned street safely and for all appearances had seized control of the target house. Then this damned Ontos had come out of nowhere and had blown them all away. What else could possibly go wrong?

About that time, L. Cpl. Charles Davis, his entire body covered with a thick coating of white plaster dust, emerged, or should I say, ejected himself out of the dust cloud that was once a house, his three team members right on his butt, in the famous "asshole-to-belly-button" formation. Davis's eyes were as big as saucers; his helmet was tilted at a ninety-degree angle and right now only covered the right side of his head. His knees were damned near smashing into his chest as he and his buddies ran for dear life out of the death house as fast as they had ever run in their lives.

In a typical Vietnam anticlimax, it turned out that they all made it back across the street unscathed, and none of them was really hurt by the Ontos attack. But they were, to a man, shaken by the experience of having a house they were standing in disintegrate around them. Their only problem was a distinct ringing in their ears that stayed with them for several days. The simultaneous explosions of six 106-mm high-explosive shells detonating in the second floor of the house had given new meaning to the expression "rattling their cages," but they were, after all, okay.

As the dust finally cleared away, we could see that the first floor of the house was still mostly intact, but the house was now a single-story structure. Fortunately for Davis and his team, the errant Ontos had put some elevation on his tubes before blasting away, and the shells had all hit the second floor and roof.

We quickly sent another fire team across the street, and they were able to hold the position. Shortly thereafter, Chief and I ran across the street with a dusted-off Davis and his team, and we consolidated our position in the nearly demolished corner house. After Chief reported our progress to Charlie Company headquarters, Scott Nelson started moving the rest of Charlie Company across phase line black immediately. The NVA on the other side of the street were gone. I guess, by now, they must have thought we were totally insane, that our immensely superior firepower had gotten out of control, and that we had taken to blowing away even houses that we had occupied.

A distinct pattern had begun to emerge in the fighting inside the Citadel. Once we had established a firm foothold in a new block, once we had successfully gotten a significant fighting force across another phase line, the enemy would quickly withdraw from the houses in that block on the entire four-block frontage, cross the next phase line, and take up defensive positions that they had prepared long before our arrival inside the Citadel. Apparently, the NVA commanders understood clearly that they could not afford to be caught with their flanks exposed, so they had decided upon a strategy which forced us to limit our tactics to the costly frontal attack, assaulting across the phase lines into the teeth of the well-prepared positions. So far, it had worked very well for them, because after eight days of fighting, the NVA still held over half of the southeast corner of the Citadel *and* the Imperial Palace.

The only comfort that we could take from any of this was that at least we were making progress. It was a very expensive progress, because at this point 1/5's fighting strength wasn't much more than 50 percent effectiveness, and we still had a long way to go, with four more phase lines to cross. But now that we had the distinct advantage of heavy firepower support and we had gained some dearly earned experience in how to cross the streets and how to clear the houses, the pace of our progress had quickened. If we could continue at the present pace, we might just crush the NVA defenders against the south wall of the Citadel or force them to move back inside the Imperial Palace grounds within a few more days. On the other hand, without reinforcements, there might not be too many of us left after a couple more days of this kind of fighting. Attrition was our worst enemy, since, so far, we hadn't seen a single replacement.

Late on the afternoon of 21 February, Charlie Company and the rest of 1/5 crept carefully into the houses facing the next phase line. I have by now forgotten the next, or fourth, phase line's color; it may have been yellow or red. By this point the colors of the phase lines had lost any meaning. I remember phase line green with an absolute clarity, an instant and persistent recall that will never leave my mind, and I remember orange and black because they followed green so closely. But the fourth and all the subsequent phase lines will remain forever in my mind without a color designation.

The Vietnamese name of the fourth phase line is Hung Vuong. Slightly narrower than green, orange, and black, it had very few trees to brag about.

Chief and I had taken up residence with one of the Charlie Three squads in a small bedroom in a narrow, two-story house facing the next street. This bedroom was situated just off a central hallway that ran without interruption from an enclosed front porch through the middle of the house to the rear. From our cautious vantage point in this middle room we could see that this house had sustained very little damage thus far. The glass of the front porch windows was all intact. The bedroom barely had enough room for a tall, full-size, brass-framed four-poster bed and a large glass-fronted hutch. The hutch was a very ornate piece of furniture that was still filled with china. It sat snugly and confidently against the bedroom wall, facing the bed and looking away from the street. There was a space of only a couple of feet separating the hutch from the bed. Chief and I were sitting on the edge of the bed, feet on the floor in the narrow space between the bed and the hutch, and I would occasionally peek out into the hallway to look through the porch into the street.

As soon as we had occupied the houses fronting Hung Vuong, the NVA had greeted us with a fierce rate of small-arms fire from their defensive positions on the other side of the street, so there was no doubt that the familiar pattern was continuing. The NVA were waiting for us on the other side of the street; this phase line would certainly be another killing ground.

Since it was late in the day, 1/5 decided to hold what we had. Travis Curd, our company artillery FO—he of the "Lost Outpost" fame—and his radio operator had entered our house a few minutes before and had climbed the back stairs to the second floor of this small house. He was trying to get into a position that offered both some cover from the enemy gunners as well as a view of the other side of the street. Battalion was becoming increasingly concerned with calling in artillery support, because as we advanced slowly toward the wall, the space that could be safely bombarded was becoming smaller, and battalion was understandably concerned about taking casualties from friendly fire. So Travis had come up to the front line to take a look-see. I asked Chief to switch frequencies on his Prick-25 so that we could monitor Travis's comments back to battalion as he described the enemy's positions across the street.

Travis called in his report. "Millhouse Three, this is Firecracker Three. Our front positions are now within six hundred meters of the south wall. We should be able to continue artillery fire support for at least two more blocks, over."

The squelch and static of the interplay between Travis Curd and Major Wunderlich, the battalion's operations officer, was very clear when Travis spoke and slightly garbled when Major Wunderlich replied, but it was still quite understandable.

Major Wunderlich said, "Roger, Firecracker. Get some target coordinates and go for it. Keep your targets at least fifty meters south of our positions, over."

Travis Curd said, "Roger, understand, Millhouse Three. The houses just across the street are very close together, and all of them are two stories high, so we have plenty of protection from any errant shrapnel. . . . Shit, what the fuck is *that* asshole doing?"

Whatever had caused Travis's momentary breakdown in radio discipline had really rattled him, because although he was obviously no longer looking for targets and communicating with Major Wunderlich, he continued to hold down the transmit button on his Prick-25 handset, so we could hear him clearly. What we heard in the next few moments made our blood run cold.

Travis Curd, his voice rising into an involuntary squeakiness, shouted over the radio, "Oh, fuck, he must be lost. This street isn't secured and here comes a fucking Ontos. Oh shit, he's coming fast, and he's pulling up right in front of us!"

By this time, Chief and I could hear the Ontos screaming up to a stop right out in front of us, and we no longer needed Travis's commentary to figure out what was going on. Here came another lost Ontos, and who the hell knew what was going to happen next.

An Ontos was definitely a "two-edged sword." Now, I never, ever wanted to be the target of the six 106-mm HEAT (high-explosive anti-tank) rounds that an Ontos could fire simultaneously, and I would much rather be *behind* an Ontos than in front of one when it decided to launch its ordnance. But every Marine that had made it through boot camp, ITR, or OCS had been drilled on the fact that a 106-mm recoilless rifle had a significant kill zone *behind* it. The gases from the fired round escaped out of a rear vent, thus eliminating much of the recoil that was related to a standard artillery piece. Our Marine instructors had placed cardboard boxes and other large objects behind a single 106-mm recoilless rifle within the kill zone, which extended about forty feet behind the breech, and we had seen these items become instantly shredded by the fiery back blast. No, you don't want to be the target of an Ontos, but you also don't want to be right behind an Ontos when he shoots. No way.

Travis Curd continued his frantic commentary, "Oh Jesus Christ, he's pivoting left. Shit, he's right in front of us! Get your heads down!!" By now Travis was screaming at the top of his lungs, so we didn't need the radio any longer to hear him clearly. Chief and I looked at each other momentarily and thought about all the glass in the front of the house and the heavy hutch sitting right next to us. We knew that we had only a couple of seconds to get out of the danger zone and that it wasn't enough time. Fortunately, we had both removed our packs and had placed them on top of the bed, and Chief had set his Prick-25 down on the floor, so we were both able to squeeze under the bed and cover our heads with our arms just as the stupid, damned Ontos let loose with all six tubes. A million shards of glass departed from the front porch and funneled themselves down the hallway.

Since this street was narrower and there was no front yard, we figured afterward that the back of the Ontos was about twenty feet in front of our house. The front porch was demolished by the force of the back blast, which also blew the hutch down, along with all the glass from it. As we heard the Ontos crank itself into reverse and start its escape, Chief and I, shaken but otherwise unhurt, looked up and realized that we were trapped under heaps of glass and the hutch.

Travis had also hit the deck in his upstairs hideaway, but despite his shouts he hadn't had much of a problem with the back blast since he was on the second floor. Fortunately, none of my Charlie Three Marines in the back part of the house had been standing in the hallway, so no one was hurt. But neither Chief nor I were going anywhere without some help.

A few moments later, Travis tromped down the stairs to see if everyone was okay, crunched through about a three-inch layer of broken glass in the hallway, and found us, trapped like a couple of chipmunks in a cage, under the brass bed.

Travis said, "Shit, Charlie Three, what the hell are you two girls doing under the bed? You know there are rules against fraternization." Travis was obviously amused by our predicament and didn't seem to be in too much of a hurry to help us out.

I looked up at him through the plumbing of the brass bed and said, frustration obvious in my voice, "Shut up, Travis, and get a couple of the guys to help pull this damned thing off us. I don't want to be under here when another Ontos decides to get lost again. Shit, why doesn't someone tell us when them damned things are going to visit our neighborhood?"

I was getting sick and tired of this; if it wasn't the NVA across the street, it was an errant chunk of shrapnel from an F-4's bomb or a damned naval gunfire short-round or a friendly sixty-millimeter mortar round dropped within six feet of me or the back blast zone of an Ontos. If the enemy didn't get me before I got out of the Citadel, my own friends were sure to.

As darkness settled uneasily over the Citadel, Chief and I left the suspect shelter of the brass bed and moved back a half block to a safer position for the night.

Chapter Sixteen

Prisoner
of War

22 February 1968

The following morning, 22 February 1968, was a dreary duplicate of all the previous days we had spent inside the Citadel. The early morning light of the sun competed with a thick, low-hanging cloud cover and just barely escaped defeat. A heavy mist threatened to turn to rain, but simply continued to dampen the city without enthusiasm.

Shortly after dawn the fighting on Hung Vuong, the fourth phase line, started up again. Although the NVA had been pushed back, they were obviously as determined to keep us on the north side of this street as they had been on the first morning when they had faced us across phase line green. Once again, Marines would have to assault across open ground into the teeth of the defender's gunfire.

There was one surprise that morning; we were visited by a young American wearing civilian clothes. It turned out that he was a reporter from the *Washington Post*.

Chief and I were hunkered down behind a small building about twenty-five feet behind Hung Vuong, monitoring and directing the small-arms fire of the Charlie Three Marines. We were providing supporting fires for Alpha Company, who was making some preliminary probes along Hung Vuong to see if they could find some weak spots in the enemy's defensive positions. Their efforts did not appear very promising, because the volume of fire from the NVA defenders was horrendous all along Hung Vuong.

Here we were in the middle of a terrible firefight, in the midst of shattered and burning buildings, keeping our heads down, and here comes this reporter. From the looks of his eyes—they were as large as saucers—he hadn't spent much time in Vietnam.

We hadn't seen any reporters at all inside the Citadel since the day we had arrived. This was probably merely due to a transportation problem, however, since the presence of reporters on the battlefield was a constant factor during the Vietnam War. A reporter who "really wanted to know what was happening" could visit virtually any spot in the country if he or she could find transportation. Most of the reporters in Vietnam stayed in the cities and took their material from the military briefings; but the really aggressive ones, the ones who came to suspect that they were being spoon-fed a bowl of pap from a military propaganda machine, were not at all restricted from going virtually anywhere they wanted to go in South Vietnam, given that they had, or could find, the appropriate transportation. But since the Tet Offensive had broken out, ground transportation had been virtually stopped up and down Highway One, and a helicopter was now a tough charter to arrange. Somehow, this young eager beaver had managed to find a means of transportation and had gotten himself inside the Citadel.

He looked to be about twenty-five years old. He was tall and solidly built, but he had an obviously new cast on his right forearm that stuck out like a sore thumb. The cast was unsoiled, virtually spotless, so he must have broken his arm within the past day or two. He had a 35-mm camera strapped around his neck and wore a photographer's vest. As he crawled up behind our position he pulled out a small, worn notebook from an upper vest pocket along with a stub of pencil.

Since our attention was focused on the fighting on the street, and since the noise from the fighting was deafening, we didn't notice him until he was right behind us. When he spoke I damned near jumped out of my skin.

"Hey, who's in charge up here?" he asked, his eyes getting even larger as he looked past us to the exchange of gunfire on Hung Vuong.

I immediately understood why he didn't recognize me as an officer, because I had long since taken my second lieutenant's insignia, my gold bars, off my collars. Since, unlike Army officers, Marine officers didn't wear cloth rank insignia on our helmets, there was no visible rank insignia on my person. One of the first things I was taught when arriving in Vietnam was that a combat commander wore his metal insignia *underneath* his collar, because a Viet Cong sniper would look for radio operators and officers to shoot first. My appearance was further confused by the fact that I was still carrying Ed Estes's M-16, and Marine officers normally only carried a .45-caliber pistol. So, at that moment, I looked like any other enlisted Marine in combat.

I looked him over briefly, decided that he was obviously an idiot (why on earth would anyone in his right mind have come here unless he absolutely *had* to?), and thought I'd have a little fun with him. I told him that I was a lance corporal, but since all the officers and NCOs superior to me had either been killed or wounded and I was the next person in the chain of command, I was the acting platoon commander of Charlie Three. As he frantically took notes, his eyes got even larger. I don't really know to this day why I created this stupid fabrication, but I did.

The young reporter spent about fifteen minutes asking us questions about what was going on. When he left he was under the impression that Charlie Company had only one officer left, the company commander, and that the highest ranking person after the skipper was a lance corporal. I didn't make anything else up, because I didn't have to. He could see the fighting for himself; he could judge for himself the fierceness of the fighting because of the destruction he had come through to get up to Hung Vuong and because he knew that we had been fighting for over a week and that we had only come three blocks. He could also see the filthy conditions that we were enduring, probably better than we could, because although none of us had changed clothes or bathed since we had left Phu Bai, we hadn't really paid much attention to our filth. He could see us as we couldn't see ourselves, and his sense of sight and probably his sense of smell must have told him that we had been living like animals. We were so dulled by our situation and our environment and the constant need to crawl about in the dirt and dust and mud that being filthy meant nothing to us.

He asked Chief a few questions as well, but Chief didn't say a word. The radio operator just looked at him with an unreadable expression in his eyes.

As the reporter asked his questions, I continued to monitor the fighting and occasionally responded to a radio query. At one point, as I was holding the Prick-25 handset to my ear and was pointing at something along Hung Vuong, I heard a camera shutter click. I turned to find that the reporter had taken a picture of Chief and me. I always wondered if that picture made the next issue of the *Washington Post*.

Later that morning Alpha Company got a squad across Hung Vuong and made another breakthrough. By the end of that day, the NVA again realized that they could easily be flanked, and they withdrew across the next street, yet another phase line, Hon Thuyen. At the end of the ninth day of fighting, 1/5 had control of sixteen blocks, a little over half of our AO. We were under 50 percent of our normal strength, but we had still not received any reinforcements. Yet we were somehow moving forward and were, by now, obviously really hurting the NVA defenders. It was becoming obvious, however, that this battle was turning into a race against time and attrition. At this rate we might not have enough men to get all the way to the southeast wall.

Late that night Charlie Three lost a KIA, one of the few casualties that occurred during the nighttime hours of the fighting inside the Citadel. Chief woke me about 0200 hours and told me that one of our squads had taken some incoming, apparently 82-mm mortars. We moved up to the squad's position in the deep darkness and met with Lattimer, who was now the squad leader. A private first class, he was doing the job of an E-5 sergeant because everyone above him had either been killed, or wounded and medevacced.

Lattimer took me to where the Marine had been killed and told me what had happened. The look on his face was one of disgust.

He said, "Shit, Lieutenant, I don't know how many times I've told these dudes to keep their damned helmets on, but no, this dude has to sit right by this window with his helmet between his legs. He took a chunk of shrapnel in the temple. That was it. If he'd had his damned helmet on, he would have had his bell rung, but his helmet probably would have saved his life. That damned 82-mike-mike round hit right in the middle of the street."

As I looked at this latest casualty of the battle for the Citadel, I also felt disgusted at the unnecessary waste of life, but there was nothing that either of us could do about it. Marines were like any other human beings, and sometimes the desire for creature comforts would outweigh good sense. The results of that particular mind warp were always consistently predictable. The only good thing that came out of an incident like this is that all the other Marines didn't have to be reminded, at least for a while, to keep their headgear on and their chin straps tight. They could see for themselves what happened when you disrespected the gods of war.

I told Lattimer to wait for first light before taking the dead Marine back to the rear for evacuation. Chief and I then made our way back to the house we had holed up in for the night to try to get some more shut-eye. As was my habit of late, I was asleep within a few seconds; I don't think Chief slept any more that night.

The next morning, 23 February, Chief roused me right at first light. I automatically heated up a C ration meal and monitored the company and battalion radio networks as the sounds of fighting, right on schedule, started up once again. My breakfast was interrupted by a radio message from Lattimer, who called Chief and told him that he needed to see me back at the house where the Marine had been killed early that morning. Lattimer said something about having a gift for me. Wondering what the hell kind of a gift Lattimer could come up with in the middle of all this destruction, Chief and I saddled up and made our way back to Lattimer's position.

Lattimer had a gift, all right. He had captured a live NVA soldier. Charlie Three had its own live prisoner of war.

As I entered the back of the house, I was met by Lattimer and several other Marines from his squad. Lattimer's face was beaming; a huge, toothy grin indicated his delight at being able to present this surprise.

He said, "This stupid fucker must have overslept, Lieutenant, 'cuz as me and Gomer were starting to carry the KIA back to the rear right at first light, we saw him. He was coming from *behind* us, walking south toward the wall. He must have been holed up in an attic or something and missed the word to fall back. Here he comes, carrying his damned AK-47 over his shoulder, just ditty-bopping right toward us. We dropped the KIA and hid in a couple of bushes, and then we jumped him. He gave up without a fight and started Chieu Hoi-ing all over the place."

Chieu Hoi was the Vietnamese phrase for "give up," or surrender. It was a well-known part of the lingo. Viet Cong and North Vietnamese fighters knew that they could *Chieu Hoi,* or surrender, and that they would most likely be treated well. They were sometimes reindoctrinated and eventually assigned to Marine handlers and then turned into spies and scouts. These turncoats were often referred to as either Kit Carson scouts or, simply, *Chieu Hois.*

From the look on his face, this NVA solider was apparently relieved to be out of the fighting, for as I made my way into the back room where he was being detained at gunpoint by several of Lattimer's men, he had a big smile on his face. He was holding his hands up in the universal gesture of surrender and was babbling nonstop in Vietnamese; every few seconds the words *Chieu Hoi* were recognizable.

As Lattimer continued his dialog and the NVA soldier continued his grinning babbling, time again warped inside my mind. The human being inside me was filled with the images of death and the shattered bodies of the young Marines who had lost their lives on phase line green. I couldn't balance those images with the image before me of this grinning NVA soldier. His entire body language made it clear that he had totally surrendered his fate into our hands. He was smiling up at me as though he was saying, "It's all over for me now; I'm out of the war. The rules say that you have to take care of me now." The automaton could not control an overwhelming rage created by the sight of this surrendering enemy, this piece of slime who had probably killed Estes or Morgan, or who had blown Sergeant Mullan's head off.

I walked up to the NVA soldier and reached out to him. His grin faded to surprise and disbelief as my hands grasped his neck and I started to strangle him. My hands took on a life of their own as they became vise-like pincers, as I tried to kill him with my bare hands. I don't remember saying anything; I didn't try to tell him what an asshole he was, or in any way try to communicate with him as to why I wanted to kill him. I just grabbed his neck with both of my hands and tried to choke the life out of him. How dare he give up and then smile up at me? Estes is dead. Estes didn't have the chance to give up. He was just dead.

The other Marines in the room were stunned by the scene of their platoon commander, a person who, up to this point, had always advocated playing by the rules, and who was now trying to commit murder right in front of their eyes. I don't know how long it took them to react, or how long it took them to pry me loose from the NVA soldier, but I do know that it was long enough for the NVA soldier to know that his fate had changed once again and that he was surely going to die. I saw it in his eyes. His look changed from one of happiness, to surprise, to shock, and then to fear. Finally, he *knew* that he was going to die. In a spastic attempt to free himself, he threw himself backward, but my hands stayed clamped to his neck as I fell on top of him. His hands grabbed my wrists, and he tried in vain to pull me off him, but my grip had somehow taken on an unlimited strength.

Finally, Lattimer and three other Marines in the room succeeded in prying me loose, and the NVA soldier, now semiconscious, curled up in a fetal position on the floor, coughing weakly. Lattimer and the others helped me up from the floor, and although these young men, these hardened combat Marines, surrounded me closely and showered concerned looks upon me, no one said a word.

Finally, Lattimer broke the uncomfortable silence by saying he would take the NVA soldier back to battalion for interrogation. Lattimer left with his prisoner of war. I went back to my running.

Later on that afternoon, one of the other companies on our left flank was pulled back into battalion reserve, and Charlie Company spread out to the left. We were facing the fifth phase line after nine days of fighting.

Charlie Three was assigned to the left flank, and Charlie Two had the right. Chief and I set up on the front porch of a large house facing the battalion's rear along the fourth phase line and waited for further orders.

About 1630 hours that afternoon we received our first reinforcements. Actually, I stumbled across these Marines (who were obviously new inside the Citadel because their green utilities were clean) sitting in the courtyard behind a house, a half block behind the fifth phase line. They were taking a break, sitting on top of three boxes that looked like nothing I had ever seen before. The small group was comprised of an E-4 corporal, a lance corporal, and a PFC. I approached the corporal and asked him what he was doing up here. His reply was as strange as his appearance.

"We just came up from Da Nang, actually from Chemical Warfare School in Da Nang. We checked in with battalion, and they told us to keep out of the way and to keep our heads down. We wanted to get out of the middle of that battalion clusterfuck, so we came up here with the grunts. I figured we'd be safer with you guys."

"Well, hell, Corporal," I replied. "We can use you. We haven't had any reinforcements since we came inside this God-forsaken city, and we're getting pretty low on manpower. What the hell are those boxes you're sitting on?"

The boxes were, predictably, painted Marine Corps green and were made of fiberglass, not wood. Actually, they weren't really boxes, because the corners were rounded. There were three of them, about two feet high, slightly less than two feet wide, and about a foot thick.

The corporal said, "These are weapons, sir. They're called E-8 gas launchers. We got them from Division Headquarters in Da Nang, where we've been at Chemical Warfare School, and we were told to bring them up here to see if they will do any good. Based on our reception at the battalion CP group they're just one more heavy thing we had to carry all the way up here." The corporal was new inside the Citadel, but he was no stranger to the vagaries of the Marine Corps.

When I asked him what these E-8 gas launchers did, he obliged my interest with a demonstration. Standing up, he bent over the E-8 gas launcher and removed the top cover, which fit snugly and was released with a suitcase-style latch.

Adopting the familiar style of a military instructor, the corporal began a dissertation about the device, "The E-8 gas launcher contains forty 40-millimeter CS-type tear gas projectiles that are fired from the backpack launcher. When you want to deploy this weapon, you remove the cover, and then you take these three base plates and swivel them around like this, and they become the tripod base. Then you tilt the launcher in the direction that you want the gas projectiles to go, judging about how far forward you tilt the launcher by how far you want to shoot the projectiles, and then you pull this cord. All forty projectiles are shot up with a trajectory something like an M-79 round. Maximum range is about four hundred meters, and this launcher is supposed to spread the tear gas over an area about one hundred meters wide and fifty meters deep."

I asked them if they had ever shot one off, and the corporal looked at me like I was crazy. "Hell, no, Lieutenant. These projectiles each have enough CS gas in them to fuck up a whole company's day. I swore after boot camp that I was going to stay as far away from tear gas as possible. I hate that shit! Besides, they only had these three units, and if we tested one we wouldn't be able to use it on the gooks."

I empathized with this corporal, because since I had gone through both boot camp and OCS and had therefore received a "double dose" of the gas chamber that all Marines, both enlisted men and officers alike, received during training, I had developed a strong sense of revulsion about chemical warfare. One whiff of CS-type tear gas could mess up your whole day.

Interestingly enough, all the 1/5 Marines had been issued brand-new gas masks when we were in Phu Bai before coming to Hue, and the rumor mill had been rampant with speculation that the NVA might try using chemical weapons against us. In the first few days of the fighting, almost all of us had taken care of our gas masks, but by this point nearly two-thirds of my men had long since lost (discarded) their gas masks along with the cumbersome carrying pouch. After nearly a week and a half of fighting the enemy at very close quarters with no incidents of chemical warfare, most of us had decided that the threat was imaginary, and we had jettisoned the extra weight. This fact got me to thinking that maybe our enemy was in a similar situation and would be vulnerable to a well-placed gas attack. What the hell, it was worth a try.

I quickly gave the corporal and his men our situation and ordered them to set up one of the gas launchers so that the forty-millimeter CS gas rounds would land about a hundred meters in front of us, on the other side of the fifth phase line. Our front line was about fifty meters in front of us, and I figured that fifty meters was a safe margin.

The corporal tilted the open launcher forward toward the NVA's positions, about fifteen degrees, and without further discourse, he pulled the firing cord. Unfortunately, since this team had missed something in their training, never having fired one of these launchers, they didn't realize that each of the forty 40-millimeter projectiles had a recoil. The first projectile's recoil caused the launcher to move back from its fifteen-degree tilt, and the launcher snapped into position aiming straight up! The remaining thirty-nine projectiles were launched within the next two or three seconds. They flew straight up in the air. After a few moments they rained down on our heads, saturating the Charlie Two positions in front of us and the entire area around us with CS-type tear gas. Needless to say, I heard over the radio from the Charlie Two Marines who were choking with the vile stuff. I'm amazed that some of them didn't come back and shoot us all for gross incompetence.

Benny Benwaring, still with Charlie Company, having been assigned to Charlie Two as a radio operator, started cussing up a storm over the company net. I had never heard Benny cuss that much at one time. His gas mask had come up missing about three blocks back.

Fortunately there was a slight breeze, so our discomfort was only temporary. After the gas dispersed, we set up the last two E-8 gas launchers, filled up a bunch of sandbags, and placed the sandbags around the launchers after tilting them forward so that the recoil wouldn't move them. We aimed them so that they would cover as much of the next block as possible, and then we pulled both of the firing cords at the same time.

Eighty forty-millimeter CS-type tear gas projectiles shot off and saturated the next block in front of us on a two-block frontage, just as night fell.

Charlie Company slept fitfully that night, thinking about the inevitable orders to cross Hon Thuyen, the next phase line. We still had three blocks to go, and then we'd still have to take the south wall of the Citadel.

Chapter Seventeen

The Effectiveness of Chemical Warfare

24 February 1968

The next morning Charlie Company received orders to assault across the next phase line, or Hon Thuyen, another street in Hue named in honor of an ancient leader. Hon Thuyen was a famous scholar.

Charlie Three was designated as the assaulting unit, with Charlie Two and the other 1/5 companies establishing supporting fire. At this point (within three blocks of the south wall of the Citadel) it was determined that artillery prep fire support was too dangerous to our own men, so we would have to assault across the street again without much supporting firepower. We were used to it.

Fortunately, we could call in a few tank/Ontos teams to soften up likely enemy positions before the assault with the vehicles' large-caliber direct-fire weapons. The teams showed up quickly and started their deadly dance.

As the last tank/Ontos team pulled back, the first Charlie Three fire team sprinted across Hon Thuyen and entered the first target house. They cleared it and found it empty. Chief and I ran across the street with

207

the rest of the squad, and we quickly moved fire teams to the adjacent houses and found them similarly abandoned. The heavy, disturbing smell of CS-type tear gas from the E-8 gas launcher attack permeated this section of the Citadel, causing our eyes to well up with tears as we moved through the houses.

The rest of Charlie Three moved across the street and leapfrogged our positions. After about fifteen minutes we had covered enough of the fifth block to be fairly sure that it was completely devoid of any enemy positions.

I called Scott Nelson on Chief's Prick-25 and reported our unopposed progress. Nelson told me that he would be moving the rest of Charlie Company across Hon Thuyen in our wake and that we should cross the next street when we were ready.

We waited for about a half hour to give Charlie Two enough time to get across Hon Thuyen and get into position to cover our movement across the sixth phase line, just in case. Without waiting for tank or Ontos supporting fires, the point fire team ran across the sixth phase line, or Dinh Cong Trong, named after a famous Vietnamese general who fought the Chinese. The point fire team crossed Dinh Cong Trong without incident and quickly established themselves inside the first target house. According to our maps the next block was larger than all the others, being about twice the depth, so it took a while to check out all the houses. Eventually, however, we checked them all out. We found them all empty.

The lingering odor of tear gas, which had pretty much covered all the territory that the NVA had controlled until the previous night, still caused our eyes to tear up, but I didn't hear one complaint. Although we weren't yet at our final objective, the south wall, it looked like the E-8 gas launchers had done the trick. Apparently, the NVA had completely abandoned the southeast sector of the Citadel.

The rest of 1/5's Marines were now following in the wake of Charlie Company, and Delta Company had started to move forward along the eastern wall of the Citadel. After about an hour and a half we were pretty sure that the NVA were gone, and Scott Nelson decided to go for the wall.

My 1:10,000 map showed that the last phase line, called Tong duy Tan, separated us from a small, triangular-shaped block which snuggled up to the southeast corner of the Citadel. Although it was cater-corner from the block we had been traveling through, Nelson and I decided to cut diagonally through this triangular block because it took us a couple hundred meters away from the Thuong Tu Porch, or tower, that was the easternmost of four southern entrances to the Citadel. If there were still NVA inside this section of the Citadel, the tower was the most likely position that they would try to defend.

Once again, maybe for the last time, the point fire team from Charlie Three sprinted across the seventh phase line, Tong duy Tan, and cleared the first house. It was empty.

Chief and I moved the rest of the platoon across the street. We fell in behind the point fire team and told them to move through the corner block and to get up on the wall, but to keep their heads down.

There was a small house in the middle of this block. As I walked up its back steps and through its back door, I stopped cold. I stood for a moment facing an old Vietnamese woman, sitting in a rocking chair, quietly rocking in her chair as if this were just another ordinary day. We had not seen a civilian in this area since the night the baby was born. American forces had been shelling this section of the city for many days, and an unbelievably fierce battle had been raging all around this old woman for days. Yet here she was, quietly rocking away the morning.

She was old, nearly ageless, ancient. She was wearing a shapeless black dress, with a shawl pulled over her frail shoulders. Covering her head was an old, tattered, black scarf. Her face was eroded, ravaged with deep wrinkles carved by the heavy wear of time. The woman sat in her rocking chair, saying nothing, staring at nothing, never even acknowledging our presence, just rocking away her final days. She must have been too old to leave when the city had been evacuated, and the NVA must have fed her and cared for her while they fiercely defended their captured territory.

No one in front of me or behind me spoke to her, although I am certain that all of us were filled with the wonder of this woman's survival in the midst of this hellish chaos. We simply walked by her, and I never saw her again.

The NVA were gone. We moved across the final block and took the short run across the narrow street that separated us from the south wall of the Citadel. Carefully and cautiously at first, we climbed the ancient brick steps to the top of the wall and peered over the bulwark.

From this new vantage point, about thirty feet above street level, we could see a vast panorama. Across the Perfume River lay south Hue and the terrible destruction that had befallen it. We could see the shattered

Nguyen Hoang Bridge, the large bridge that had previously allowed travelers on Highway One to cross the Perfume River. Looking to the west, we observed the Thuong Tu Porch, or tower, sticking out like a sore thumb another twenty feet higher than the wall. Although this tower was about four hundred meters away, we could sense that the NVA were there, and we clearly remembered the devastation rained down upon us from the NVA occupying the Dong Ba Porch on phase line green. So we crouched back down below the bulwark, unwilling after all we had been through to give an NVA sniper an easy target. Behind the tower, another three or four hundred meters further away, stood the walls of the Imperial Palace. The palace was most likely the next defensive position of our enemy, and some of us started to speculate about how difficult it would be to take the palace away from the NVA. Mostly, however, we were just happy that we had been able to move through the final three blocks without a shot being fired.

Apparently, the NVA could not deal with our "secret weapon," the E-8 gas launchers, a weapon so secret that even *we* didn't know anything about it until the previous evening. That started me to thinking about the "what ifs." What if we had brought the E-8 gas launchers and had used them the very first day? Would they have worked as effectively, or had the NVA soldiers, like our Marines, been equipped with gas masks and then discarded them over the past few days when it appeared that they would be unnecessary? I stopped thinking about that quickly, though, because there was no way to know the answers.

It was enough to realize that it had taken 1/5 nearly ten days of bloody fighting to progress four blocks toward our objective; that we had lost over 50 percent of our manpower through casualties during the process; and that it had taken less than three hours to progress the remaining three blocks, during which time we had not been shot at once. The only lesson that could be learned from this was that nothing is ever certain in war. In war, everything is always totally unpredictable.

The sounds of late morning were unsettling as we sat up there on the wall, because it was just too damned quiet. I hadn't heard a shot fired during our three-block walk, a period of slightly over two hours. After living through the constant fighting during the daytime of the last ten days, the quiet was unsettling. I pulled off my pack and helmet and sat down, using my helmet as a low stool. After rummaging around in my pack and finding a C ration meal to cook, I then told Chief to call Scott Nelson to let him know that the objective was secured.

As I prepared yet another unappetizing but necessary C ration meal, I looked around at the Citadel wall. For the first time, I began to understand why Delta Company had experienced such a tough time taking the tower. Behind the bulwarks, or parapets, of the wall, there were many fighting holes built into the wall itself. The fighting holes were about three feet square and three to four feet deep and were spaced only a few feet apart. If this theme continued throughout the Citadel's defensive complex, the towers would be a maze of fighting holes. I began to realize just how lucky we were that the NVA hadn't overrun the First ARVN Division compound. If we had been forced to attack the enemy from the *outside* of the Citadel, we would have paid a terrible price just to get inside.

After we had been sitting on the wall for about a half hour, a commotion down below us, coming from our rear area, got my attention. I looked up just in time to witness one of those classic wartime events that make the front pages and are awe-inspiring to the civilians who read the hometown news, but which are laughable to the combat soldiers who were there. Evidently, the 1/5 CP group had finally decided to put in an appearance with the front line troops and were surrounded by a covey of reporters and photographers.

The battalion CP group was "assaulting the Citadel wall" en masse, led by a crusty radio operator who worked for the forward air controller. Most of the combat Marines happened to like the FAC radio operator, because he could get on his magic radio and call in the big birds of death, but in this case he had gone just a little too far. As this cluster of battalion CP group Marines "stormed the Citadel wall" for the reporters, led by the FAC radio operator who even had an American flag on a six-foot flagpole in his hands, the Marines of Charlie Three, the men who had done all the work and had dealt with all of the death and destruction, started to get angry.

"Shit, Lieutenant," said PFC Robert Lattimer, "look at them fuckers. We haven't seen those dudes since we left the ARVN compound, and here they are getting their pictures taken for the press, taking credit for the whole damned thing. Maybe we should give them some realism, you know, shoot a few M-16 rounds over their heads, make them duck a little."

I looked away from the media circus, got eye contact with Lattimer, and replied, "Leave them alone, Lattimer. They don't know any better." The truth was, I just didn't give a damn. I knew who the heroes were, and if the press and the public wanted to feel better by looking at a few pictures of some rear-area dudes charging the wall that we sat on, so be it. We could always tell our grandchildren the truth, that we were sitting on the wall looking down at these silly people, and that the heroes never seemed to get the credit that they deserved.

A couple of hours later Lima Company from 3/5 passed through our positions and assaulted the Thuong Tu Porch tower. They met with some fierce resistance initially, but persisted. Within minutes Lima Company's Marines had overwhelmed the remaining NVA defenders, and the southeast sector of the Citadel was finally secured. The NVA had most certainly withdrawn from the southeast section of the Citadel and had escaped into the Imperial Palace.

That afternoon, as more fresh Marine units arrived inside the Citadel, Charlie Company was finally able to pull back. We were moved back to phase line green and assigned to cleanup duty. This meant that we had to search every house meticulously for any NVA stragglers and to pick up any bodies that the NVA had left behind. It also turned out that we had to keep the civilians out of their homes until the Citadel was declared safe again, which would not happen until the NVA were completely routed. And it was soon evident that the NVA were still holed up inside the Imperial Palace. NVA snipers on the Imperial Palace wall started shooting at targets of opportunity, which became more and more abundant as replacement troops started to join 1/5.

The new guys stood out like a sore thumb, because their uniforms were almost bright green (if you could ever define Marine Corps green as being bright) and very clean, but mainly because they didn't know enough about city fighting to keep their heads down. At one point, upon witnessing three clean Marines walking boldly down the middle of the street, I lost my cool and hollered at them without thinking. "Hey, you stupid assholes, get outta the middle of the fucking street! Where the fuck do you think you are, fucking Disneyland? There are plenty of NVA snipers still around here to welcome you to the Citadel if you keep strolling down the street like that!"

I guess I got their attention, because all three of them scurried out of the middle of the street and hunched down just a little bit. They didn't say anything to me in response, either, although I noticed as they walked by my position that one of them was a captain and the other two were senior staff NCOs. I still had my second lieutenant's gold bars hidden under my collar, so they probably thought I was a stupid private and didn't know any better, and since they couldn't bust me for disrespect, they decided to leave me alone. But maybe it was the tone of my voice and my appearance. . . .

Charlie Three took up residence in the house that Estes had died in. It had an actual sit-down toilet and a couple of functional beds, so it was a good choice, but I think we homed in on the place because we had all lost something there. We stayed there for a few days as the mop-up operation continued and as the Vietnamese Black Panther Battalion was given the assignment to assault the Imperial Palace.

This time, even though the Imperial Palace really *was* sacred ground, there was plenty of heavy support brought to bear on the NVA inside the palace grounds. The tanks and Ontos made many passes on the palace wall until a large hole had been blown in it, giving the Black Panthers an entrance to use that could not be as well defended as the tower-dominated entrance.

I had mixed emotions when I was first told that someone else would be making the final assault into the Imperial Palace, that the Marines of 1/5 would not be involved. Part of me was resentful that anyone else would be given the "honor" of delivering the "coup de grace" and driving the NVA out of the Citadel once and for all. A different, saner part of me was relieved, however, because surely this battle would be as bloody as any that had occurred thus far. It would be vicious, because now that the NVA were trapped inside the Imperial Palace, they had nowhere to go. We had been told that the Citadel was completely surrounded by American and ARVN forces and that all avenues of egress were completely sealed off. With the NVA cornered, they were now going to be given the simple choice of surrendering or dying. We didn't think that the NVA would surrender. And so, for two more days the tanks and Ontos delivered their deadly loads onto the NVA inside the Imperial Palace to support the Black Panthers in their final assault.

Meanwhile, the Marines of Charlie Three filled up the toilet in our commandeered home with puke and shit (the toilet was a modern sit-down version with a flushing tank, but it had long since ceased to function; this had no deterring affect on any of us who desired the simple pleasure of a seated defecation). And we continued to search out the houses and to police the area of bodies and unexploded ordnance.

On the afternoon before we departed the Citadel, one of the Marines of Charlie Three remembered the dead NVA body that had been run over by the tanks.

"Hey, Lieutenant," he said, "do you remember where that dead gook was that the tanks ran over?"

"Yeah, I remember," I said. "It was a couple of blocks over and a block up." With that in mind and with a couple five-gallon cans of gasoline, about a half dozen of us walked off in search of the dead NVA body that the tanks had run over. Although we were on the right street within a few minutes, it took us a while to find this particular body, because it wasn't much of a body any more. It was more like a grease spot. It was a spot on the side of the street, about three feet long and about a foot wide, covered by a few tattered shreds of green cloth. It was him, all right, but there wasn't much left of him. This particular NVA body had become symbolic of the frustration of the tank and Ontos drivers during the battle for the Citadel and had probably been run over hundreds of times over the past few days.

I grabbed a gas can, twisted the cap off, and poured about a gallon of the flammable liquid over the grease spot. Replacing the gas can's cap, I stepped a few feet away from the spot and nodded to Chief, who pulled out a book of matches and lit the spot on fire. Without thinking about it, I pulled off my helmet and stood watching the flames, contemplating this act and the fate of the dead NVA soldier who had been run over so many times. In some ways, this burning NVA grease spot was symbolic of the participants of this terrible battle, and now that the fighting was over, the symbol was being burned from existence.

I hadn't noticed it when we torched the grease spot, but as the fire dwindled down and I replaced my helmet and prepared to leave the spot forever, I looked up and saw that everyone else in the vicinity had also stopped and removed his helmet. Looking around me, I saw that there were many Marines within eyesight of our small group who had seen what we had done. They had also stopped what they were doing, had removed their helmets, and had spent a few moments of thoughtful silence.

It was the closest thing we had to a memorial service.

The next morning, 1/5 was relieved of our responsibilities inside the Citadel fortress of Hue. We walked out the Thuong Tu Porch, the south tower's gate, across the ancient moat, through the business district that fronted the Citadel and separated it from the Perfume River, and made our way to the edge of the river. Mike boats were waiting for us to move us back south across the river. A Mike boat, as the smaller "cousin" of the Whiskey boat, could comfortably carry at least fifty combat-loaded Marines, so there was room to spare.

When we climbed into the Mike boats, I could take a silent head count, because there were so few of us left in Charlie Company. Of the original fifty-one Marines of Charlie One who entered the Citadel, only seven of us rode in that boat.

Docs Lowdermilk and English were sitting together in the bow area of the boat, looking as though they were having a quiet, private conversation. Lines of fatigue and despair shadowed both their faces, as the weight of their responsibilities and their memories of giving immediate medical assistance to their buddies continued to weigh heavily upon them both. Both these young men had performed their duties in an extraordinary way and had been directly responsible for saving many lives during those days inside the Citadel. In Doc Lowdermilk's case, he was also a part of a birth. He had experienced the full cycle of life and death and had helped to alleviate the suffering of others. Like all the corpsmen I served with during my time in Vietnam, these docs were critically important members of our team, and I always thought of them as fellow Marines.

PFC Robert Lattimer hung out with his buddy, Gomer, in the rear of the boat. They weren't talking about anything. They had both succumbed to exhaustion and sat in a lump on the deck.

Benny Benwaring was rummaging through his pack, trying to find something to eat, without much success. Benny also sat on the deck, and his pack sat between his long, spindly legs, which were drawn up so that his heels competed with his butt.

Lance Corporal Charles Davis sat by himself along the left side of the deck of the large boat, staring at the other side of the boat.

That was it. Out of the forty or so Marines who comprised Charlie Company on the day we left the Citadel, there were seven of us on that boat who had originally been a part of Charlie One. All the Marines of Charlie Company were on this one boat, so I was sure of my tally. Seven.

Although I was not then completely aware of the details, eleven Charlie One Marines died inside the Citadel fortress of Hue, and thirty-three Charlie One Marines were wounded badly enough to require medical evacuation.

The last two Marines to board the Mike boat for the short trip to the south bank were The Gunny and 1st Lt. Scott Nelson, the Skipper. The

Gunny really didn't look too much different than he had looked two weeks before, because he had already been a grizzled veteran before we entered the Citadel. He just looked tired and dirty as he sat down on the tail of a mule, leaned back on a stack of C ration cases there, and lit up a slightly rumpled Lucky Strike.

Scott Nelson had earned the title, Skipper. After Hue, I never again thought of him as 1st Lt. Scott Nelson; he was the Skipper. I'm certain that all the other men in that boat that day felt the same.

I didn't envy him his position; I still don't, to this day. As the commanding officer of the company that was thrust into the center of the deadly cauldron of house-to-house fighting inside the Citadel of Hue, he was a key part of the military equation that meant, in many instances, life or death to the Marines in his charge. At the same time, he was the man who had to communicate with the upper levels of command, the critical supporting elements, and our sister companies. In this particular battle, he also had had to deal with the initial rules of engagement that had restricted our heavy support and had cost so many lives. It was like being inside a pressure cooker with an incredible amount of pressure coming from a dozen directions at once. Scott Nelson had been the one Marine that I had observed inside the Citadel who had not cracked under this incredible pressure at least for a moment or two.

He stood alone at the bow of the Mike boat as the crew raised the bow ramp. The boat slowly and deliberately backed away from the muddy bank of the Perfume River and began its slow turn toward the south bank. The Skipper's expression was unreadable. If you hadn't known him before, you wouldn't have known that he had been through the gauntlet, except that he was also tired and dirty. But there was no grin on his face. His expression was neutral. He stood there and, removing his helmet, gazed off into the distance, tugging absent-mindedly at his mustache.

No one looked back. There was no curiosity displayed about the Citadel any longer. We had seen enough. More than that, I think most of us felt that if we had looked back at the Citadel, we would all turn into blocks of salt. It was over.

Chapter Eighteen

Aftermath, and a Dying Pig

5 March 1968

Charlie Company and the rest of 1/5 made our second crossing of the Perfume River at the end of February 1968. For the next few days, until 5 March 1968, the company roamed the countryside east of Hue, chasing the remnants of the NVA forces that had overwhelmed the population centers of South Vietnam during the Tet Offensive. The NVA's offensive had initially been very devastating, but we had ultimately kicked their asses, and they had been totally fragmented into small groups running for their lives.

The South Vietnamese Black Panther Battalion finally assaulted the Imperial Palace at the end of February. They found that the tight cordon that American and ARVN forces had established around the Citadel was leakier than a sieve. The NVA had completely disappeared from the Imperial Palace grounds, but the Black Panther Battalion had their victory, however hollow it had turned out to be.

My memories of those long and dangerous days following the horrendous fighting inside the Citadel are now as fragmented as the NVA forces were, following their ejection from the Citadel.

I remember being ambushed by a large force of NVA, probably a reinforced company, from a position that we had been told was firmly under the control of U.S. Army forces. Several enemy rockets and a huge volume of small-arms fire erupted from across a narrow river, blowing up a mule carrying a 106-mm recoilless rifle. The mule driver's left arm was blown off at the shoulder. I remember watching while the corpsmen worked on this young man and being amazed when the mule driver realized that it was his left arm that was missing. I can remember hearing him ask someone to fetch it, because his wedding ring was on the third finger of the hand of that now useless arm. The arm was found, the swollen ring finger was removed, and the ring was returned to its rightful owner. It seemed to give him some comfort as they carried him away on a wooden door. . . .

I remember being nearly killed by a U.S. Air Force F-4 Phantom jet that hastily and mistakenly dropped two 250-pound snake-eye bombs right on top of us. It happened after we had been pursuing a sizable force of NVA, when they decided to stop and fight. A significant firefight had broken out between us and the NVA, who were about three hundred meters away across a dry rice paddy, in a tree line. Fixed wing support was called in by our forward air controller, and the O-1 spotter plane shot his first spotter rocket at us instead of the enemy. The F-4 pilot, seeing the smoke from the spotter rocket wafting up about twenty feet in front of our position, dropped in and unloaded two bombs before the forward air controller could straighten him out. I remember hunching down behind a low cinder block wall, seeing the spotter rocket hit and the smoke starting to drift up, and then turning around and looking behind us. The F-4 was committing a classic error, making his pass perpendicular to our front lines from behind us instead of parallel to them from one side or the other, as close air support doctrine dictated. I remember seeing the two 250-pound snake-eyes dropping off the airplane, seeing the stabilizing wings deploying and the distinctive wobbling of the bombs as they dropped, seemingly in slow motion, out of the sky. There seemed to be no way they could miss us. I was sure I was a dead man. Chief and I hunkered down behind that low wall and tried to get as small as possible. Both bombs blew up about twenty-five feet on the other side of the wall, and the concussive force of the two near-simultaneous explosions was shattering. My ears rang for several days afterward, but fortunately no one was injured. The FAC radio operator told the Air Force F-4 pilot to return to base, regardless of the fact that he had not dropped all of his ordnance. I remember that the FAC, in the process of kicking the Air Force jet jockey out of the sky, wasn't very polite. . . .

I remember chasing squad-, platoon-, and company-sized units of NVA for click after click across the countryside east of Hue. A distinctive pattern emerged in these running fights. We would proceed cautiously down the trails and narrow roads east of Hue, inevitably establish contact with the NVA, call in fire support, artillery, and air support, get the NVA on the run, and chase them as fast as we could. At one point, Charlie Three got way out in front of the rest of Charlie Company and our point element started to come under heavy enemy fire. We were stopped, so we called back to Scott Nelson and requested fire support. Our request was approved, but we were told to withdraw to put some distance between ourselves and the enemy positions, because some fast movers were going to put heavy bombs, probably 500-pounders, and napalm in on the target. I remember that I gave the word to pull back, but that Chief and I stayed in our position for a few more moments to make sure that the enemy wasn't going to try to counterattack or some other foolish nonsense. When we suddenly realized that we were all alone, Chief and I took one look at each other and then took off running to the rear. We quickly caught up with the rest of Charlie Three, but Chief's and my withdrawal was so rapid that to anyone in the rear, it looked like a rout. I remember seeing the look on The Gunny's face as Chief and I approached the Charlie Company CP group at a dead run. The Gunny's eyes got large as he summed up the situation, and it was obvious from the look on his face that he was certain that a large force of NVA were close behind us. He even started to turn and run before he noticed that Chief and I were stopping. . . .

Finally, on 5 March 1968 Charlie Company received orders to return to Phu Bai. We were told to march several clicks back to the small blown-up bridge on Highway One, where we were to be picked up by a truck convoy for the short ride back to Phu Bai.

Charlie Company marched back south, taking up the familiar ten-meter staggered interval that was the standard operating procedure for forced marches. Stay ten meters behind the man in front of you; two staggered columns, one on either side of the road.

Because south Hue had been long since secured, we didn't even put out a flanking element, which we knew would only slow us down. We had been shot at and shit on for nearly three weeks and had forgone the luxury of hot meals and showers during that time. Most of us were black with accumulated filth, and we were all looking forward to getting back to Phu Bai and into a hot shower.

Moving through the destruction of south Hue, we took a more circuitous route than the one we had taken on our way in. We crossed Highway One, continued west for a couple of clicks, and walked close by a large, heavily damaged structure, which we found out later was a Catholic cathedral. Shattered buildings and rubble littered the streets.

As we walked up a short hill just past the cathedral, I noticed a single combat boot sitting upright on the left side of the road. Since I was the third man back in the column on the right side of the road, I couldn't see the boot clearly until I was nearly adjacent to it. Once I got to that position, I immediately noticed two things about the boot: first, it was clearly an American combat boot; and second, there was a leg bone sticking up out of it. The policing details in this part of Vietnam would be working overtime for a long time to come.

As we approached the brow of the hill, I tore my gaze away from the boot and looked forward again. I tried to concentrate my vision on the back of the man in front of me and to just put one foot in front of the other. Soon we would be back in Phu Bai, and although it wasn't as good as going back to the World (a thought that someone like me, with over nine months left to go on my thirteen-month tour, could ill afford to consider), the prospect of hot food and hot water beat the hell out of what we had just been through.

Just as I was able to focus back on these thoughts, a disturbing noise ahead made me look past the man in front of me. There was a medium-sized pig lying on its side on the right side of the road. The noise I had just heard sounded like a grunt/oink, like the pig had just made a one-word protest at having its sleep disturbed. The Marine walking point on the right side of the road was now a couple of paces past the pig. Perhaps the pig had been sleeping on the side of the road and the Marine's passing had woke it up. Insanely, once again, time ground to a halt, and my forward vision ratcheted down into slow motion.

My mind and soul were numb; my body was exhausted. The automaton who controlled me continued to command my legs to put one foot in front of the other.

The mystery of the grunt/oink noise was solved as the Marine in front of me reached the pig. Although he could easily have stepped around the pig without causing it further distress, he kicked it in the stomach. Grunt/oink.

The Marine in front of me didn't go out of the way to kick the pig overly hard; the noise that it made—grunt/oink—was the same level of noise that the point man had gotten out of it. The pig continued to lie on its side. It was sick, helpless, and probably dying of starvation.

This poor, defenseless animal had nothing to do with our recent experiences, and kicking the pig would change nothing. Of that I was certain.

There would be no satisfaction in this sadistic act; there would be no easing of my soul's torment. Estes was dead; Morgan was dead. Sergeant Mullan's head had a hole in it; Sergeant Odum's face was destroyed. Sixteen Marines from Charlie Company who had entered the Citadel and fought the politician's fight would be returning home in body bags. The bulk of those men had been from Charlie One. The politicians would make speeches about how these men had died a noble death. Their families, in the agony of their mourning, would simply wonder about the quick equation of the life of a young man that became, too easily, the death of a Marine. None of this would be changed, or even diminished one iota, by the equally mindless act of kicking this pig.

I continued to walk forward, one step at a time, and without missing a beat, I kicked the pig.

Unlike many who fought in South Vietnam, my tour lasted the full thirteen months. After we returned to Phu Bai, Top Stanford took one look at the Charlie Company survivors and got busy arranging as many R&R flights as he possibly could. After about two hours in a hot shower, which was still insufficient to remove the deeply ingrained filth of Hue, I ventured into the Charlie Company hooch, and Top Stanford handed me orders for R&R.

Top Stanford also handed me my official notice from the U.S. Marine Corps that they had accepted my request for a regular commission. The date on the notice was several weeks old. It had obviously taken a while for Headquarters Marine Corps to track me down and let me know about their decision. I was being accepted into the fraternity of the leadership of the greatest fighting force on the planet, the United States Marine Corps.

I took one long look at the papers, noting that there was a place for my signature, which was, of course, required for certification that this terrific offer had been accepted. I took a second look at Top Stanford, who regarded me with an inscrutable look. Then I proceeded to tear up the notice into narrow strips of confetti. I never said a word to Top Stanford, Scott Nelson, or anyone else about my decision to get out of the Marine Corps at the earliest possible moment. I just tore up the paper and turned away.

I was on a commercial jet from Da Nang twenty-four hours later. After a too-short R&R in Sydney, Australia, which can easily and economically be described as spending six days in paradise in an alcoholic haze, I returned to South Vietnam and reassumed command of a new group of young Marines, the platoon called Charlie One.

While en route to the beautiful city of Sydney, I had stopped in the main PX in Da Nang and bought a camera. I had seen many amazing sights and beautifully scenic vistas during the first months of my tour, but other than six of the snapshots that appear in this book, I had no photographic record of my experiences. And since I was on my way to Sydney, a location that I probably would only visit once during my life, it made sense to buy a camera. I bought a 35-mm Olympus Pen half-frame camera, which was small in size but heavy on quality. Since it was a half-frame camera, I could get two images on every frame; a twenty-four-frame film canister would yield forty-eight images. Since it was very compact, I could carry it with me in the bush when I returned, in an ammo pouch on my web gear.

I bought a roll of Kodak color film, top quality, thirty-six frames, as soon as I arrived in Sydney. Despite my alcoholic stupor, I managed to shoot up half the roll while I was there. Since the one roll of film had cost me eight dollars and since I was on a budget, I tried to conserve. When I returned to the bush on 13 March 1968, I had half a roll left, and I expended the last thirty-six shots during the next week. Charlie One left immediately on a long-range patrol in the foothills of Phu Bai, and we traveled through some utterly, almost disturbingly beautiful areas, so I had plenty of photographic opportunities. Deserted villages, abandoned shrines, and the distinctly unique graveyards that dotted the lush countryside were all captured on the second half roll of film.

As Charlie One took a quick break on some long-forgotten trail adjacent to an unused, muddy rice paddy, I took the last of seventy-two photos and decided to take the film out of the camera. I would put it in the depths of my pack, in its own plastic wrapping, to make sure that even if the camera got wet, at least the film would be safe. I depressed the little button on the bottom of the camera, lifted the tiny hand-crank, and started to turn it. Before the end of the very first rotation, the film canister began to free-wheel; there was no resistance from the film at all. With my heart sinking to the bottom of my stomach, I released the back of the small camera, and my worst fears were realized. The film was all the way inside the film canister. When I had loaded the precious film a couple of weeks before in Sydney, the little square holes had not engaged properly with the drive sprocket, and I had taken seventy-two photos on the same frame. The film had never advanced. Then, I had compounded my stupidity by rewinding the film all the way inside the canister, so that I couldn't reuse the film without destroying the canister.

Without thinking, I threw the Olympus Pen as I would a hand grenade with its pin already pulled, as hard and as far as I could. It landed about fifty meters away and, with a soft splosh of mud, disappeared from my life forever. It is probably still there, buried in the mud or water of that distant rice paddy, an unrecognizable hunk of metal and celluloid.

I continued to serve as the platoon commander of Charlie One for four more months. But it wasn't the same. The original group of Marines called Charlie One haunted my mind as I accompanied this new bunch. I never again got close to any of the men after Hue. I couldn't. I simply could not bear to learn about these young men, to understand a little about their lives, to get to know their families, even at a distance, only to see their dreams shattered and their worst nightmares fulfilled. After Hue, I could only deal with my men from a military point of view.

Although there was no written SOP covering this aspect of a Marine officer's Vietnam experience, most junior Marine officers during their first tour in Vietnam could expect to spend about half of their time in a job that required them to be in the bush, and then they could expect to be reassigned to a rear-area job to finish out their thirteen-month tour. After eight months as Charlie One Actual, after receiving a promotion to first lieutenant, I was reassigned as the executive officer for Alpha Company. Scott Nelson, who had been replaced by a senior captain as the skipper of Charlie Company shortly after Hue, had been reassigned as the company commander of Alpha Company. And, although a company executive officer typically ran the company's affairs from the battalion rear, which in our case was Phu Bai, Nelson decided that I could best be used in the field, as a sort of "co-company commander." To be clear on this point, we both understood that Scott Nelson was in command and that he would call the shots and make the critical decisions. But it seemed to be somewhat comforting for him to have me close by, at least to share the communications and control responsibilities during the long nights. So the relative "cushy" life of a rear-area Marine was not to be for me.

In early September 1968, 1/5 left the Phu Bai area and moved south of Da Nang to the area around An Hoa, which was about forty or fifty clicks southwest of Da Nang, and I was reassigned as the company commander of Headquarters and Service (H&S) Company. Now, finally, after ten months in the bush, I would be setting up shop in a relatively safe rear area.

H&S company commanders have a lot of responsibility. They are in charge of everyone in a Marine infantry battalion save the infantry companies and the battalion CP group itself. H&S companies are comprised of the 81-mm mortar crews, M-60 machine gun teams, and the other heavy weapons assigned to an infantry battalion, as well as a lot of the administrative functions of a Marine battalion. On paper, an H&S company was much larger than an infantry company, with well over two hundred men. However, in reality this command was much less significant than an infantry company, since most of the time the M-60 machine gun teams were attached to the infantry companies, and sometimes even the 82-mm mortar crews were detached and under some other command. In a way, I was disappointed that I had not been assigned as an infantry company commander; but in all honesty most of me was relieved. At least now I could enjoy some of the creature comforts of a large firebase, such as An Hoa, and I would not be in constant danger.

Two days after arriving at An Hoa, 1/5 was picked up by five waves of CH-46 helicopters and dropped across the river, into a hotly contested landing zone in the middle of what was called the Arizona Territory. The Arizona Territory was one of the few "free-fire" zones in I Corps, where everyone there who was not instantly recognizable and therefore considered friendly was considered the enemy. In a "free-fire" zone, the rules of engagement allowed us to shoot first and ask questions later. Everywhere else that we had been, permission had to be given to fire unless we were under enemy fire ourselves. In the Arizona Territory, there were plenty of targets to shoot at.

For two months, 1/5 slogged through the rice paddies and villages of the Arizona Territory, where we were in almost constant contact with the enemy. As 1/5's H&S company commander in the bush, my job was to travel with the battalion CP group and provide them with security. Since most of my men were attached to the infantry companies, my duties were very similar to those of a platoon commander of a large rifle platoon. Although I tried not to think of it, as fast as the time of my tour was running out, I was constantly afraid that my luck was also running out. One of the few other junior officers in 1/5 who had survived the battle of Hue, a platoon commander in Delta Company, was killed in the Arizona Territory about a week before he was supposed to rotate back to the World.

Lieutenant Colonel Thompson was honorably relieved as 1/5's battalion commander during our first day in the Arizona Territory. I had mixed feelings about (then) Major Thompson. Whether or not it was warranted, I had initially resented him, perhaps detested him. To me, he represented the problems with the military chain of command and its paralyzing dependence on public opinion and politics back home. As a result, only too late did we receive the support so desperately needed during the battle inside the Citadel. However, on that dreary day in September 1968, as I sat in a hastily dug foxhole with bullets zinging over my head in the middle of a shattered grove of trees near our landing zone in the Arizona Territory and watched him leave, part of me was scared to death. This man, a man whom part of me once detested but whom I had also come to think about during the months after the battle for Hue, with respect, as the "old man," was leaving us. At that moment, I felt a disturbing sense of loss and abandonment. It turned out, however, that our new battalion commander, although he had the usual amount of combat experience—none—did have a pretty good head on his shoulders and didn't make any serious blunders while I was working for him.

Finally, after a total of twelve months in the bush, I was reassigned as 1/5's battalion legal officer and sent back to the rear area in An Hoa to wait out my last few weeks in relative safety. I got my orders to return to the World on 8 December 1968, and I was packed and ready to go early on the morning of 9 December.

My good-byes were brief. There was really no one to say good-bye to except the company clerk and the first sergeant of H&S Company.

As I waited for the first available chopper at the dusty edge of the airstrip in An Hoa, with my mind refusing to think about anything save my exit from this hellish existence, I heard someone calling my name. I turned to see Lattimer running toward the airstrip.

Robert Lattimer had earned a Bronze Star with "V" for valor for his heroic acts during the battle for Hue, and he had since earned three "battlefield" promotions. I was responsible for instigating all three of them. PFC Robert Lattimer was now E-5 Sergeant Lattimer, and as he ran toward me, waving his arms, I considered the growth and maturing process that this young man had endured and survived. Lattimer had also recently been reassigned to a rear-area job in An Hoa, and he had only a couple more weeks to wait to rotate back to the World himself. I had seen him from time to time over the past few weeks, but I hadn't even thought about looking him up to say good-bye. I didn't really feel *that* close to this man, although he had certainly saved my life on more than one occasion, and he had surely saved me from making terrible mistakes on many occasions as well. It was just that I was, simply, unable to feel closeness to anyone. That part of me had been seared from my soul on that morning on phase line green, 13 February 1968, when Ed Estes had died. No, I didn't feel close to Lattimer; I simply felt respect.

As he approached me, a wide smile covered his handsome face, and he playfully chastised me for not letting him know that I was leaving.

"Hey, Lieutenant, did you think that you could sneak off without saying a proper good-bye? I didn't even know that you had gotten orders until I accidentally bumped into the Top a few minutes ago."

As I looked at him for those few moments, the distant pain of our shared experiences subsided just long enough so that I could see him in a different light. Here, standing before me, was a shining example of everything that was good about the military experience. Lattimer had grown well beyond the casual, easy-going point man that we had relied upon. He was a man. More than that, he was a leader of men. He was tall, strong, confident, ready for whatever life would throw at him. And here he was, making an effort to say good-bye to me. I was more than surprised; I was stunned.

He looked me in the eye and stuck out his hand in an effort to grasp mine in his. He looked, for all the world, as if this farewell greeting was the most important thing in life to him at this moment.

I grasped his hand, but was unable to speak. He said it for both of us.

"I just wanted to say, 'Thank you.' I think you did a good job in a bad situation, and I'm glad you're not one of those who is going home from this place zipped up in a body bag. I wish you luck, Lieutenant."

With that, Lattimer smartly stepped back one full pace, came to a perfect position of attention, and saluted me. I could not bring myself to speak, as my emotions were just barely under control. Had I spoken, I would most certainly have embarrassed myself and besmirched the character of an officer in the United States Marine Corps. I simply looked him in the eye, came to attention, and returned his salute.

I hope I was able to show Lattimer my thanks through the expression on my face, as that was then, and remains to this day, the most meaningful moment of my life.

As the Huey landed on the metal landing strip about fifty meters away and threw red dust over us both, I managed a weak smile, grabbed his hand again, and shook it firmly.

I said, "Keep your head down, Lattimer." And then I grabbed my bags, turned around, and ran into the noisy dust cloud that would take me home.

Commanding Officer's Comments

Charlie Company, 1/5, was part of the Marine Corps attack force that recaptured Hue City, after this very important cultural and political center was overrun by thousands of NVA and Viet Cong forces during the infamous Tet Offensive of 1968.

The First Platoon of Charlie Company, known to me as Charlie One, was an integral element of Charlie Company's attack strategy. During the battle for Hue City, which housed the formidable Citadel Fortress and the Imperial Palace within it, as the commanding officer of Charlie Company, I relied heavily on the fifty-one brave Marines of Charlie One and their platoon commander, Nick Warr. This reliance was, in fact, a dubious honor, because Charlie One was often assigned as the company "point" element, which like any backhanded compliment, is not always a good thing. Obviously, the situation on point is tough and dangerous. It's kind of like being a human lighting rod. Charlie One got the job because the Marines of Charlie One had a sixth sense about it, a sort of innate awareness of direction and cause. They were dedicated, tough, and dependable. They were also very human, and they managed to somehow maintain a sense of humor, despite the often difficult and sometimes downright terrifying situations they were confronted with. And they were very vulnerable, because, after all, they were for the most part just kids. Nick was a kid, a blunt, skinny kid himself who often reminded me of a scholar or professor. He seemed not to want to be there, like many of those who served during the Vietnam War, but he made the very best of it. He looked out for the welfare of his Marines, and he was alert and tactically sound. As a Marine platoon commander, he spoke his mind, and while I didn't always agree, I listened.

As the house-to-house, street-to-street fighting progressed inside the Citadel, Charlie One, along with all the Marines of Charlie Company, paid a heavy price for every foot of real estate that we wrenched away from the enemy. First of all, this was not the typical jungle warfare we had trained for, and secondly, during the initial stages of the battle, our staggering superiority of supporting arms, artillery, air strikes, and naval gunfire was limited because of the fire restrictions on the Palace walls. That hurt, and it cost lives.

Nevertheless, the Marines of Charlie Company didn't let up. Once the full force of our supporting arms kicked in and we effectively began using the awesome firepower of the six recoilless rifles atop each Ontos, along with the overwhelming blast power of the tanks, the tide of battle turned. Rather than the traditional "search and destroy" mission so commonly practiced to hunt down the elusive Viet Cong, the battle for the southeastern corner of the Citadel became a bluntly effective "destroy and search." House by house, block by block, the defensive structures of the NVA, previously the beautiful homes of upper-class Vietnamese, were systematically destroyed, and along with them the NVA defenders.

Toward the end of the battle for the Citadel, the remnants of Charlie Company took an NVA position near the Imperial Palace. I remember pulling down from a spindly pole, a blue, yellow, and red NVA flag. This was not the imposing flag that had taunted the Marines from a distance atop the Imperial Palace walls, but rather a smaller regimental-sized flag that hung precariously from its flimsy pole near the entrance to the Imperial Palace. In a word, the taking of this flag spelled defeat for the NVA aggressors. There was not a lot of joy or excitement at this "deflagging." Rather, a begrudging sense of accomplishment and pride exuded from all present. Appropriately, the flag had several holes in it and was sprayed with spots of dried blood. This impromptu ceremony was not recorded by the press, although they had filmed some scenes during the previous days, and my family in Florida recalled seeing some news of Charlie Company, First Battalion, Fifth Marines, on the TV. It was only then that they knew why I had not written for almost a month. I also remember leaving Hue City, our mission accomplished, only to be ambushed outside of the city, yet another bloody encounter with an enemy that was down, but not out. Obviously, the war did not end with the recapture of Hue City.

In fact, in my opinion, the war really ended *before* the tumultuous battle to retake Hue City began. It ended early on in the minds and hearts of the American politicians and many of the American people, the dissenters, who unfortunately did what hundreds of thousands of NVA and Viet Cong could not do. They broke the military's will to win, restricted the military's ability to act effectively, and in many ways diminished the sacrifices of those who served and the fifty-eight thousand who died protecting the rights and privileges of those of us who remain. Charlie One did everything they could do to reverse that tide, but it was already too little, too late. Too bad.

Finally, I must say that it is a privilege to add in some small way to Nick's chronology of this battle, entitled *Phase Line Green*. It is a poignant, personal story of real Marines in real battle. No holds barred. Over the years as a twenty-six-year veteran of the FBI, I've fought other skirmishes in other places, but never any so gut-wrenching, never so prolonged, never so final. Many distant memories, some good and some bad, were resurrected by reading *Phase Line Green*, and they've become a working part of my persona. So has Charlie One.

My gratitude to those who died. My hope for those who remain.

Semper Fi
Scott A. Nelson

Index

About the Author

Nicholas Warr grew up with his four brothers near Coos Bay, Oregon, on a small working farm maintained by their parents. The boys attended Marshfield High School, from which Nick graduated in 1963. He attended Brigham Young University and the University of Oregon before enlisting, at age twenty, in the Marine Corps in June 1966. Nick was recommended for the Enlisted Commissioning Program by his boot camp drill instructor; he attended OCS in Quantico, Virginia, and was commissioned in March 1967. His first assignment as a second lieutenant sent him to WestPac from November 1967 until December 1968.

Writing *Phase Line Green* has been an odyssey of healing for Nick Warr. The experience at Hue City and the images of the men who served with him have disturbed Nick's sleep and colored his days since. "I hope the publication of this book will help me locate other survivors of Charlie Company, and that they will contact me. I would very much like to see them again." Nick feels the same about his youngest brother, Joe, Jr., who was drafted into the army and returned from Vietnam psychologically damaged. He has been lost to his family for many years and his whereabouts are currently unknown.

Nick was awarded the Presidential Unit Citation for participation in Operation Hue City and was honorably discharged as a first lieutenant in March 1970. Today, he enjoys a successful career in computer technology sales. Nick resides in Alpine, California, with his wife, Pamela, and continues to work on writing projects.